THE A-Z OF
JUDGE DREDD

THE *A-Z* OF
JUDGE DREDD

THE COMPLETE ENCYCLOPEDIA

FROM AARON AARDVARK TO ZACHARY ZZIIZ

Mike Butcher

HAMLYN

Commissioning Editor: Julian Coningsby-Brown
Assistant Editor: Michelle Pickering
Designer: Richard Scott
Assistant designer: Sue Michniewicz
Production controller: Heather O'Connell
DTP Production: Andy Tough
Researchers: Steve MacManus, Martin Morgan and Kevin Brighton

Title page illustration: first appearance of Judge Dredd in 2000AD

First published in Great Britain in 1995
by Hamlyn
an imprint of Reed Consumer Books Limited
Michelin House, 81 Fulham Road,
London SW3 6RB
and Auckland, Melbourne, Singapore and Toronto

Reprinted in 1996

ISBN 0 600 58408 9

A catalogue record for this book is available from the British Library

Produced by Mandarin Offset
Printed in Hong Kong

INTRODUCTION

How do you sum up 18 years of Judge Dredd in a mere 160 pages? That's less than nine pages for every year. Or more than nine weeks' worth of comics on every page! Drokk it, we thought ... let's do an A-Z and stick to the important stuff. Okay, so the third Judge from the left in panel 4 of page 6 of the story appearing in *2000AD* Prog 432 missed out on his own entry. Tough break for him, but we had to draw the line somewhere. Instead, the tome you hold in your hands right now is the Complete A-Z of Judge Dredd. It's complete with references to every character, place, vehicle and weapon that has had a major impact on the series over the years. As Judge Dredd enters the celluloid world for the first time in the Summer of '95, this book tells you everything you ever wanted to know about "Old Stoney Face" and his world – and probably a lot more.

There are a few things you should know before you plunge into the feast of facts that lies ahead, however, and the first of these concerns our radical approach to the previously sacrosanct realm of the alphabet. Admittedly, we do use the same 26 letters as everyone else, but in deference to the relative informality of the 22nd Century you'll find characters listed by the first names in this book, rather than their surnames. Believe me, it works better that way. The exceptions to this rule are the Judges and anyone else with an official title (like Mayor or President), who are indeed listed with reference to their respective surnames. This seemed expedient when we realised that the J section would account for around 75 per cent of the book if we didn't make this exception. To summarise, you'll find Judge Dredd under D, but Fink Angel under F. It's simple really – even a Mega-City One Game Show Host could understand it.

The second thing to look out for is the regular cross referencing, which should help you get around the book and find out more about certain things when the mood takes you. Then, there's our handy colour coding system – especially designed to give you the reader an instant handle on any given entry. There are eight categories of entry in this book – THE PEOPLE, THE JUSTICE DEPARTMENT, TECHNICAL, ARTIFICIAL INTELLIGENCE, NON-HUMAN CREATURES, LOCATIONS, EVENTS and MEGA-CITY LIFE. Check out the colour key below to find out which is which and the kind of things each heading covers.

THE PEOPLE
CITIZENS, GROUPS, ORGANISATIONS

THE JUSTICE DEPARTMENT
JUDGES, DIVISIONS, CITY OFFICIALS

TECHNICAL
VEHICLES, WEAPONS, DEVICES

ARTIFICIAL INTELLIGENCE
ROBOTS, COMPUTERS

NON-HUMAN CREATURES
ALIENS, MUTANTS, MONSTERS, ANIMALS, PLANTS

LOCATIONS
BUILDINGS, LOCATIONS, SECTORS, CITIES, WORLDS

EVENTS
CONFLICTS, CRIMES, PROCEDURES, EVENTS

MEGA-CITY LIFE
AFFLICTIONS, CRAZES, GAMES, FOODSTUFFS, LANGUAGES

A

Aaron A. Aardvark

CITIZEN: Mega-City One

AARON A. AARDVARK – THAT'S
AN UNUSUAL NAME, CITIZEN.

Y-YES, CHIEF JUDGE. MY NAME USED
TO BE ERIC PLUNKET. I-I CHANGED IT
TO BE FIRST IN THE VID-PHONE BOOK!

When the mad Chief Judge Cal sentenced the entire population of Mega-City One to death (for the first time!) he ordered the citizens to show up for execution in the order they appeared in the Mega-City One Vid-Phone Directory. Incredibly, millions of them did, and first in line was the number one named person in the book – Aaron A. Aardvark! Not surprisingly, Aaron – formerly Eric Plunket – had changed his name to achieve this dubious honour and he paid for it with his life.

See ZACHARY ZZIIZ

2000AD Prog 95 (dies)

The Academy of Law

BUILDING: Judges' training school, Mega-City One

Training a Judge takes fifteen long, hard years and many of the entrants to the Academy of Law never make it to the streets of Mega-City One as a full Judge. Cadets are either cloned from proven genetic stock or enter the Academy at the age of five or under. They are then expected to learn the basics of law enforcement very quickly and any failing during their rigorous training is likely to lead to expulsion. It is therefore quite some achievement for a Cadet just to reach Rookie Judge status and be given his or her half eagle and white helmet.

Cadet Judges attend regular classes on all aspects of policing and controlling a 22nd Century Megalopolis.

Both practical and mental skills are vital to their progress at the Academy, so they are subjected to continual assessment by their Judge-Tutors.

The Academy of Law is a self-contained environment for prospective Judges – affording them somewhere to live, train both physically and mentally, and to be tested . . . up to a point. Cadet Judges do, however, have to go outside in groups for their Hotdog Run and, of course, Rookie Judges must pass a "final street test" before they can graduate. Only when they have satisfied a serving Judge that they can handle themselves on the streets of Mega-City One can a Rookie leave the Academy with his or her black helmet and full eagle.

See also INSTITUTE FOR ETHICAL VIOLENCE

Introduced: 2000AD Prog 27

Psi-Judge Kit Agee

JUDGE: Psi-Division, Mega-City One

Already one of Psi-Division's most sensitive operatives, Kit Agee had been working hard to enhance her abilities when she was overwhelmed by a powerful vision of the Sisters of Death. The other-dimensional creatures were using the mind of an unfortunate citizen called Xena Lowther to bridge the gap between their world and Mega-City One when Agee tapped into their fearsome presence. As much as the apparition was disturbing to the Judge, it was welcomed by the evil Sisters – since they needed a much stronger mind to make their bridge permanent. Combining the strong will of a Judge with her extremely powerful psi-powers, Kit Agee was the ideal candidate for the job, so they used the former Judda, Kraken – in the guise of Judge Dredd – to lure her into a trap. She was overpowered by him, under the Sisters' control, and then subjected to a massive psychic assault that she could not possibly resist, allowing the creatures to make their presence felt in Mega-City One. While the Sisters of Death were creating their Necropolis – or "City of the Dead" – Agee was their unwitting conduit and, when Psi-Judge Anderson discovered this, she knew that killing her friend would be the only way to free the city. Despite the Sisters' best efforts to hide Agee from her, Anderson managed to use her own powers to locate her and Judge Dredd – the real one this time! – ordered a massive attack on the apartment in which she was being held. Thus, Psi-Judge Agee was released from her torment at last and the Sisters' hold on Mega-City One was broken.

See also SISTERS OF DEATH, XENA LOWTHER

2000AD Progs 676–683, 693–695 (dies)

Aggro Dome

BUILDING: Leisure Complex, Mega-City One

An attempt to cash in on the level of aggression seething through the city, the Aggro Dome was a specially designed environment where citizens could relieve their pent-up feelings of violence. In theory, everything that happened there would be so carefully controlled that there was no danger to any of the clients, but things got out of hand. Encouraging violence proved to be a disastrous policy. Citizens started attacking each other and took the place apart before the Judges could quell the riot and close the place down!

Introduced: 2000AD Prog 183

Aggro-Drug

DRUG: Powerful hypnogenic, Mega-City One

Developed by the Mega-City One Justice Department, the Aggro-Drug induces an overwhelming sense of menace in anyone under its influence and provokes terrifying and highly realistic hallucinations that could test the strength of even the strongest mind. In anticipation of future dangers likely to beset her City – according to the predictions of Psi-Division – Chief Judge McGruder authorised the use of the drug on selected Judges in order to toughen them up and prepare them for the crisis ahead.

Introduced: 2000AD Prog 854

Agros

WORLD: Hadean System, Deep Space

Home to twelve separate warlike races, Agros is a scene of regular carnage, as its wars are controlled like sports events. Every day a war is organised on one of the planet's designated battlefields between at least two of the native races. Imported weapons of all varieties are used and thousands are killed, but each war is packaged carefully for television – with expert commentators, referees and even a half-time break! Judges Dredd and Hershey visited Agros during their quest to find the Judge Child and unwittingly became participants, finding themselves classified as "natural hazards".

Introduced: 2000AD Prog 167

Alien Catcher General

MUTANT: Citizen, Cursed Earth

One of the most feared denizens of the Cursed Earth, the Alien Catcher General's job was to recapture any alien slave that escaped their human masters. Along with his "Slay-Riders", a vicious band of mutant marauders, he saw that the offworlders were returned to captivity or killed as an example to any other enslaved aliens. While tracking down the alien Tweak, the Alien Catcher General came up against Judge Dredd who prevented him from killing the innocent and highly intelligent alien.

See also TWEAK

2000AD Progs 69, 70, 85 (cameo)

Alien Zoo

BUILDING: Menagerie, Mega-City One

Containing examples of alien species from all over the Universe, the Alien Zoo is one of Mega-City One's most popular attractions. Housing such weird and wonderful creatures as the Wurlitz Wooflebest, the Duck-Billed Yabba-Dabba and the Antarean Tentatee, the Zoo is a showcase for creatures which earth people would be unlikely to ever see in their home environment – although inter-galactic conventions mean that only aliens classified as having extremely low intelligence can be kept in captivity in a Zoo of this kind.

Introduced: 2000AD Annual 1982

Mega-City One freedom fighter America Jara

Alien Seeds

ALIEN: Bred on orbiting space farm

A peculiar fusion of plant and animal, Alien Seeds were released in Mega-City One in their thousands during one of the city's most damaging crazes. They seemed innocuous – small creatures grown from seeds – but they just got bigger and bigger. And as they grew, they became hungry and sometimes dangerous animals. The alien creatures soon became a menace and the Justice Department was forced to act. The distribution and ownership of Alien Seeds was quickly outlawed, but a few of them are believed to have survived in the back alleys of Mega-City One.

Introduced: 2000AD Prog 148

America Jara

CITIZEN: Democracy Activist, Mega-City One

When America's parents came to Mega-City One, they named their daughter after their new country. Having seen the way that the Judges acted at a very young age, America Jara had none of the illusions of her parents and she reacted against the oppression of the Justice Department.

She went on the Democratic March with her boyfriend, but he was killed and she was arrested. When released, America fell in with Total War, a democratic pressure group believing in extreme action and she soon had the blood of four Judges on her hands. During a Total War set-up, she crossed paths with Bennett Beeny, a childhood friend, who witnessed the killing of a Judge. Bennett was shot in the throat and left by America's associates to die but she was horrified and went to see him. She asked Beeny for money to buy explosives to blow up the Statue of Liberty but he was troubled by her plan. He gave her the money, but informed the Judges and America was shot in an ambush. Pronounced dead on arrival at the hospital, her body survived intact and so Beeny arranged for a full body transplant and had his own brain put into her otherwise healthy body!

See also BENNETT BEENY, TOTAL WAR

Judge Dredd the Megazine Volume 1: 1-7 (dies)

Psi-Judge Cassandra Anderson
See page 10

The Angel Gang
See page 12

See page 12

Ankhhor

MONSTER: Luxor City

Ankhhor – "the dead-in-life" – discovered a method whereby his physical body could survive beyond his death in ancient Egypt. When he was discovered by Luxor City Judge Kamun in 2115, having rested for three thousand years in a state between life and death, the time had come for Ankhhor to be reborn and take his place as the God-King of a New Dynasty in the World! Kamun pledged allegiance to him and helped him to absorb the Ka – the genetic essence – of a number of Judges to make him strong. Ankhhor's influence grew, but he needed the genes of one last victim to make him all-powerful, a victim with a DNA strand of the highest quality who was visiting Egypt as part of a cultural exchange ... Judge Dredd! Not surprisingly, when served up as food for an Egyptian God-King, Dredd proved extremely unpalatable and he finally killed off the creature who could not be killed by putting him through the Luxor version of Resyk and Ankhhor was shredded beyond even his powers of recovery!

See also JUDGE KAMUN

2000AD Progs 859-866 (dies)

Anti-Mugging Suits

WEAPON: Heavily armed suit, Mega-City One

When Anti-Mugging Suits with their fully-automated anti-personnel weapon systems were first introduced into Mega-City One, they were adjudged too dangerous to be used by the citizens and the Judges banned them. However, the Guard-o-Ped fiasco convinced Chief Judge McGruder that the suits, while dangerous, were essentially a defensive weapon and considerably better than the alternatives being offered to the citizens in the name of personal security.

See also GUARD-O-PED

Introduced: 2000AD Prog 354

Apocalypse Monument

MONUMENT: Tribute to those lost in the Apocalypse War, Mega-City One

Following the Apocalypse War against East-Meg One, 65% of Mega-City One was left in ruins and casualties ran to some 400 million people, so work units were formed to begin the long rebuilding process. The first priority of these work units was to construct a massive "mushroom cloud" monument as a tribute to all the Judges and citizens who died during the war.

Introduced: 2000AD Prog 271

Above:
Memorial for 400 million, the Appocalypse Monument

Ape Gang

GROUP: Intelligence-enhanced apes, Mega-City One

Led by Don Uggie Apelino, Fast Eeek and Joe Bananas, the Ape Gang consisted of highly intelligent apes with the power of speech. The Ape Gang operated in an area known as "The Jungle', modelling itself on the gangster mobs of 1930s. When a massive gang war broke out, the Judges stepped in to end the violence and the leading members of the gang were arrested. They were confident, however, that they would go free since, as apes, they were exempt from the law, but they reckoned without the 1987 Animal Nuisance Act so they were packed off to serve their time at the Mega-City Zoo.

2000AD Prog 39/2000AD Sci-Fi Special 1979

Left:
Egyptian God-King Ankhhor puts Judge Dredd on the menu

Psi-Judge Cassandra Anderson

JUDGE: Psi-Division, Mega-City One

As one of Mega-City One's most accomplished Psi-Judges, Judge Cassandra Anderson has been involved with many celebrated cases and missions. She came to prominence when brought in to investigate Judge Death's first appearance in Mega-City One. Her powerful Psi mind was a great attraction to the Dark Judge and he possessed her when his corporeal body was destroyed. Subjugated by his will, Anderson was still able to suggest the means of Judge Death's defeat, even though it meant she would be encased in solid Boing forever. In order that the Dark Judge could never escape, she was thus immobilised with Judge Death trapped inside her and her body was placed in the Justice Department's Hall of Heroes.

In fact, Judge Death was released a a year later by the other Dark Judges – Fire, Fear and Mortis. Anderson was freed at the same time and, despite her incarceration, was found to be in good health. With Dredd's help she was able to force the Dark Judges to retreat to their own dimension, but Anderson was determined to end their menace once and for all. Dredd and Anderson pursued them to Deadworld and, with the Psi-Judge acting as a conduit for the psychic pain of the Dark Judges' billions of victims, Judges Death, Fear, Fire and Mortis were apparently destroyed.

Cassandra Anderson's next two major challenges both saw her team up with Judge Dredd against seemingly impossible odds. Part of Dredd's hand-picked "Apocalypse Squad', she helped to achieve an unlikely victory over East-Meg One. Shortly after this, Anderson accompanied Judge Dredd on a trip 13 years into their future in Proteus, an experimental time vehicle, Proteus, to investigate the coming doom, predicted earlier by dying Psi-Judge Feyy. Dredd and Anderson found the Mega-City One of 2120 dominated by vampires, zombies and other monsters under the control of an evil being called the Mutant. All of Judge Anderson's past success almost counted for nothing

when Judge Death managed to influence her into unwittingly freeing the Dark Judges' spirits from their own dimension. Her actions saw her suspended and looking stretch on Titan, but she defied her suspension to deal with the evil Judges, banishing them to limbo using some experimental dimension jump devices.

Anderson's suspension was subsequently lifted, allowing her to take on a series of ever more dangerous and often quite bizarre cases. Psi-flashes of a wolf troubled her for a while, but this was a warning that

East-Meg assassin Orlok was about to be freed from the Iso-Cubes by a band of East-Meg "sleeper" agents. Anderson was badly injured by the sleepers, but she was finally able to round them up, though Orlok escaped to plot his revenge. His plans were ultimately thwarted by Anderson, but he remained at large.

From first contact with a group of aliens on the look-out for large quantities of salt to an unfortunate monk whose search for Nirvana appeared likely to end with the release of Judge Death from limbo, Anderson's cases showed no signs of becoming any less weird over the following months. Meanwhile, she formed a firm friendship with fellow Psi-Judge Corey and their nights on the town helped Cassandra to retain her sanity through a trying period.

Judge Corey's suicide, then, was a shattering blow for Anderson and her parting sentiments – that she could no longer face using her talents for such ugly purposes – caused Anderson to reconsider her life once more.

Personal matters were temporarily put to one side when Judge Death returned once more to transform Mega-City One into a Necropolis. Anderson played a significant part in saving the city. Not long afterwards, Anderson went through a major trauma in the Cursed Earth as one of her earliest memories had been stirred. Unknown to her throughout her adult life, Cassandra Anderson had been abused by her father at the age of three and the first manifestation of her Psi powers had been his murder. The Judges at that time had considered her incapable of handling the memory, which was why it was buried.

For Anderson the crunch came when she was party to the arrest of Jon Baptiste, a Christian whose pure faith and honest goodness touched her deeply. Baptiste was treated roughly during his interrogation by Judge Goon and Cassandra objected, lashing out at her colleague. Having gone out on a limb for the Christian, his subsequent faked "suicide" was too much for her to take. If this was what being a Judge was all about, she wasn't sure she had a future with the Justice Department.

An unconventional mission to Mars followed, during which she encountered an all-powerful alien race and formed an unholy alliance with Orlok. She then tendered her resignation as a Judge. She travelled the universe in search of some other meaning to her life and enjoyed freedom she had never experienced as a Judge. Encountering all manner of strange creatures on many different worlds, she even ran into Orlok again. Anderson finally decided to return to earth, however, when she received a vague psi-flash warning her of a great catastrophe due to hit Mega-City One. Believing she could make a difference, Anderson requested her badge back and was accepted on a trial basis.

See also PSI-JUDGE AGEE, THE APOCALYPSE SQUAD, JON BAPTISTE, PSI-JUDGE COREY, THE DARK JUDGES, JUDGE DEATH, THE MUTANT, ORLOK THE ASSASSIN, NECROPOLIS

2000AD Progs 150, 151, 224, 226-228, 263-267, 269, 270, 393-400, 402-406, 416-427, 468-478, 520-531, 607-609, 612-622, 629, 635-647, 657-659, 669, 670, 674-717, 758-763

Judge Dredd the Megazine Volume 2, Nos. 8, 10, 11, 14, 22-24, 27-37, 50-60

Judge Dredd Annuals 1985–1988; Judge Dredd Yearbook 1993; Judge Dredd Mega-Special 1988, 1991, 1992; 2000AD Sci-Fi Special 1989; 2000AD Annuals 1984, 1987, 1988, 1990; 2000AD Yearbook 1993; 2000AD Winter Special 1988; Judgement on Gotham 1-3; 2000AD Progs 160, 161, 173, 176, 177, 179-181, 195; Judge Dredd Annual 1983 (cameo)

2000AD Graphic Novel: Childhood's End

The Angel Gang

CITIZENS: Criminal family, Texas City Badlands

The most infamous and feared band of thugs ever to come out of Texas City, the Angel Gang were responsible for a near endless string of crimes with one overriding common factor – they were all quite unnecessarily violent! Never ones to commit a murder when a vile atrocity would do, the Angels were led by Elmer "Pa" Angel and comprised three of his four sons – Link, Mean Machine and Junior. Their most audacious act was the kidnap of Owen Krysler – the so-called "Judge Child" – although they were forced to flee into space to evade the attentions of Judge Dredd, who was pursuing the boy. The value of a child who could see and perhaps even influence the future was obvious, but the Angel Gang had to travel a long way before they could find a way to turn a decent profit from his capture. They finally arrived on the Planet Xanadu, where a mysterious and dangerous robot called the Grunwalder ruled over his own independent Kingdom. Pa Angel was keen to do a deal with the robot, hoping to exchange Owen Krysler for considerable riches – as well as protection from the Mega-City One Judges! However, Dredd caught up with the Angel Gang on Xanadu and he was prepared to kill them all in his quest for the Judge Child. Link was the first to fall, followed by Mean Machine, then Junior and finally Pa. By the time the Judge returned

to earth only one Angel was left alive – Fink, the loner of the family and Pa's eldest son, was never a true member of his Pa's gang, but he was mighty angry when news came to his hole in the Cursed Earth that he was now an only child!

See also PA ANGEL, MEAN MACHINE ANGEL, FINK ANGEL, JUNIOR ANGEL, LINK ANGEL, JUDGE CHILD, GRUNWALDER

2000AD Progs 160, 161, 173, 176, 177, 179-181, 195

Judge Dredd Annual 1983 (cameo)

Left, from top to bottom: Pa, Junior, Link, Mean Machine and Fink

Right: The Angels make Sadie Suggs an offer she can't refuse

Top right: Mean's so mean he butted himself on a trip to the past

Apocalypse Squad

GROUP: Elite unit, Mega-City One Judges

Formed to carry out a last ditch attempt to end the Apocalypse War by destroying East-Meg One, the Apocalypse Squad was an elite group led by Judge Dredd. Accompanied by eight other Judges – Kwan, Ocks, Anderson, Hershey, Costa, McDonald, Hamble and Morant –Dredd first set out to capture a Sov Strato-V Assault Craft, which was moored in his city during a terrible hurricane. They captured the craft successfully and headed for East-Meg One, infiltrating one of the missile silos just outside the city. The Sov-Judges manning the Bostok 7 Silo never knew what hit them as the Apocalypse Squad used the element of surprise to take control of their missiles. Re-targeting them on East-Meg One, Judge Dredd ordered a full-scale assault with one simple intention – the city's complete annihilation! With just 14 seconds to marshal their defences, the Sov-Block's first city had no chance of survival and over half a billion people were wiped out in minutes. Dredd and his comrades had no choice but to give themselves up to the Sovs in the wake of their actions, but the damage to their attackers was done. The East-Meg One invaders in Mega-City One lost their will to fight and Judge Dredd was soon released so that he could kill War Marshal Kazan and accept the Sov forces' unconditional surrender.

See also EAST-MEG ONE, JUDGE OCKS,
WAR "MAD DOG" MARSHAL KAZAN
2000AD Progs 263-267, 269, 270

The Apocalypse Warp

DEVICE: Force Field, East-Meg One

Developed by some of the Block's top Tek-Judges, the Apocalypse Warp enabled the defence force of East-Meg One to protect itself almost completely from Mega-City One's retaliation during the Apocalypse War. To maintain such a large shield effectively required an awesome amount of power.

The force field worked by actually "warping" the Mega-City One's oncoming nuclear missiles into a parallel dimension – saving East-Meg One at the cost of millions of lives on some previously undiscovered alternate earth!

Introduced: 2000AD Prog 249

Arachnid Gene Virus

AFFLICTION: Genetic disease, Mega-City One

An extremely rare virus, AGV – or the Arachnid Gene Virus – attacks its victims' genes directly, rearranging their structure into something resembling the genetic make-up of a spider. If caught very early on, it is possible to burn the virus out of any afflicted area in the human body, but it takes hold of the major organs very quickly and soon becomes inoperable. Manifesting itself slowly. AGV first causes unsightly hair to form on its victim's body and gradually alters their posture. Mental processes are affected next and the sufferer begins to realise they are not fully human anyway. Eventually, the entire body shape is changed and the victims limbs become arachnoid in nature. Any citizen of Mega-City One unfortunate enough to contract the disease has one added indignity to bear – incurable AGV is classified as a genetic abnormality under the terms of the Mutant Segregation Act, so any sufferer is liable to be exiled from the city by compulsory order of the Justice Department! It is common then for AGV victims to seek any means of remaining in the city, even if this requires their relatives to break the law by helping them hide from the Judges. Unfortunately, when the virus reaches its final stages the sufferer undergoes a total physical and mental transformation into a giant spider-like creature, making it difficult for them to avoid the Judge's attention.

See also ELEANOR GROTH
Introduced: 2000AD Prog 603

Above:
**Armitage with
Rookie Judge
Treasure Steel
to his right**

Detective Judge Armitage

JUDGE: Brit-Cit

Despite the fact that almost everyone in the Brit-Cit Justice Department hates him, they still have to admit that Armitage is by far the best plainclothes Detective Judge they've got. Little is publicly known about him - not even his real name - and he never carries a gun. Yet Armitage's knowledge of weapons is extensive, mainly due to his activities during the Brit-Cit Civil War of 2092-99, when he fought on the losing side. After the war, Armitage joined up as a Judge, but he become cynical and morose when his lover Liora was killed by the crime lord Efil Drago San, in revenge for the Detective Judge crippling him. Armitage soon acquired a reputation for being impossible to work with and having no respect whatsoever for authority, but he was an outstanding Judge and brought tremendous investigative abilities to the Brit-Cit Justice Department's plainclothes homicide division. When Rookie Judge Treasure Steel was assigned to Armitage for a year-long assessment, they didn't get on at all, but they soon developed a grudging respect for each other and Steel has become one of his closest friends and allies.

See also ROOKIE JUDGE TREASURE STEEL

Judge Dredd the Megazine Volume 1: 9-14

Judge Dredd the Megazine Volume 2: 10-21, 31-33, 63-70

Judge Dredd Yearbooks 1993, 1994

Arnold Stodgman

CITIZEN: Fattie, Mega-City One

I SAID – **GIMME THE PIE!**

THIS IS INCREDIBLE! ABDOMINAL ARNIE IS TRYING FOR THE **MAGIC TON!**

Times were tough for Fatties like Arnold Stodgman in Mega-City One after the Apocalypse War. With food shortages a major problem, he was rounded up along with everyone else weighing over 300 kilos and put into a special Segregation Block on a forced diet. Arnold's great achievement was that he managed to put on weight in the Block – somehow eating his way from 983 to 986 kilos despite the blocks strict regime – and this attracted Charley Bruno to him. Charley was a trainer of heavyweight eaters and broke him out of the Segregation Block so he could compete in the World Heavyweight Eating Championships. Arnold duly won the contest by eating more than a ton of food – a new world record – but the effort killed him, so he had pigged his last!

2000AD 331-334 (dies)

Atlantic Division

DIVISION: Mega-City One Justice Department

Charged with the responsibility of patrolling the heavily polluted waters of the Black Atlantic, the Mega-City One Judges' Atlantic Division have what is potentially the dirtiest job in the Justice Department! They have jurisdiction over all the vessels operating in Mega-City One waters and they are also responsible for the policing of the incredible Atlantic Tunnel link with Brit-Cit, which is highly vulnerable to any form of terrorist attack. In fact, they do this in conjunction with their fellow Judges from Brit-Cit and each force is nominally responsible for the safeguarding of their half of the tunnel against any possible catastrophe.

See also BRIT-CIT

Introduced: 2000AD Prog 197

Judge Kwame Assengai

JUDGE: Leader, Pan-African Judge Squad

Following the Credit Wars in the late 21st Century – and a nuclear conflict which devastated the continent – Africa is slowly being put back together, but the presence of dozens of widely differing governments and philosophies has made this process very difficult indeed. The Pan African Compromise pledged free trade and passage between most of these regions and created a Pan-African Judge force to prevent crimes all over the continent. Kwame Assengai is the experienced leader of one of the many Judge Squads which patrol the dangerous African terrain, hunting down ivory poachers and trying to maintain law and order in general. His Squad has an unusually diverse spread of cultures, beliefs and nationalities, which gives them an edge in many situations – something they often need desperately, since many of the Pan-African states still refuse to recognise the Judges' authority.

See also JUDGE BECKY STEEL

Judge Dredd the Megazine Volume 2: 45-49

Judge Dredd Yearbook 1994

Below: **Pan-African Judge squad leader Kwame Assengai**

B

Banana City

CITY: South America

Ciudad Barranquilla, better known as "Banana City", is one of the poorest and most corrupt cities in the World. Run by an elite and often brutal Judge force who live in luxurious conditions while their people starve, Banana City is a tough place to live unless you are lucky enough to be very rich. Most of the city's wealth and property is in the hands of a powerful criminal class and the Judges themselves, who have profited from the growth of crime through an institutionalised system of bribery and corruption. Under "Banana Law" it is actually possible to buy years off your sentence at a special appeal session with the city's Judge Supremo if you have enough credits to offer!

Introduced: 2000AD Prog 623

Barney

COMPUTER: City Hall Computer, Mega-City One

All non-Justice Department matters are recorded and controlled by Barney, Mega-City One's mainframe computer. He has been programmed to be extremely user-friendly, with a cheerful and generous personality to boot, but on one occasion his kindness became a problem. He declared an early Christmas in Des O'Connor Block and offered everyone exactly what they wanted as a gift, however impossible it might to deliver it in reality. Utter chaos ensued and, as usual, the Judges had to pick up the pieces when the citizens were disappointed by his false promises. Realising the error of his ways, Barney shut himself down in preparation for some major repairs.

Introduced: 2000AD Prog 144

Below:
The Basking Soggies bid a musical farewell to Mega-City One's premier lawman

Basking Soggies

ANIMALS: Mutated fish, Emerald Isle

Unique to the waters around the Emerald Isle, Basking Soggies are rather large talking fish. Mutated by the radiation of the Atomic Wars of 2070, these creatures are not actually intelligent, but being attuned to human radio waves they are remarkable mimics and often sing songs for the amusement of visitors to the Isle. Unfortunately for the trusting and plentiful Soggies, they also make a pretty tasty fish finger!

2000AD Progs 728, 732

Judge Supremo Batista

JUDGE: Banana City

As the "top banana" in Ciudad Barranquilla, Judge Supremo Batista is an extremely wealthy man. He makes no apology for the corrupt Justice Department he presides over and his position has enabled him to become Banana City's biggest landlord – Batista owns almost half the city's slum properties. Charging exorbitant rents to his unfortunate tenants, anyone not paying up in time is liable to receive a Judicial visit – with anything from a one-off demonstration of Judicial violence to a five year stretch in the 'Cubes as the deterrent against missing another payment. Needless to say, most of his tenants pay up on time.

See also BANANA CITY

2000AD Prog 625

16

Battle of Armageddon

CONFLICT: Final showdown with Legion of the Damned, Death Valley

In the wake of the short-lived Atomic Wars, a civil war between the Judges of the Mega-Cities and the deposed President's robotic army raged across the country. Even though Robert L. Booth had been sentenced to 100 years in suspended animation, his Presidential Guard was programmed to fight on and their struggle culminated in a last stand in Death Valley in 2071, which came to be known as the Battle of Armageddon. More than 100,000 Judges and Mega-Troopers were killed in this final conflict, but the so-called Legion of the Damned was finally defeated and ceased to be a major threat to the three Mega-Cities.

See also PRESIDENT BOOTH, LEGION OF THE DAMNED

2000AD Prog 625

Bella Bagley

CITIZEN: Mega-City One

When Judge Dredd rescued Bella Bagley from a couple of muggers, he had no idea that she would fall in love with him. She became obsessed with him and wrote him dozens of love letters without receiving a single reply. Finally, she arranged to meet him under false pretences and declared her love for him – only for Dredd to arrest her for wasting a Judge's time! Bella then attempted suicide and Dredd was forced to rescue her for a second time, only to pack her off to a Psycho Cube for treatment. Six years later she contacted Dredd again, claiming to be having his baby! When she took a number of hostages, Dredd had no choice but to swear his undying love for her – before head butting her into unconsciousnes!

2000AD Prog 444; Judge Dredd Mega-Special 1991

Bennett Beeny

CITIZEN: Entertainer, Mega-City One

Bennett Beeny's parents died when he was young, so when growing up he became attached to a girl called America Jara. He loved her, but she saw him more as a brother and, as they got older, they grew apart. He became a popular recording artist. Meanwhile, America was getting involved with the Democratic Movement in Mega-City One. Barely a day went by when Bennett didn't think about her. One night, in a sleazier part of the city, he witnessed America Jara's involvement in the murder of a Judge. The man she was with shot Bennett in the throat to prevent him from identifying either of them. Beeny survived, but his singing career was over. Being rich, he was soon fixed up with an artificial voice-box, but he knew that his voice could never be the same again. Some time afterwards America turned up at his house to see that he was alright, asking him for money to buy explosives to blow up the Statue of Liberty; he could not refuse but decided to tell the Judges. He made them promise not to hurt anyone, but they lied and America was killed. Bennett srranged to have her body kept alive and had his brain transplanted into her body. The singer resumed his career, but where he had always specialised in comedy songs, now he could only sing sad ones.

See also AMERICA JARA, TOTAL WAR

Judge Dredd the Megazine Volume 1: 1–7

Bert Dubinski

CITIZEN: Mega-City One

The man with the dubious honour of being the first ever perp arrested by Judge Dredd – during the lawman's final street assessment as a Rookie alongside Judge Morphy – Bert Dubinski did a thirty-five stretch in the Iso-Cubes when his uncontrollable anger saw him commit a double murder. When he finally got out, Bert went to see Dredd, believing there was some kind of bond between them, but the Judge made it clear that he had no time for the killer. Outraged by this snub, Bert Dubinski's temper got the better of him once again and he made the mistake of trying to shoot Judge Dredd. This time Bert was spared a further stretch in the 'Cubes and had to settle for a bullet in the brain instead!

2000AD Prog 775

Bethann Rosie

CITIZEN: Civil rights activist, Mega-City One

Leader of the Committee for the Restoration of Civil Liberties, Bethann Rosie was prevented from joining the Democratic Charter March when the Judges levelled trumped up charges against her, accusing her of bigamy. The charges were spurious, based on a ridiculous technicality, but her reputation was damaged beyond repair and she had to withdraw from public life.

See also COMMITTEE FOR THE RESTORATION OF CIVIL LIBERTIES

2000AD Progs 531-533

Psi-Judge Bhaji

JUDGE: Psi-Division, Delhi-Cit

One of Delhi-Cit's most powerful Psi-Judges, Bhaji came to Mega-City One on a cultural visit at a particularly bad time, since it coincided with former Judge Grice's devastating attack on the city with a killer virus. As soon as he arrived, the Delhi-Cit Judge experienced a very bad psi-dream, warning him that something very bad was about to happen and that Judge Dredd would be the man left to pick up the pieces. His prediction proved uncannily accurate as the Judges lost control of their city to ex-Judge Grice and Bhaji had to join the fight to recapture Mega-City One from his renegade group. The visiting Judge worked well with Psi-Judge Janus during the struggle and their combined efforts helped save the city from the virus and contributed to the ultimate defeat of Grice.

See also JUDGE GRICE, PSI-JUDGE JANUS

2000AD Progs 842-846, 848, 852, 853

Big Smelly

RIVER: Undercity, Mega-City One

Before the building of Mega-City One much of the Eastern Seaboard had become horribly polluted, so the new city was simply built on top of it. The Ohio River had suffered badly from the problem, becoming so full of toxic material it became known as the "Big Smelly". With the construction of the first Mega-City, the Ohio River was covered up too and it now runs through the Undercity below, as badly polluted as ever.

Introduced: 2000AD Prog 99

Right:
It's big and it's smelly ... it's the Big Smelly!

THE BIG SMELLY.

Bill Bailey Block City-Def

GROUP: City-Def Unit, Mega-City One

Having taken refuge in a well-fortified nuclear bunker at the height of the Apocalypse War, the last surviving members of the Bill Bailey Block City-Def Unit didn't emerge for nine long years. Their City Block had been razed to the ground during the fighting and it was obvious that the Sov forces would be triumphant, so they felt justified in their strategic withdrawal.

When they did finally leave their shelter they knew the Sovs would be in charge, so they were determined to fight a guerrilla war against the enemy and, if necessary, to sell their lives very dearly indeed. They were unaware that Mega-City One had won the war after all and that the appearance of normalcy all around them was not an East-Meg deception, so they began a terrorist campaign in earnest. This soon brought them into conflict with the Mega-City One Judges and, despite repeated attempts by Judge Dredd to convince them of their mistake, the Bill Bailey Block City-Def members refused to surrender to people they saw as "collaborators" with the Sovs. Hence, the misguided City-Def Unit perished finally in one last brave but sadly futile act of defiance.

2000AD Progs 723-726

Bingoholism

AFFLICTION: Gambling Addiction, Mega-City One

Scientists in the 22nd Century have masterminded the colonisation of distant planets and sent probes through the heart of the sun, but they still cannot find a cure for bingo! The compulsion to play the game is felt most acutely by the elderly and there are plenty of criminals willing to set up illegal bingo halls to cash in on the tragic problem of bingoholism in Mega-City One.

Introduced: 2000AD Prog 372

Biochip

DEVICE: Personality Chip, Lesser Lingo

Banned in Mega-City One, Biochips allow their users to live forever – or at least until the money runs out! At the moment of death, a person's personality is programmed onto a tiny Biochip which can then be inserted into a prepared socket in a hired body. The technology can result in a pretty anarchic unstable society, as demonstrated by Lesser Lingo, one of the few planets where the use of Biochips is legal and most people rent out their bodies for at least part of the time!

Introduced: 2000AD Prog 164

Birdie

DEVICE: Lie Detector, Mega-City One Justice Department

One of the most useful items in a Judge's kit, this hand-held device can detect the slightest voice fluctuation, while monitoring a suspect's heart-beat, respiratory functions and even brain electricity. Combining all these elements in its miniaturised and highly sophisticated computer brain it becomes a near-infallible lie-detector. A simple read-out then ensures that a little "Birdie" can tell a Judge instantly if a perp is lying to them. The Lawman is then able to employ other means to discover the truth.

Introduced: 2000AD Prog 133

Bishop Snodgrass

CITIZEN: Bishop, Mega-City One

When vid-channels are looking for a non-controversial spokesman from the Church to appear on one of their talk shows, Desmond Snodgrass is usually top of their list. Completely unflappable, the Bishop was at Channel 48 during the famous hijack of the station by the Democratic Tendency. On the strength of this, he was asked to appear on a show covering the big democratic referendum almost six years later, despite the fact that he had no idea whatsoever what the election was about!

See also DEMOCRATIC TENDENCY

2000AD Progs 460, 751

Above:
Jaw Wars
at a typical
Bite Fight

Bite Fighting

CRIME: Underground sport, Mega-City One

One of the most barbaric entertainments in Mega-City One involves two burly fighters being pitched into a "Bite Pit" with their arms tied behind their backs, ready to bite each other into submission! Bite fighting is strictly illegal, but it remains a popular "sport" - although individual fighters are usually quite easy to spot, since they generally have their teeth filed down to sharp points for extra efficient chomping in a fight. Naturally, they are also covered in bite marks all over their bodies.

Introduced: 2000AD 337

Black Atlantic

LOCATION: Formerly the Atlantic Ocean

As pollution became an increasingly more alarming problem world-wide during the 21st Century, vast waterways – oceans as well as rivers – were filled with all manner of toxic materials. The Atlantic Ocean was soon redubbed the "Black Atlantic", since it had become so filthy that this was a fairly accurate description of its colour. Certainly exposure to its waters became likely to prove lethal to any human unfortunate enough to take a swim in it. Giant Anti-Pollution ships patrol the ocean, but their cause is a lost one, since the waters of the Black Atlantic are generally believed to beyond redemption.

See also ATLANTIC DIVISION

Introduced: 2000AD Prog 128

Black Museum

LOCATION: Grand Hall of Justice, Mega-City One

Whereas the Hall of Heroes honours Mega-City One's finest Judges and most worthy citizens, the Black Museum is a macabre reminder of the city's darkest hours and its most dangerous enemies. The likes of Judge Death, Captain Skank, War Marshal Kazan and Sabbat are all remembered here and relics pertaining to such menaces are exhibited.

Introduced: 2000AD Prog 149

Black Plague

ANIMALS: Mutant Spiders, Cursed Earth

Having been mutated by radiation, these giant spiders were both poisonous and carnivorous and roamed the Cursed Earth in a massive swarm in search of food. One bite from them would knock you cold, while a second bite would finish you off! When the Black Plague threatened the town of Atom Gulch, a local resident sought help from Mega-City One to beat them off. Judge Dredd helped to protect the town with a wall of fire and made it so hard for the spiders to overrun the place that they decided to look for easier pickings in the big city!

Again fire was the key weapon against the mutant spiders, as the Judges bombarded them with tremendously powerful incendiary shells. This time, though, the creatures sheltered underground and most of them survived to climb the city walls and invade Mega-City One's streets. In very quick time the Black Plague had overrun an entire Sector of the city. The creatures were delighted with their opportunity to feast on the Mega-City One citizens and Judge Dredd was forced to give the order to burn the whole area down. Unable to burrow into solid concrete, the spiders were duly exterminated as a result of this extremely drastic manoeuvre!

See also HENRY FORD, MOZE BIGLEFTEAR

2000AD Progs 140-143

Blobs

CRAZE: Face-change surgery, Mega-City One

In the quest for the completely unidentifiable perp, "Cyclops" Pete Runcie came up with idea of promoting the "Blob Look" - where people had face-change surgery to remove all distinguishing features. By making this the height of fashion, he was able to send out his henchmen in Blob guise to pull off crimes and then they could simply blend into the crowd to avoid detection by the Judges! Runcie's tactics were effective for a while, but then the Judges passed a new law which required Blobs to carry an indelible serial number on their forehead and the real criminals were quickly rounded up.

2000AD Prog 290

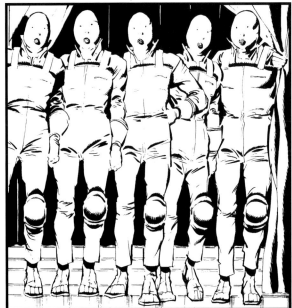

It's fashionable, it's fun and it's very, very stupid – it's the Blob Look!

Blitz Agencies

ORGANISATIONS: Contract killers, Mega-City One

Mob "Blitzers" in Mega-City One have a strict code of honour – once a contract has been taken out on someone's life it cannot be cancelled, whatever the circumstances. Also, for the protection of a Blitz Agency, all their professional hitmen must consent to having a "suicide box" fitted into their bodies, before he is accepted as a "Blitzer". The box is sensitive to emotional changes and prevents a Blitzer from surrendering to the Judges by blowing him up, thereby preventing compromising information about the Agency being passed on at the same time.

See also BONNY STAPLES

Introduced: 2000AD Prog 215

Block Mania

AFFLICTION: Massive Block War outbreak, Mega-City One

Although Block Wars are common enough in Mega-City One, when three quarters of the city started fighting each other, the Judges knew that there must be some outside force inspiring the violence. Indeed the madness, which came to be known as "Block Mania", was caused by a Sov drug which had been put into Mega-City One's water supply by Orlok, the East-Meg One assassin. As the Western Judges were about to find out, Block Mania was just a prelude to the Apocalypse War, as the Sovs began their nuclear assault on a weakened Mega-City One.

See also BLOCK WAR

Introduced: 2000AD Prog 236

Block War

CONFLICT: Inter-Block War, Mega-City One

In an overcrowded city like Mega-City One, tensions and rivalry between neighbouring City Blocks are inevitable and, very occasionally, these feelings spill over into full-scale wars. Because each City Block is an independent unit in its own right, a sense of patriotism is often attached to them by their residents and wars can break out with "enemy Blocks" over the most trivial matters. For the Judges, a Block War is one of the toughest situations to police, simply because there are usually so many people involved and arrests generally have to be made in vast numbers before things can be properly cooled down and peace restored.

See also CITY BLOCK

Introduced: 2000AD Prog 182

Mega-City One's
Leading
Democrat,
Blondel Dupré

Blondel Dupré

CITIZEN: Civil rights activist, Mega-City One

As leader of "The Democratic Urge", Blondel Dupré was a central figure in the formation of the "Democratic Charter Group", which unified the various democratic pressure groups in Mega-City One. She went on to play a major part in organising the ill-fated Democratic Charter March in 2109 and, thanks to the machinations of the Justice Department, Dupré was the only leader allowed to participate in it. When the march was broken up by the Judges, she was arrested along with thousands of others and set up as a scapegoat for the violence she was caught in the middle of. Sent to the Iso-Cubes for breach of the peace and assault, Dupré remained defiant, still convinced that democracy would eventually win the day.

No-one was more surprised than Blondel Dupré, however, when Judge Dredd – who was having severe doubts about the Judges' handling of the march – ordered the release of all remaining democrats still doing time. Some time later, following the horrors of the Necropolis, she was even more astonished when the Judges announced a referendum to be held on the issue of democracy in Mega-City One.

Suddenly, Blondel Dupré was thrust once more into the political limelight, but this time it seemed she would be triumphant. As the leading exponent of democracy, she put her case against Dredd's assertion that the citizens should stick with "the devil you know". The Judges were fully expected to lose the vote, but they actually won by a landslide and Dupré was forced to concede the defeat as a fair one, rather than risk a violent reaction from her followers who believed the ballot had been rigged. Despite her disappointment with the result, the democrat leader was convinced that Judge Dredd was a man of his honour and that the referendum reflected the genuine views of the people.

See also DEMOCRATIC CHARTER GROUP

2000AD Progs 531, 533, 668, 751, 754-756

Bob Nicely

CITIZEN: Illegal Game Show Host, Mega-City One

The game show "You Bet Your Life" may well have been popular back in 20th Century America, but the Mega-City One version introduced a whole new meaning into the title. Bob Nicely was the smiling host of the show, broadcast illegally on a pirate TV station, and his job was to get his contestants to quite literally bet their own life, or the lives of other members of their families, against their ability to answer a question. What made it worse for his victims – er, contestants – was that Bob's questions and games were loaded against them, making it virtually impossible for them to win. As a result, the show had few survivors, though its supply of plainly very stupid contestants was plentiful. Bob himself, as well as his wife and co-host Morticia Nicely, also failed to survive the show in the end, as their studio was finally tracked down by Judge Dredd, and the smiling duo were killed as a result of the Judge's efforts to ensure that at least one gullible contestant might live to answer questions another day!

2000AD Prog 25 (dies)

Bob Wezzell

CITIZEN: 21st Century America

The rather obscure "people's" philosopher, Bob Wezzell came up with a few pertinent observations on life that have particular relevance to life in a 22nd Century Mega-City. Most notable among his sayings was Bob's Law: "All it takes is one person to do something stupid and all the rest are sure to join in."

When Mega-City One's boundaries were drastically rearranged following the devastation of the Apocalypse War of 2076, Bob's Law certainly held as the citizens went berserk rather than accept the new classifications. In the end, Chief Judge McGruder was forced to fall back on Bob's Second Law: "If all else fails, bribe 'em!" So she offered every citizen a one hundred credit incentive to agree to start calling their Sector by its new number, then brought in a Clean Air Tax – a one-off payment of one hundred and five credits – to cover the cost of the bribe, plus five credits for administration! This admirably went on to prove Bob's Third Law: "What the Justice Department gives it can just as soon take away again."

2000AD Prog 355

Boing®

MATERIAL: Miracle rubber, Mega-City One

One of the most sensational developments in rubber technology ever, Boing is a spray-on rubber coating that solidifies into a giant ball around the object it is sprayed on. A person can even be turned into a human pinball with it, since you can breathe through it even when you are solidly and safely encased in its rubber coating. When encased in Boing you only have very limited control over your bouncing, however, so the use of the material outside in Mega-City One is illegal – with twenty years in the 'Cubes the penalty for improper use of the stuff. Special Palais de Boing leisure domes have therefore been built where Boing may be used safely and legally.

A more serious use for Boing has emerged since its invention, as it has been discovered that the material is capable of holding the physical and spirit forms of the Dark Judges from the Death Dimension. Encased in Boing they retain the ability to think and to transmit their thoughts to a limited degree, but they are otherwise rendered harmless.

See also DARK JUDGES, JUDGE DEATH, PINBOING

Introduced: 2000AD Prog 136

Bonny Crickle

CITIZEN: Mega-City One

When she strayed from the path and fell into a chem pit, young Bonny Crickle suffered horrific injuries and the medic robots were only able to save her brain. Bonny's parents weren't very well off, but they used every penny they had and borrowed as much as possible to ensure that their little girl could have an operation to attach her brain to a mechanical body. Unfortunately, the operation was only partially successful and some of the connections between Bonny's brain and her new body didn't work, so she was nothing like she was before the accident. Judge Dredd encountered Bonny in the course of his duties and her story touched him. He authorised payment for a second operation to fix the connections and the girl was cured. Tragically, when Bonny realised her full predicament – her brain was trapped inside a rather odd-looking mechanical body – she freaked out and ran in front of a truck. Judge Dredd received this news with great sadness and the experience shook his convictions somewhat, since it seemed he had made a rather bad error of judgement in the Crickle case.

2000AD Progs 388 (dies)

Mob Blitzer Bonny Staples

Bonny Staples

CITIZEN: HITMAN, Mega-City One

A blitzer for the Stallone Mob, Bonny Staples went freelance when Papa Stallone was put away by the Judges and he ended up working for the Sons of Erin – an Emerald Isle liberation group. He transformed this predominantly non-violent group into an extremely violent terrorist movement – albeit, a rather inept one. During a single action organised by Staples, all of the group's members were either killed or captured, so he made a break for it with as much money as he could "liberate" from them! Unfortunately for Staples, Judge Dredd and Judge-Sergeant Joyce caught up with him as he was trying to leave Murphyville and forced him to give himself up. Being a blitzer, however, he was fitted with a suicide box and this was triggered by his surrender, causing him to explode before he could be taken into custody!

See also SONS OF ERIN

2000AD Progs 727-732 (dies)

President Booth

CITIZEN: Cursed Earth, former U.S. President

When President Robert L. Booth pressed the button and initiated the Atomic Wars of 2070, he brought catastrophe upon his country and he was deposed. Having so discredited his office, Booth was destined to be remembered as the last President of the United States and a terrible war criminal to boot. Punishment for his crimes came in the form of the famous "Judgement of Solomon", which decreed that he should serve a 100 year term in suspended animation, locked up in the deepest vault in Fort Knox. Three medic robots were assigned to look after the sleeping ex-President and they were programmed to check and change his blood on a regular basis. Unfortunately, when a bomb hit Fort Knox years later, he was inadvertently revived. Judge Dredd sentenced him to "life", working on a Kentucky farm.

See also LEGION OF THE DAMNED

2000AD Progs 67, 68

Brain Blooms

ANIMALS: (Or, more strictly) Bio-organic plants, Mega-City One

Not truly animals, nor exactly plants, Brain Blooms are bio-organically grafted creatures, which grow in the ground rather like turnips! Unlike, such regular fleshy vegetation, however, these can speak and indeed imitate any sound. Most particularly, they are capable of emitting an hypnotic hum, rendering their victim highly susceptible to any suggestion. Despite their name, Brain Blooms themselves have no independent thought, and simply respond to the wishes of their grower. Their cultivation, sale or possession is highly illegal in Mega-City One and the penalties are harsh.

2000AD Prog 18

Brian Skuter

CITIZEN: Reporter, Mega-City One

Right:
Investigative journalist (or seedy hack?) Brian Skuter

As a freelance writer, Brian Skuter was always on the lookout for a big story, so when he received a telephone call from Judge Death he had to follow it up, despite the risk. He found the Dark Judge in a reflective mood and keen to explain himself to the citizens of Mega-City One – since he believed he was greatly misunderstood and under-appreciated by them. Having spilled out his secret origin to the reporter, Death sent Brian Skuter off to write up his story. Unfortunately, he couldn't sell the tale as a serious account of the Judge's life, as no-one would believe him. Skuter was forced to trivialise the story and break it down into typical tabloid pap before anyone would agree to publish it – this infuriated Judge Death. Summoned into the presence of the Dark Judge once more, Brian Skuter was foolish enough to turn up and this time he didn't live to report on what happened!

Judge Dredd the Megazine Volume 1: 1-5, 7-12 (dies)
2000AD Graphic Novel: Young Death

Judge Bram

JUDGE: Retired, Mega-City One

A good Judge, but one whose decisions were becoming erratic, Bram took the Long Walk into the Undercity beneath Mega-City One to take law to the lawless there. Unfortunately, he was infected by Cassidium, a radioactive chemical substance which turned him into a werewolf. In his crazed wolf form he found his way back into city above, where he was killed before his true identity could be discovered.

See also WHITE WEREWOLF, MED-JUDGE CASSIDY
2000AD Prog 323 (dies)

Brit-Cit Babes

JUDGES: Brit-Cit Vice

Shea Coran was one of Brit-Cit's best Vice Judges, operating on the decidedly seamier side of the city. When she got involved with trying to smash a slavery racket, however, she saw her young protégé K.C. killed and the attitude of her superior officer convinced her to quit the force.

Judge Dredd the Megazine Volume 1: 16-20

Brit-Cit Brute

JUDGE: SAS, Brit-Cit

Seen as a last resort in the Brit-Cit Justice Department, the SAS is only called in when all else has failed. Nicknamed the "Demolition Squad", due to the destruction it generally leaves in its wake, the SAS now consists of just one active member – Judge Newt – who is best known by the name of "Brit-Cit Brute", due to his rather uncompromising attitude!

Judge Dredd the Megazine Volume 2: 31-33, 60-62

Brit-Cit

City: Britain

Run by its own Justice Department, Brit-Cit is a society still riddled with class conflicts and dominated by privilege, despite the effects of the Atomic Wars of 2070 which saw a similar change in the style of government as was seen all over the World. The Brit-Cit Judges are still organised along the lines of the old police force, so each sub-department retains a degree of autonomy and has a representative at their New Old Bailey Headquarters. Inter-departmental cooperation is often sadly lacking and the Justice Department suffers from a deeply ingrained streak of racism and sexism.

Introduced: 2000AD Prog 485

The Brotherhood of Darkness

Group: Mutants, Cursed Earth

One of the more audacious of Cursed Earth mutant groups, the quasi-religious sect, the Brotherhood of Darkness actually organised raids into Mega-City One to capture slaves to put to work in their forced labour camps. Long before the huge City Wall was erected this was an easier prospect, but the Brotherhood was thwarted when they captured the son of the then City Father, Washington, and Judge Dredd was alerted to their activities. He set off into the Cursed Earth and destroyed their slave camp, freeing all their surviving captives.

During Dredd's quest to reach Mega-City Two by land across the Cursed Earth, he encountered them once more – the Brotherhood attacked his group as they passed Mount Rushmore. They were warded off only when the Judge threatened to destroy the image of their leader, Brother Morgar, which had been carved into the rock face along with those of the old U.S.A.'s honoured Presidents. Undeterred, the Brotherhood of Darkness pursued the travellers and soon renewed their attack, with Brother Morgar determined to claim the life of Judge Dredd himself. Morgar was finally killed by Novar, a mutant with telekinetic powers who helped defeat the Brotherhood once and for all.

See also NOVAR

2000AD Progs 4, 65, 66

The Brotherhood of Marshals

Group: Lawmen, Cursed Earth

Deriving their way of life from an old "Lone Ranger" book, the Brotherhood of Marshals modelled themselves on Tonto and brought a kind of law to the lawless in the Cursed Earth. Unfortunately, most of the Brotherhood were wiped out when their water supply was contaminated by Tek-Judge Eckson's genetic virus, as he carried out an unauthorised and illegal test on them. Keen for revenge, they dispatched one of the few survivors of the incident – calling himself just the Marshal – to Mega-City One to punish the Judge responsible.

See also TEK-JUDGE ECKSON, THE MARSHAL

Introduced: 2000AD Prog 802

2000AD Graphic Novel: Tales of the Damned

Below: Brother Morgar leads his mutant band to Mount Rushmore

25

The Brotherhood of Trash

The Brotherhood of Trash

GROUP: Mutant cult, Cursed Earth

Possibly the most bizarre of all the quasi-religious groups operating in the Cursed Earth, the Brotherhood of Trash was founded by Filmore Faro, the self-proclaimed "Garbage God". His cult became very rich and powerful by digging for antiques in their "garbage mine" - actually an abandoned town preserved under a sheet of radioactive dust – and selling them on to collectors. Using their wealth and a good deal of slave labour, the Brotherhood set about recreating some of the monuments of ancient Egypt -like the pyramids – while never forgetting the true object of their worship ... garbage!

See also FILMORE FARO

2000AD Progs 157-159

Right:
Sports Day with the Brotherhood of Trash

Below:
Bruce arrests Dredd during his visit to Oz

Oz-Judge Bruce

JUDGE: Sydney-Melbourne Conurb, Oz

Typical among the Oz-Judge, Bruce was an efficient lawman, but more laid back than any of his Mega-City One counterparts. When Chopper came to Oz to compete in Supersurf 11, he was still a wanted man in the Big Meg, so Judge Dredd was determined to arrest him. It was Oz-Judge Bruce who placed Dredd himself under "protective arrest" so that Chopper could compete and he later gave the skysurfer his chance to get away. Dredd was not too put out by Bruce's actions, however, since his "arrest" was all part of an elaborate trap to snare a member of the Judda. When Bruce and Dredd met again, they met on good terms.

See also CHOPPER, JUDDA

2000AD Progs 554, 557-561, 563, 565-568, 570, 794-796

Judge Dredd the Megazine Volume 1: 4

Buggo

ALIEN: Cave painter, Planet Ombra

Buggo was a primitive cave-dwelling alien Judge Dredd encountered during his quest to find the Judge Child. Dredd's arrival on his planet distracted Buggo's enemy, Black Boab, just enough for Buggo to beat him in combat and so win the hand of the fair Uglika. Forever grateful, Buggo painted Dredd on his cave wall to remind him of the "dreaded face of God"!

2000AD Prog 163

Left: Renegade Judge Bundy makes her escape from Titan

Judge Bundy

JUDGE: Renegade, Mega-City One

When Judge Bundy fell in love, she couldn't really have picked a worse partner than dangerous perp, "Psycho" Starling. The relationship alone would have wrecked her career, but the fact that they held an entire City Block hostage and killed thirty Judges, booked her a one-way trip to the Titan Penal Colony for crooked Judges. Bundy had gone way over the edge, so they tried burning out large parts of her brain on Titan in an effort to calm her down, but the operations just left her more unhinged than ever. She was an ideal compatriot for the deranged Judge Grice when he engineered an escape from the prison, and she became his chief henchperson when he took control of Mega-City One on their return to Earth. Grice and his fellow renegades' grip on the city was not all that firm, however, and they soon found themselves under attack by a weakened but determined Judge Dredd. Bundy seized her opportunity to beat on Dredd, but she miscalculated badly when she let him get near a gun and he blew her away with an armour-piercing bullet!

See also JUDGE GRICE

2000AD Progs 836-841, 843, 845-847, 849-851 (dies)

Supreme Judge Bulgarin

JUDGE: Supreme Judge, East-Meg One

One of the main architects of the Sov's attempt to conquer Mega-City One during the Apocalypse War, Supreme Judge Bulgarin oversaw the whole plan – right from the incident involving Captain Skank to placing Orlok in the enemy city so that he could cause "Block Mania" to the sending in of War Marshal "Mad Dog" Kazan after the initial nuclear assault on Mega-City One. Bulgarin reckoned without Kazan's ambition, however, and as the War Marshal commenced hostilities in the American city, he also ordered the murders of the Supreme Judge and his fellow members of the East-Meg One Diktatorat.

See also WAR MARSHAL "MAD DOG" KAZAN,

ORLOK THE ASSASSIN, CAPTAIN SKANK

2000AD Progs 200, 245-250, 259 (dies)

Left: Supreme Judge Bulgarin gets ready to press the nuclear button

Cadet Judges

SOCIAL CATEGORY: Trainee Judges, Mega-City One

From their entrance to the Academy of Law, either as a clone infant, or as a child, age five or under, Cadet Judges face a tough regime of training and testing until they either flunk at any stage and find themselves expelled or they attain the status of Rookie Judge almost fifteen years later. Until a Cadet attains the status of Rookie he or she is banned from leaving the Academy unsupervised by other Judges for any reason whatsoever.

See also ACADEMY OF LAW, ROOKIE JUDGES

Introduced: 2000AD Prog 30

Judge Cahill

JUDGE: Mega-City One

A forty-year man, Judge Cahill was one of Mega-City's most experienced lawmen when Sabbat's zombies besieged the city. Unlike so many of his comrades, Cahill survived that particular battle, but he did suffer an apparently insignificant bite from one of the zombies while defending the City Wall. Some months later the Med-Judges informed him that he had picked up a rad-cancer from the bite, but by then he had just a few hours to live. Devastated but unbowed by this news, he died, as he had lived, taking out perps on the streets of Mega-City One during one final – and eventful – patrol alongside Judge Dredd.

2000AD Prog 790, 792, 823 (dies)

Chief Judge Cal
See page 30

Call-Me-Kenneth

ROBOT: Carpenter Robot K12, Mega-City One

When his obedience circuit malfunctioned, the carpenter droid known as "Call-me-Kenneth" began a violent rampage across Mega-City One. Utilising his carpentry attachments and high-level intelligence, his capacity for killing was considerable, but this also made him easy for Judge Dredd to track down. He was disabled by a combination of electrocution and having his head blown off! The remains of Call-me-Kenneth were subsequently delivered to the optimistic robotics specialist, Arnold Wisenheimer. He set about reassembling Call-me-Kenneth, even arranging for the final stages of his work to be broadcast live on TV. Unfortunately, a sudden surge of electricity reactivated the droid before his obedience circuit was repaired. The new Call-me-Kenneth took advantage of the live TV link-up to call on robots all to join him in his war against the "Fleshy Ones". The Robot Wars had begun! As battle ensued, Judge Dredd and Walter the Wobot managed to infiltrate Call-me-Kenneth's base, only to be captured. However, with the help of Walter, Dredd escaped and succeeded in turning more than half of Call-me-Kenneth's robots against him. Forced to make a hasty exit, the rogue robot led a team of giant Heavy Metal Kid robots on a last-ditch assault on the Grand Hall of Justice itself. The attack threatened to overwhelm the Judges until Dredd arranged an impromptu electrical storm. Call-me-Kenneth escaped, but he was pursued once again by Dredd, who finally put paid to the droid by exploding a flying Texas City Oil Tanker right beside him.

See also THE ROBOT WARS

2000AD Progs 10–17

Judge Dredd the Megazine Volume 2: 45 (cameo)

Judge Dredd Annual 1983 (cameo)

Captain Skank

MUTANT: Black Atlantic Pirate, Cuban Wastes

A crazed mutant with deadly metallic coils instead of hair, Captain Skank was a troublesome pirate operating in the waters of the Black Atlantic between the Cuban Wastes and Mega-City One. He became a bigger problem when he kidnapped a Mega-City nuclear scientist capable of updating and activating the nuclear warheads aboard his sea fortress – a formidable undersea vessel left over from the Atomic Wars of 2070. Skank's subsequent nuclear attack on Mega-City One saw the Bob Oppenheimer City Block completely annihilated and more than four million people killed, despite the city's highly effective Laser Defence Network. The Judges acted quickly – tracking down his vessel, boarding it and regaining control of its weaponry – and Skank was killed along with a giant mutant squid which he believed to be his mother! Only then did the Judges discover that the Captain had been manipulated by his second-in-command, Tuskerosa the Vicious, who was secretly an East-Meg One agent.

See also TUSKEROSA THE VICIOUS

2000AD Progs 197-200 (dies)

Judge Dredd the Megazine Volume 2: 45 (cameo)

Judge Dredd Annual 1983 (cameo)

Med-Judge Cassidy

JUDGE: Med-Division, Mega-City One

AW, C'MON – I HAD TO CALL IT SOMETHING.

Called in to examine the dead body of former Judge Bram, who had become a werewolf while bringing law to the lawless in the Undercity, Med-Judge Cassidy worked hard to isolate the cause of his affliction. He discovered the presence of a radioactive chemical substance in Bram's blood and – never one to miss out on any credit for his efforts – he named it Cassidium. Cassidy's discovery suggested a problem of major proportions, since there was clearly a large supply of this substance somewhere in the Undercity, so Chief Judge McGruder sent Judge Dredd there to find and destroy it. This he did, along with dozens of werewolves, but not before he was infected by the Cassidium himself. Brought back to Mega-City One as a werewolf, Dredd was cured by Med-Judge Cassidy who had quickly developed an antidote.

See also WHITE WEREWOLF

2000AD Progs 325, 328

Judge Laverne Castillo

JUDGE: Mega-City One

Having frozen in a combat situation on the streets of Mega-City One, Judge Castillo was held partly responsible for the fact that her partner had been shot. She was brought up before Chief Judge McGruder, who removed her from regular duties and gave her an administration job. Castillo soon became McGruder's personal assistant and accompanied her on the mission to try and sell robotic Judges on Hestia. When their spacecraft crashed on the planet, Judge Castillo acquitted herself admirably during the battle for survival and she felt ready to go back on the streets when they returned to Mega-City One. Some of her fellow Judges were sceptical, believing she would freeze up again, but Judge Dredd vouched for her and she proved she was up to the job.

2000AD Prog 891, 894, 904-915

Judge Dredd the Megazine Volume 2: 58-68

Above:
Captain Skank

Below:
Judge Laverne Castillo

Chief Judge Cal

Although not a class-mate of Judge Dredd's, Cal was certainly a contemporary of "Old Stoney Face", sharing as they did several Judge-Tutors at the Academy of Law. Cal was a capable but rather misunderstood Cadet and his views did not always endear him to his fellows. His admiration for great dictators from history like Adolf Hitler was considered odd, if not entirely inappropriate for a Judge. Shortly after his graduation, Judge Cal joined the feared Special Judicial Squad – the Judges who judge the Judges – and found this kind of service very much to his liking. The Squad's autonomy and power within the Justice Department appealed to Cal and he excelled in the role of an SJS Judge, quickly working his way up to a senior position. By 2100 Cal had been appointed head of the SJS and took his place on the Council of Five in this capacity. His nomination as Deputy Chief Judge followed almost immediately, though he already had his eyes set on the top job itself.

Frustrated by Chief Judge Goodman's longevity in his post, Cal began to plan the older man's demise and the apparatus of the SJS was to prove vital to his schemes. Under Cal's leadership, the Special Judicial Squad grew ever more secretive and more independent of the Judges' other Divisions, until he was ready to make his move. Then he hit upon his masterstroke. The SJS were responsible for the Judges' Daily Crime Briefing and, by placing a subliminal message on the tapes that were played to every Judge when they went on duty, Cal was able to instil blind loyalty to himself in all of them. Judge Dredd was one of a handful of Judges who missed out on this indoctrination because he was on a mission in the Cursed Earth, so Cal framed him for murder to keep him from interfering with his plans. Having accessed Dredd's personal file at the Justice Department, the SJS leader was able to arrange for an extremely lifelike Judge Dredd robot to be built and the murders committed by this simulacrum appeared to provide irrefutable proof that Dredd had become a homicidal maniac. When Chief Judge Goodman was compelled to add his vote to a Council of Five condemnation of one of his most senior Judges, it almost destroyed him and Cal took advantage of the old man's confusion to tighten his grip on the Justice Department. Even when Judge Dredd demonstrated his innocence, the Chief Judge was incapable of regaining control and Cal found it a simple task to organise his murder.

With Chief Judge Goodman brutally slain by undercover SJS Judges, Judge Cal seized power and immediately began implementing his own brand of law. His first act as Chief Judge was to reintroduce the death penalty for a whole range of offences – including criticism of the Chief Judge! – and he also imposed a 6pm curfew in Mega-City One. The final proof of his insanity was to follow, however, when he appointed his pet goldfish as his successor as Deputy Chief Judge. Meanwhile, Judge Dredd and a handful of other Judges unaffected by the mad Chief Judge's brainwashing formed a small but organised resistance to him. When they managed to storm the Justice Department – with the support of thousands of armed citizens – Cal's reign looked to be over, but the arrival of the Kleggs turned the battle. The alien mercenaries had been in orbit for a while, awaiting the Chief Judge's call should the need arise for some reinforcements, and they helped beat back the resistance forces in short time.

NO, NO INDEED! AM I NOT *WITHOUT MERCY*? AM I NOT THE *CRUELLEST MAN WHO EVER LIVED*? HA, HA, HA, HA!

Alongside his new allies, Chief Judge Cal renewed his grip on Mega-CIty One and pronounced a death sentence on all its citizens in retribution for the failed uprising. Several million were executed before the death of Judge Fish, which Cal took to be a sign that the city should be spared. However, the poor turnout for the goldfish's state funeral enraged the Chief Judge, and when citizens began deserting Mega-CIty One in their droves to seek refuge in the Cursed Earth, his fury was all-consuming. Having appointed the Klegg leader, Grampus, as his new Deputy Chief Judge, Cal put him in charge of stopping the exodus, authorising him to employ whatever violent means he deemed necessary. Shortly after this, work began on the Mega-City Wall. Although in subsequent years the wall would form a valuable defence for the city against attacks from outside, it was originally erected by Cal, using citizens as slave labour, to stop his own people from getting out! Judge Dredd's resistance were still a thorn in the Chief Judge's side throughout this period and they severely disrupted the work on the wall on numerous occasions. Cal had already offered a one million credit reward for information leading to the arrest of the renegade Judge, but he seemed to have finally solve his problem when Dredd and his fellow rebels were involved in an horrific roadliner crash – resulting in the vehicle smashing its way down through city bottom and into the Undercity. Believing his enemies to be dead, Cal decreed that crime would be legal for a day of celebration, but the incidences of crime actually fell! Enraged once more by this snub, he decided to outlaw happiness – banning laughter, smiling and even conversation.

With this edict and the banishment of hope among the people after the apparent death of Dredd, Cal's rule entered a smoother and more satisfying phase for the mad dictator. After 100 days as Chief Judge, he decided that he had created the perfect society in Mega-City One and that the only way to preserve this perfection was to gas the citizens, leaving the empty city as a permanent monument to what he had achieved. Judge Dredd, who had in fact survived the roadliner crash along with most of his rebels, was therefore forced to speed up his plans to overthrow Cal. Dredd managed to substitute a replacement tape at the Judges' Daily Crime Briefing and thus freed the bulk of them from the Chief Judge's control. With most Judges switching their allegiance away from Cal and the Kleggs leaving earth in large numbers in order to avoid the planned gassing of the city, the resistance forces soon gained the upper hand. Unfortunately, Cal had already placed

nerve gas canisters around Mega-City One and had set up a release mechanism at the top of the Statue of Judgement. Dredd was unable to stop Cal from ascending the statue and it became a desperate race against time to prevent him from carrying out his plan. In the end it was Fergee, an Undercity denizen befriended by Dredd during his unscheduled stop there, who ensured the survival of the city he no longer lived in by carrying the tyrant off the top of the Statue of Judgement – sacrificing his own life in the process.

Cal, who was convinced he could talk to all his predecessors as Chief Judge and believed himself to be the greatest of them all, demonstrated his madness right up to the end. During his plummet from the top of the statue, so convinced of his power was he that he commanded his fall to stop. Strangely enough, it didn't and Mega-City One breathed a mighty sigh of relief as he hit the ground.

See also FERGEE, JUDGE SLOCUM

2000AD Progs 86-108 (dies), 182 (cameo)

Judge Dredd Annual 1983 (cameo)

Chester Whut

CITIZEN: Juve, Mega-City One

During a school expedition to the Mega Disposal Plant, Chester Whut became fascinated by the omnivorous Fang Worms used to consume waste there. In his efforts to get his hands on one to take home he first dropped a classmate in amongst them and then pushed one of his teachers into their vat, too. The resulting feeding frenzy saw his whole class consumed by the beasts and Chester was the only survivor! He came up with an explanation for the whole affair and related it to Judge Dredd, but the Judge had his Birdie lie-detector to hand and packed the boy off to the Juve Cubes without hesitation.

See also FANG WORMS

2000AD Prog 598

The Chieftain

CITIZEN: Former Chieftain of Covert Assassination Squad, Cal-Hab

Below:
The Chieftan (Andy Dunn) heads to Mega-City One with his killer bagpipes

Andy Dunn was the leader of a Ranger assassination squad in Brit-Cit's Caledonian Habitation Zone several years before his family were killed in a revenge attack. Dunn pursued the murderer to Mega-City One and found that he was working for Wartech, an arms manufacturer involved with some highly illegal arms dealing to his home country. Despite the attention of the Mega-City Judges, the Chieftain managed to kill his target and exposed Wartech's activities at the same time. Then, his mission now completed and to avoid capture, Andy Dunn committed suicide by throwing himself off the top of Wartech's towering HQ before any of the Judges could stop him.

2000AD Progs 832-834

Chief Judge

SOCIAL CATEGORY: Ruler, Mega-City One

The position of ultimate executive power in each of the US Mega-Cities is held by a Chief Judge. The post was created in 21st Century, when it was recognised that newly-built Mega-City One needed an new kind of police force. Originally, the Chief Judge was intended to serve as the head of the new force, the Judges, but the Atomic Wars of 2070 saw a major shift in the balance in power when President Booth was forced to step down because of his role in initiating the war. Mega-City One's citizens petitioned the Judges to assume power and, in due course, the Chief Judges of the Mega-Cities were elevated to the status of city leaders.

See also PRESIDENT BOOTH

Introduced: Prog 34 (term)

Chiller Black

CITIZEN: Game Show Host, Mega-City One

Hailing from Brit-Cit, Chiller was the host of one of Mega-City One's most popular games shows, "Blind Mate". When Dredd came to investigate one of her contestants she made the big mistake of asking him to appear on her show – landing herself a spell in the 'Cubes for making an improper suggestion to a Judge!

2000AD Prog 825

Chopper
See opposite

Chump Dumping

CRIME: Dumping of aliens in Deep Space

A common sideline for most Perp Runners is the practice of "Chump Dumping". Rather than take their spacecraft back to Earth completely empty, the Perp Runners often convince aliens to take the trip with them. They tell their customers what a wonderful life they could have on Earth, but in fact dump them in space during the return journey, so they never have to live up to their extravagant promises!

See also PERP RUNNING

Introduced: 2000AD Prog 212

Chopper

CITIZEN: Scrawler and skysurfer, Mega-City One

Marlon Shakespeare was just like any other Juve - no money, no job and no future. When he finally found a way to be somebody by becoming Chopper - the city's "King Scrawler" - the Judges arrested him for his trouble. While on a Juve Rehab programme, he was given his first opportunity to use a power board and he soon become an expert skysurfer. Warned not to do any illegal low-level flying, Chopper realised that this was where the excitement lay, so he started training for the annual Supersurf competition, the skysurfers' unofficial World Championship. Chopper triumphed in Supersurf 7, which was staged in Mega-City One, but he was arrested by Judge Dredd at the end of the race.

Ironically, the next two Supersurfs were staged legally in the Sydney-Melbourne Conurb, with the backing of the Oz Judges, and as Supersurf 10 approached, the clamour for Chopper's release was growing. To be on the safe side, the Judges decided to transfer him to a secret location, but when he was mobbed by fans on the way, Chopper escaped. On the back of a power board, he made an historic journey all the way to Oz and arrived in time to compete in the Supersurf. Although he lost the race narrowly to Jug

McKenzie in the end, they had a terrific battle and Chopper at least had the satisfaction of beating the Australian in a one-on-one rematch they staged for their own amusement a few weeks later. First, though, he had to escape from Judge Dredd, who was determined to take him back to Mega-City One to serve the remainder of his sentence, and he managed this with the help of a well-timed collision between McKenzie and Dredd along with the cooperation of the Oz-Judges, who allowed him free passage into the Radback.

Chopper and Jug McKenzie became good friends and the Australian even introduced him to Charlene, who soon became the young skysurfer's girlfriend. Chopper's life had taken a definite turn for the better, but he still spent thought about the prospects of becoming World Champion again. Unfortunately, his dreams were tarnished when the race was bought by a new sponsor, Stig, who planned to stage it in Mega-City Two and introduce unreasonable levels of danger into it. Jug McKenzie wisely refused to take part, but Chopper couldn't resist and signed up for the race, despite the fact that Stig had snipers along the route! Not surprisingly, Supersurf 11 turned into a bloodbath and Chopper was the only surfer to reach the finish, though even he sustained near fatal injuries and collapsed before he crossed the line. Returning to Oz, Chopper took quite a while to recover from the physical and mental scars caused by his last Supersurf, but he was happy to retire from competitive skysurfing and live with Charlene and Jug in a drop-out commune in the Radback there.

See also JUG McKENZIE

2000AD Progs 206, 207, 428, 429, 545-550, 553, 555-558, 564-570, 572, 594-597, 654-665

Judge Dredd the Megazine Volume 1: 1-5

Judge Dredd the Megazine Volume 2: 36

Judge Dredd Mega-Specials 1988, 1990

Judge Dredd the Poster Prog 4

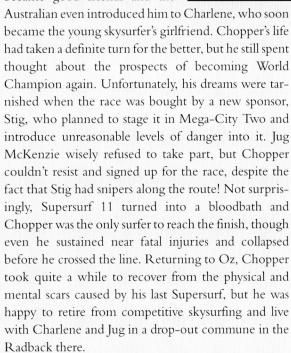

Church of Almighty Dredd

GROUP: Religious Cult, Mega-City One

Founded and led by its high priest Biggie Shanks, the Church of Almighty Dredd worshipped Judge Dredd and sacrificed 62 people to him by stabbing them with knives emblazoned with the Eagle of Justice. They were in for a shock when Dredd actually tracked them down, however, and put them all under arrest for their crimes. At first, Biggie Shanks thought the Judge must be an impostor, so they all resisted arrest, but when they saw him in action they realised he was the one true Dredd. Biggie himself was killed in the struggle, along with most of his followers, and only a few of the cult members survived their very own "Judgement Day"!

2000AD Progs 780-782

Below:
The congregation assembles at the Church of the Almighty Dredd and are introduced to High Priest Biggie Shanks

Citizen Snork

CITIZEN: Mega-City One

James Fenemore Snork wanted nothing more than to stand out in a crowd and, if he couldn't do it himself, he was determined to make sure that his nose did it for him! Inspired by an item on the popular vid-show "Just Plain Stupid", Snork decided to grow his nose so that it became the biggest one in Mega-City One. Using hormone injections, electro therapy and rigorous nose exercises he succeeded in cultivating a 119 centimetre long hooter and became an instant celebrity. Fame brought him many rewards, but it also attracted the attention of a man known as the "Collector", who stole all sorts of unique items and coveted Snork's nose. The man's first attempt to get it saw him chop off the 118 centimetre nose belonging to Snork's nasal rival Herbivore Bung by mistake, but when he had a second try at the nose-napping, Judge Dredd was waiting for him. The Collector was killed trying to make a hasty escape, while the unfortunate Snork got his nose caught in a garbage grinder during the struggle and Dredd was forced to shoot it off to save his life! Noseless, and so anonymous once more, Citizen Snork settled back into a life of obscurity, having selected a petite "Robsmith" artificial nose to adorn his face where once his mighty snout had been!

2000AD Progs 356-358
Judge Dredd the Megazine Volume 2: 45 (cameo)

Citizens' Committee for Compassion to Criminals

CITIZEN: The Judges' headquarters in Mega-City One

Run by Mrs Marjory Blackshack and Councillor Frank Petty, the C.C.C.C. believed that the Judge system had become too harsh and that love and understanding would be a better answer to crime. In the period following the reign of Cal, Chief Judge Griffin felt obliged to co-operate with such groups up to a point and he authorised an observation of a Judge in the course of his daily duties. Hence, Judge Dredd was accompanied by Mrs Blackshack and Councillor Petty on patrol, but their "compassion" got the better

of them. Duped into releasing a dangerous criminal after Dredd had captured him, Mrs Blackshack was kidnapped by the villain. Her experience as a hostage – while often more harrowing for her captor! – convinced poor Marjory that the Judges' methods might sometimes be preferable to her own. Unfortunately, she and the Councillor had six months to reflect on this lesson, since Judge Dredd sent them both to the Iso-Cubes for their part in the criminal's escape!

2000AD Progs 111, 112

Citizens Watchdog Committee

ORGANISATION: Judge monitoring group, Mega-City One

Having secretly made vid-slugs of the Judges in action, the self-appointed Citizens Watchdog Committee organised public viewings to illustrate the excesses of the Justice Department. Most of the citizens in attendance seemed to enjoy the violence in the vid-slugs, however, and the Judges soon rounded up the C.W.C. leaders on a charge of using the image of a Judge for entertainment purposes!

2000AD Prog 739

City-Def Units

ORGANISATIONS: Civil defence groups, Mega-City One

Each City Block has a City-Def Unit, to which any resident is eligible. These Units are intended to look after the interests of the citizens of their Block in times of crisis, but many have become paramilitary with an altogether different agenda. Some City-Def Units have armed themselves, frequently for offensive rather than defensive purposes.

See also **BLOCK WARS**

Introduced: 2000AD Prog 198

City Blocks

BUILDINGS: Self-contained tower blocks, Mega-City One

The majority of Mega-City One's 400 million citizens live in specially constructed City Block. These are fully self-contained living environments, equipped with al the necessay facilities, including schools, hospitals, shopping malls, leisure complexes and even civil defence organisations. These "cities" within the embrace of the "mega city" are able to provide everything a citizen may need from the cradle to the grave without ever stepping outside of their extraordinary confines. Somewhere in the region of 750 crimes are committed every day in each City Block, however, and stastically speaking 87 of these are likely to be major ones, so they are potential powder kegs and the Judges have to work hard to ensure they keep a lid on any trouble in each of them.

See also **BLOCK WARS, CITY-DEF UNITS**

Introduced: 2000AD Prog 117

Colt Widowmaker SNG Shotgun

WEAPON: High-powered rifle, Mega-City One Justice Department

As life has become harder on the streets of Mega-City One, the weaponry needs of the Judges have increased. The old Lawrod, therefore, has become rather outdated and the Colt M2000 was designed to replace it. Issued at first to Senior Judges only, the new shotgun proved highly effective and has now gone into mass production.

Introduced: 2000AD Prog 790

Condos

SPACE STATIONS: Space Living Communities, Earth Orbit

Part of Mega-City One's ongoing battle to house its overflowing population involves building vast space condominiums, capable of housing over 200,000 citizens. These Condos have their own oxygen plant, waste recycling system, factories, schools and hospitals, as well as large areas of rich artificial farmland. They are therefore close to being self-sufficient and even operate their own legal system, affiliated to the Justice Department. Although the Space Condos offer a good standard of living for their inhabitants, they do have one serious drawback – they are vulnerable to sabotage and a complete evacuation of one is near impossible in an emergency. This was demonstrated with the destruction of three Condos in the Gemini series.

Introduced: 2000AD Prog 319

Comic Running

CRIME: Supply of 20th Century comics in Mega-City One

The thrilling comics of the 20th Century (such as *2000AD*!) are banned in Mega-City One, due to their addictive nature. Hence, criminal gangs have arisen who supply this kind of material on micro-film slugs to addicts who are willing to pay high prices.

Introduced: 2000AD Prog 20

Committee for the Restoration of Civil Liberties

ORGANISATION: Civil rights activists group, Mega-City One

One of Mega-City One's many pressure groups in favour of a new democratic government, the Committee for the Restoration of Civil Liberties were one of the subscribers to the Democratic Charter March of 2109. Its leader, Bethann Rosie, was falsely discredited by the Judges before the March itself and she was forced to take a back seat as the remnants of her organisation were absorbed by the Democratic Charter Group following the tragic failure of the protest.

See also DEMOCRATIC GROUP, BETHANN ROSIE

2000AD Prog 531-533

Conred Conn

CITIZEN: Actor, Mega-CIty One

Often described as "the handsomest man in the world", Conred Conn was famously cast as Chief Judge Cal by Cal himself, when the mad Chief Judge planned a celebration of his life in movie form. He had earlier retired from the movie business after making such classics as "The Beasts That Ate Mars" because he wanted to be alone, but Cal made it quite clear that his head and body might be going their separate ways if he didn't accept the role. Fortunately for Conred, the tyrant was deposed before the film could be made, though the surviving rushes from the incomplete epic command a lot of creds on the Mega-City One vid-slug black market!

2000AD Prog 101, 838

Cool Johnny Cool

CITIZEN: Deejay, Mega-City One

Despite being Radio Radio Radio's top Deejay, Cool Johnny Cool was one of the most irritating guys to ever hit the airwaves. When a blow to the head awakened Johnny's latent psi-talent he was swamped by the negative feedback from people all over Mega-City One and, finally, unable to bear this influx of hatred, he stuck his head in a garbage grinder!

2000AD Prog 560, 740 (dies)

Psi-Judge Corey

JUDGE: Psi-Division, Mega-City One

New to the streets of the city, Psi-Judge Corey was called in to assess the motivations behind the Exploding Man. Being a true empath, Corey found the man's agony hard to bear and Judge Dredd was unimpressed by her consequent show of emotion. When assigned to help Dredd investigate a religious grouping, worshipping Gaia, he asked for a replacement Psi operative because she refused to carry out a Deep Psi-probe on one of Gaia's followers. Dredd's resolution was to ban the religious grouping, but the incident had awakened an interest within Corey and instilled a massive doubt in herself as a Judge.

In the meantime, she had become good friends with Psi-Judge Anderson. Eventually, Corey couldn't bear the pain of existence any longer. Her suicide note, written to her only friend, affected Judge Anderson deeply, causing her to re-evaluate her own life.

See also EXPLODING MAN

2000AD Progs 471, 614-622, 641, 644, 760 (cameo)

2000AD Sci-Fi Specials 1988, 1989 (dies)

Corn O'Connor

CITIZEN: Game Show Host, Mega-City One

As host of game show "Any Confessions?", Corn O'Connor enjoyed the second highest ratings of any vid-show in Mega-City One. Contestants had to confess to ever more serious crimes in order to win a large cash prize – and a Judge was waiting in the wings to arrest them! Judge Dredd opposed the show on the grounds that it incited crime, but the Council of Five endorsed it, since it was a valuable aid to their crime clear-up rate. Only when Deputy Chief Judge Pepper was gunned down by an aspiring contestant did Corn O'Connor find his show off the air.

2000AD Prog 201

Judge Corzo

JUDGE: Banana City

Part of the corrupt Judge system in Ciudad Barranquilla, Judge Corzo first met Dredd and Hershey when they visited his city in search of the renegade Judge Kurten. He later participated in the final assault on Sabbat when Judges from all over the world tried to survive the Necromagus's "Judgement Day". Corzo was captured and killed by the black magician.

See also BANANA CITY, SABBAT

2000AD Progs 623-625, 794, 795

Judge Dredd the Megazine Volume 2: 8 (dies)

Cosmus

ALIEN: Supremely powerful being, high above Mega-City One

Convinced that the people of Mega One were too pathetic to deserve him as a God, Cosmus made a bet with his sister, Venus Muncia. Having bestowed incredible power upon an ordinary citizen, Cosmus was convinced he would make a mess of things, though Venus had more confidence. Sure enough, the citizen proved a hopeless failure and Cosmus won his bet. However, Judge Dredd warned him not to meddle in the affairs of his city in future.

2000AD Prog 600

Council of Five

JUDGES: Ruling Executive Body, Mega-City One

The Council of Five consists of five Senior Judges – the Deputy Chief Judge, plus the heads of the Special Judicial Squad, Psi-Division and Tek-Division, along with one other Senior Judge. Meeting in the Grand Hall of Justice to deliberate over the most important issues affecting Mega-City One, each member represents certain interests within the Justice Department – between them, the Deputy Chief Judge and the Senior Judge look after the interests of ordinary Street Judges, the Academy of Law and the Judge-Warders, while the head of Tek-Division has responsibility for all scientific aspects of the Department's work, including Med-Division and Genetic Control.

Following the terrible reign of Chief Judge Cal, the Council was imbued with the power to challenge the Chief Judge in extreme circumstances, but in most situations they must yield to his or her wishes. The Council of Five has in fact only just been reformed, having been previously disbanded by the now departed Chief Judge McGruder.

Introduced: 2000AD Prog 86

Above:
Dredd goes before the Council of Five - accused of murder!

Crime Blitz

PROCEDURE: Legal Search, Mega-City One

Crime Blitzes can be carried out by the Judges at any time on any citizen, with or without cause for suspicion, according to the Mega-City One Criminal Code, Section 59(D). Forcing entry to a citizen's home, the Judges are empowered to make a thorough search without warning knowing that no-one is completely free of all crime. Invariably some kind of offence is discovered, but penalties for minor infringements are fairly lenient in these circumstances, since the fear of committing future crimes inspired by this random search is more valuable to the Judges than an arrest.

Introduced: 2000AD Prog 128

Cosmic Punks

GROUP: Punk Gang, Mega-CIty One

When the Chief Judge Cal was deposed law and order broke down in parts of Mega-City One. Southside Sector 41 was declared a no-go area for Judges by the Cosmic Punks, a dangerous group of lawbreakers led by Gestapo Bob Harris, File-Tooth and Brainstorm. They worked from their own "Hall of Justus" and dispensed their own form of justice to anyone they came across. Judge Dredd was determined to stamp the authority of the Judges on the city once more, so he took on the Punks all by himself. By arresting them all and banishing them from Mega-City One for ten years, he proved that the Judges were back in firm control of the city!

See also GESTAPO BOB HARRIS
2000AD Progs 110, 124, 125

Cursed Earth

LOCATION: Atomic wasteland, former U.S.A. heartland

Following the Atomic Wars of 2070 most of the U.S.A. became a nuclear wasteland. With only the three Mega-Cities surviving, the remainder of the country became known as the "Cursed Earth". Although considered unfit for human habitation, the Cursed Earth is populated by all manner of creatures, scraping a living in a tough environment. Since the Atomic Wars, genetic mutations appeared, but mutants are banned from living in the cities, so they are forced to make their homes there. The area is largely deindustrialised and the communities are mostly poor, rural groupings, often dominated by quasi-religious doctrine. In more extreme cases, these communities become cults well enough organised to threaten Mega-City One as a revenge for the way the city has treated these outcasts.

Introduced: 2000AD Prog 4 (concept), 61 (term)

Judge Dana

JUDGE: Renegade, Mega-City One

Facing a corruption rap, Judge Dana realised he was about to be arrested, so he took desperate steps to avoid being sent to the harsh Penal Colony on Titan. By putting Huckleberry Pym under deep hypnosis and arranging for some hasty face change surgery, Dana was able to successfully switch identities with the hapless citizen, who wound up being convicted in his place. The switch was only discovered four years later, when Dana became very short of credits and decided to commit a robbery. His combat prowess gave him away as a Judge and, when he was captured, his true identity was soon uncovered. Dana then had to swap places with Pym once more, as the unfortunate citizen was freed from the Titan Penal Colony and the crooked Judge was sent there to begin a life sentence!

2000AD Prog 369

The Dark Judges

JUDGES: Deadworld

Judge Death, Judge Fear, Judge Fire and Judge Mortis are collectively known as the Dark Judges. Hailing from a planet in another dimension which is now only known as Deadworld, they were so effective in their mission to eliminate crime there that they exterminated all potential perpetrators, too. None of the Dark Judges are truly "living" creatures anymore either, since the mystical Sisters of Death transformed all four of them into supernatural entities – ethereal beings inhabiting non-living host bodies. Consequently, they are impossible to kill.

The Dark Judges were satisfied with their success on Deadworld, so when a group of inter-dimensional travellers inadvertently brought them dimension jumping technology, they were happy to kill the visitors and leave it at that. Judge Death alone was intrigued at the prospect of finding new worlds to "Judge", so he went against the opinion of his colleagues and travelled to Mega-City One without them. When he didn't return, the other Dark Judges decided to go and look for him. They found him trapped inside the body of Psi-Judge Anderson, who was in turn trapped inside a casing of solid Boing, on display in the Justice Department's Hall of Heroes. They arranged for Anderson and Death to be released, then Judge Death led the Dark Judges into battle in the

Billy Carter Block. They claimed thousands of victims before Judge Dredd and Psi-Judge Anderson managed to outmanoevre them and they were forced to retreat to their home dimension. The Mega-City One Judges then used a Dimension Jump Globe which had been liberated from the Dark Judges to follow them. On Deadworld, Anderson was able to channel the torment of their billions of victims to exorcise all four of the evil Judges and it seemed as though their threat was over.

In fact, the Dark Judges had merely been weakened by this assault and four years later they had mustered enough strength to dupe Anderson into returning to Deadworld to restore their power. She unwittingly helped them regain their physical forms and they repaid her by leaving her for dead, as they set off to Mega-City One once more. They returned to their task of eliminating the cause of crime – life! - and thousands more victims were claimed before Anderson made it home and hit upon an idea to defeat them. The Justice Department's own Dimensional Studies Laboratory had come up with a D-Jump device, an imperfect version of the Dimension Jump Globes used by the Dark Judges, Anderson used to dispatch Judges Death, Fear, Fire and Mortis off to limbo.

When the Sisters of Death launched their own attack on Mega-City One, they took control of Judge Kraken – the former Judda who was given the unenviable tastk of of posing as the new Judge Dredd – and made him force his way into the Dimensional Studies Laboratory. He was able to retrieve the four Dark Judges from limbo and they were delighted with their best opportunity yet to bring their "justice" to the city. They even appointed the hapless Kraken an honorary Dark Judge and had him accompany them, wearing his Dredd badge! The Sisters of Death were eventually defeated, however, and the evil Judges were unable to maintain their control of Mega-City One without them. Judge Mortis's and Judge Fire's bodies were soon destroyed and their ethereal forms were kept in check by Psi-Judge Anderson, until they could be trapped in Boing. Judge Fear suffered a similar fate, although his physical form was imprisoned along with his non-corporeal one. Judge Death alone remained at large once the city had been freed from their evil influence, but the menace of the Dark Judges was over – at least for a while!

See also BOING, JUDGE DEATH, JUDGE FEAR,
JUDGE FIRE, JUDGE MORTIS, SISTERS OF DEATH

2000AD Progs 224-228, 416-424, 672, 684, 688-690, 694, 696-699, 734
Judge Dredd the Megazine Volume 1: 10-12
Judge Dredd the Megazine Volume 2: 45 (cameo), 50
Judge Dredd Annual 1983 (cameo)
2000AD Graphic Novel: Young Death

Dave the Orang Utan

ANIMAL: Mayor, Mega-City One

When Billy Smairt's constant companion, an orang utan called Dave, managed to pick the winner of the Superbowl while all the so-called experts got it wrong, he was signed up to appear on the vid-show "Tipsters Tonite". A run of success followed for the ape and he achieved a 61% average success rate with his predictions – twice the rating of his nearest human rival! Dave was not without his detractors, however, and they believed he would be exposed as a fraud when they asked him to pick the winner of the upcoming Mayoral election. The orang utan was given pictures of all the candidates, but he rejected them all and selected a publicity still of himself instead. His critics were delighted with this apparent mistake, but his choice got Dave's fans thinking. Within a few hours, the ape had enough nominations to enter the race for Mayor and his candidature was readily accepted by the Justice Department. Not altogether surprisingly, the orang utan stormed to victory in one of the biggest landslides in Mega-City One history and the city gained its first true "banana republican"!

Sadly, Dave's reign as Mayor lasted less than two years, as he and his owner, Billy Smairt, were both murdered in the street on the way home from Salmonella's Bar, their favourite drinking spot. Political motives for the killings were suspected, but it turned out that Billy was the real target, since the murderer was his best friend – barman Mo Molinsky – who misguidedly believed that he stood to collect an enormous life insurance payout on Smairt's death. Thus, poor Dave was the innocent victim of a motiveless killing, but he is still widely regarded as Mega-City One's finest Mayor!

2000AD
Progs 366-368, 443 (dies)

The Dead Man

JUDGE: Judge Dredd himself after taking the Long Walk into the Cursed Earth

When Yassa Povey found the gnarled remains of a body in the Cursed Earth wilds just outside Bubbletown no-one was more surprised than he that the man was still alive. Young Yassa christened him "The Dead Man" and the boy's parents took him into their home to tend the man's injuries, fully expecting him to die soon anyway. But the Dead Man refused to die. Although he had been through some terrible trauma causing him to lose his memory, he knew one thing – he must not die! There was a very important reason for him to stay alive and the only way to discover what that could be was to recover his memory and find out who he was. To this end, he and Yassa set out across the Cursed Earth in search of the scene of whatever had happened to turn him into the Dead Man. Following an arduous journey, they made it to the deserted town of Crowley where they found the wreckage of a Judge's Lawmaster Bike and a Judge's badge.

The Dead Man's memories came flooding back as he recalled the nightmare events that caused the destruction of the town and his own disfigurement. The Sisters of Death – fellow evil entities from Judge Death's world – had projected their terrifying countenances at the place to kill everyone. However, their power was dependent on the minds of their victims giving in to them, so there was just one strong-willed survivor from their assault – Judge Dredd. Having previously resigned as a Judge and taken the Long Walk into the Cursed Earth, Dredd had spent some 100 days bringing law to the radioactive wasteland before his run-in with the evil Sisters. With his memory restored, 'The Dead Man" knew that his destiny lay back in Mega-City One, fighting against whatever horror the Dark Judges and the Sisters of Death might have created there in his absence.

See also JUDGE DREDD, SISTERS OF DEATH,
YASSA POVEY

2000AD Progs 650-668

Deadworld

WORLD: The Dark Judges' homeworld, Death Dimension

Deadworld was once an ordinary world not unlike Earth, populated by people not unlike Earth people. They even had Judges, too – but there the similarity ended. These Judges, led by the appropriately named Judge Death, developed their own moral code, their own special brand of law. To the Dark Judges of Deadworld, life itself was a crime. After all, who could deny that all crimes were committed by the living – that only the dead could be truly innocent of the intent to perpetrate criminal acts? The solution to law and order, on Deadworld was obvious to Judge Death and his most trusted lieutenants. Eliminate life, eliminate crime. It was as simple as that. Deadworld's original name is unknown, but the Dark Judges and their mystical compatriots the Sisters of Death have ensured that the place lives up to its current name perfectly. Even they have left now, seeking more people to judge – and more life to extinguish – in other dimensions, Deadworld became a desolate place, tormented by the departed souls of the Dark Judges' victims.

See also JUDGE DEATH, DARK JUDGES,
SISTERS OF DEATH, PSI-JUDGE ANDERSON

Introduced: 2000AD Prog 149

DEADWORLD!

LONG AGO ITS JUDGES REALISED ALL CRIME WAS COMMITTED BY THE LIVING. THEREFORE, LIFE ITSELF WAS DECLARED ILLEGAL.

THEY JUDGED THEIR PEOPLE WITHOUT MERCY. THEY WIPED THE CURSE OF LIFE FROM THEIR WORLD. NOW ONLY THE FOUR DARK JUDGES REMAINED – AND THE TORMENTED SOULS OF THE JUDGED!

DROKK! WHAT A NIGHTMARE!

Judge Death

JUDGE: Deadworld

When a young boy called Sidney on a planet quite like Earth started displaying sadistic tendencies by torturing his dog, little did his parents suspect the kind of horror they had spawned. Sidney went on to kill his dog and tried to murder his sister as he explored his fascination with death. It certainly didn't take him long to work out that the dog no longer got him into trouble once it was dead. Sidney's father was a dentist and had his own sadistic streak, so when he knew the boy shared his interest, he took him along to work to observe the agony of his patients. Eventually, Sidney's father started killing his patients, however, so the boy shopped him to the Judges and then helped them to execute him! Dentistry had a certain appeal for Sidney, but he had set his sights on a higher calling. Signing up with the Judges, he looked forward to getting his licence to kill, but he got in as much practice as possible beforehand anyway. Once he got his badge and gun there was no stopping Sidney – or Judge "Death" as his fellow Cadets had christened him – and he declared that life itself should be deemed a crime, since all crime is committed by the living. Not all of his colleagues supported his views, but three other young Judges could see the wisdom in Judge Death's philosophy and they became his most trusted lieutenants. A chance meeting with two weird sisters, Phobia and Nausea, provided Death with the final piece of his

"justice jigsaw" when they offered to kill him. Realising that he could not be pure while he still lived, Death agreed and the Sisters used their mystic potions to transform him into an undead creature with awesome supernatural powers. They did the same for his lieutenants – Fear, Fire and Mortis – and the Dark Judges were born. Judge Death then killed the Chief Judge, took his job and declared life illegal on the planet he soon "Deadworld". When a group of inter-dimensional travellers inadvertently brought dimension jumping technology to Deadworld, Judge Death was intrigued at the prospect of finding new worlds to "Judge", so he travelled to Mega-City One to start dispensing justice there. Despite endless defeats by Anderson and Dredd since then, Death's zeal for "Justice" remains undiminished.

See also PSI-JUDGE , ANDERSON,
BRIAN SKUTER, DARK JUDGES,
SISTERS OF DEATH

2000AD Progs 149-151, 224-228, 416-424, 520, 612, 613, 672, 679, 684, 694, 696, 697, 700, 701, 734, 901, 902

Judge Dredd the Megazine Volume 1: 1-12

Judge Dredd the Megazine Volume 2: 15, 44, 45, 50

Judge Dredd Annuals 1983 (cameo), 1987 (cameo)

Judge Dredd Yearbooks 1994 (cameo), 1995 (cameo)

2000AD Yearbook 1992 (cameo)

Judgement on Gotham 1

2000AD Graphic Novel: Young Death

Death Aid

EVENT: Sponsored Hunt, Mega-City One

Above:
**Special Death
Aid T-shirt**

Following the horrors of Judge Death's Necropolis in Mega-City One, the Hunters Club wanted to show the charitable side of their natures and do their bit for the orphans of the city, so they organised "Death Aid", a special sponsored hunt! Each member went out to stalk and kill as many people as possible, in order to clock up the sponsor money and they could even poach each other's scores by killing their fellow members.

In fact, the Chairman of the Hunters Club, Elmort Devries, had the competition sewn up from the start because the Death Aid badges he gave out at the start of the hunt to his members were wired to explode on his command, so he was able to claim any of their scores whenever he wanted to!

See also ELMORT DEVRIES, HUNTERS CLUB

Introduced: 2000AD Prog 711

Judge Degaulle

JUDGE: Renegade, Mega-City One

When Judge Dredd was investigating the vigilante activities of the so-called Executioner, he formed the impression that she might be a Judge and DeGaulle seemed to fit the bill. He interrogated her mercilessly, but his lie detector checked out the fact that she was clean. Judge DeGaulle was highly resentful over his treatment of her, however, and almost five years later she had her opportunity to pay him back. Working temporarily with the SJS, she was asked to perform a strip search on Dredd when he was selected for a Random Physical Abuse Test, enabling her to inflict the kind of humiliation on him that she had previously suffered at his hands.

Tragically, DeGaulle's career on the streets of Mega-City One came to an abrupt end after fifteen years of active service when she was horrifically injured in a Las-Blaster attack. Badly crippled, she was transferred to Justice Control, where she could still perform a valuable role despite her disability. Bitterness ran deep in DeGaulle following this incident and she was only too happy to aid Judge Grice when he tried to sabotage the Democratic Referendum organised by the Judges in 2113 to decide the future government of Mega-City One. When her involvement in Grice's plans was uncovered, Judge DeGaulle was sentenced to the mandatory twenty years on Titan, along with her fellow conspirators. Life was even harder for her than for most of the other inmates of the Penal Colony, due to her disability, and DeGaulle was a broken woman in more ways than one. When Grice led his mass breakout from the prison, she was left behind and left for dead by her former allies.

See also JUDGE GRICE, RANDOM PHYSICAL ABUSE TEST

2000AD Progs 293, 518, 754, 834–837

***Above:*
Renegade
Judge Degaulle**

Judge Dekker

JUDGE: Mega-City One

Regarded by Judge Dredd as his best Rookie, bar none, Judge Dekker graduated with honour from the Academy of Law on his recommendation. She was always likely to impress him, since her standard

DREDD – DECKER! GUNFIRE BACKSTAGE! INVESTIGATING!

reference text at the Academy was Dredd's Comportment, the Senior Judge's own seminal guide to becoming a good Judge. Dekker distinguished herself on the streets of Mega-City One in the years which followed her attainment of the full eagle and she worked alongside Dredd himself on many occasions. In fact, she accompanied her mentor when he was rounding up the conspirators who had plotted to murder him and sabotage the Democratic Referendum of 2113. Having survived the dangers of being a Judge on the streets of Mega-City One for more than eight years, Dekker was killed when Sabbat the Necromagus launched his zombie attack on the city. She was defending Gate One against a seemingly inexhaustible supply of reanimated corpses intent on invading the city, when she ran out of ammunition and the monsters broke through. Realising that the only way to stem the tide of their invasion was to blow them up with a grenade, Judge Dekker took this option, knowing full well that she would perish in the blast too.

See also DREDD'S COMPORTMENT,

SABBAT THE NECROMAGUS

2000AD Progs 370–373, 746–748, 754, 790, 791 (dies)

The Democratic Tendency

ORGANISATION: Civil rights group, Mega-City One

Although there have been many other political groups advocating different forms of "democracy" for Mega-City One, none of them have influenced events and opinions in the city more than the Democratic Tendency. This is mostly due to one act of "terrorism" - or "selfless bravery", depending on how you look at it – which occurred on 13th March 2108. In a deliberate and calculated action, Hester Hyman, Franklin Lund, J. William Williams and Roofer Tuttle stormed the studios of Channel 48's popular breakfast show. They were armed and ready to fight, but hurt no-one as they broadcast the demands of the "Democratic Charter". They called for: 1) "An immediate return to democratic principles. The people must control the Judges! The Judges should not control the people!"; 2) "The return of basic freedoms taken away over decades of oppression!"; and 3) "A repeal of the harsh penalties for minor infringements!"

When they blasted their way into the studio to recapture Channel 48 from the Democratic Tendency, the Judges had no way of knowing how much trouble they were bringing down upon their own heads. By killing Hester Hyman and her cohorts when they refused to surrender, the Judges gave the democratic movement what it sorely needed... four martyrs around whom to unite. Shortly afterwards the Hester Hyman Trust was formed, and this group was instrumental in forming the Democratic Charter Group – uniting many of the democratic organisations in Mega-City One. Consequently, a little more than a year after the Channel 48 incident, the Democratic Tendency had been transformed from another irrelevant splinter group into the inspiration for a democratic movement powerful enough to mount a realistic challenge to the Judges' rule.

See also HESTER HYMAN, GORT HYMAN, THE HESTER HYMAN TRUST, DEMOCRATIC CHARTER GROUP

Introduced: 2000AD Prog 460

Democratic Charter Group

ORGANISATION: Democratic Pressure Group, Mega-City One

Inspired by the sacrifices made by the members of the Democratic Tendency when they seized control of Channel 48, the Democratic Charter Group was formed around a year later. A coalition between the Hester Hyman Trust, the Sons of the Constitution, the Freedom League, the Democratic Urge and the Committee for the Restoration of Civil Liberties, the Group had as its central aim the fulfilment of the Democratic Charter as proposed by the Democratic Tendency. To this end, the Democratic Charter March of 2109 was organised and some sixteen million citizens took to the streets of Mega-City One in support of democracy. Although the Judges successfully broke up the March, the ideas of the Democratic Charter Group had gained enough of an echo to eventually trigger the Democratic Referendum of 2113.

See also DEMOCRATIC TENDENCY, HESTER HYMAN TRUST, FREEDOM LEAGUE, DEMOCRATIC URGE, COMMITTEE FOR RESTORATION OF CIVIL LIBERTIES

2000AD Progs 531-533

The Democratic Urge

ORGANISATION: Civil rights group, Mega-City One

Led by Blondel Dupré, the Democratic Urge was at the centre of the unification of most of the civil rights groups arguing for democracy in Mega-City One. It ceased functioning as an organisation in its own right when Dupré announced the formation of the Democratic Charter Group and it instead provided a good deal of the structure which went into the newly created coalition.

See also BLONDEL DUPRÉ, DEMOCRATIC CHARTER

2000AD Progs 531-533

Dennis the DNA Man

CLONE: Product of illegal cloning experiments

Like his more famous namesake, Professor Milton D. Frankenstein was obsessed with the creation of life and the DNA Man was the result of his experiments using his own DNA. Although the technology involved with successful human cloning had long been perfected by the Judges of Mega-City One, this was a fairly tightly guarded secret and private experimentation in this area had long been outlawed. Frankenstein defied the law to create a series of clones, but "Dennis" was the only one to possess truly "human" qualities. Willing to continue his work at any cost, the Professor was unconcerned about the feelings of his creations, or even of his assistant who he ordered Dennis to murder. When Frankenstein's activities were finally exposed by the Judges, his creation was forced to try and protect him, even at the risk of his own life. However, when Frankenstein tried to flee the city, Dennis – a flawed clone, but an otherwise innocent pawn of the evil Professor – turned on his master and perished along with him, having tasted life for only the briefest of periods.

See also PROFESSOR MILTON D. FRANKENSTEIN

2000AD Progs 113-115 (dies)

Judge Dredd Annual 1983 (cameo)

Deputy Chief Judge

SOCIAL CATEGORY: Deputy to the Chief Judge, Mega-City One

A position which has not always been filled, the job of Deputy Chief Judge in Mega-City One is a rather peculiar one. Despite its grand title, little real responsibility comes with the post, since the Chief Judge rules the city either on a purely individual basis, or sometimes in consultation with the Council of Five. Although the Deputy Chief Judge sits on the Council, he or she has no more power than the Divisional heads and other Senior Judges alongside them. Even if something should happen to the Chief Judge, the Deputy Chief Judge is only entitled to assume power temporarily, while a new leader is selected. In this sense, the post is relatively unimportant, since in the absence of a Deputy Chief Judge, any Council member can be nominated to become acting Chief Judge in an emergency.

Introduced: 2000AD Prog 86

Devlin Waugh

CITIZEN: Investigator, Vatican City

One of the World's most eccentric characters, Devlin Waugh is not only a sometime investigator for the Vatican Judges, he also acts as a spiritual envoy for them and enjoys full diplomatic status. On top of that, he is a freelance exorcist, a part-time cat breeder and a full-time hedonist! Spending the majority of his time in the pursuit of pure pleasure, Devlin regularly partakes of alcohol, tobacco and steroids, and he has a large collection of "Vintage European Erotica". A man of considerable stature, he was an Olympic athlete until he was banned for illegal steroid abuse, so his size and strength make him a formidable opponent in a scrap.

Left:
Vatican Investigator Devlin Waugh

Devlin Waugh needed all of his many and varied talents when the Vatican Justice Department sent him to investigate reports of an outbreak of vampirism at Aquatraz – an underwater prison deep beneath the Black Atlantic near Mega-City One. There were indeed vampires there, but even the experienced exorcist found himself unable to stop them from overwhelming the staff and prisoners in Aquatraz. They were swiftly transformed into members of the bloodsucking undead and Devlin himself was eventually infected with the vampire virus, too. He still managed to overcome the creatures in the end, when the whole prison was destroyed, and he was soon rescued from the disgusting waters of the Black Atlantic. As a vampire, he now has to feed every day on blood to stay alive, a fact that has played havoc with his previous attraction to the delights of fine cuisine. He is also vulnerable to direct sunlight, so he mostly travels by night.

Strangely enough, Devlin's talents are even more in demand now that he is a fully-fledged member of the undead, but he resists the requests for his services whenever he can, in order to pursue his own interests. His diplomatic status is a positive boon to his unconventional lifestyle, though, since it allows him free movement in most parts of the World, even when his activities contravene local laws. It was a cause of great chagrin to Judge Dredd when he was unable to refuse Devlin admission to Mega-City One for an international cat breeders' show, despite the fact that he was carrying thirty-nine prohibited items with him, along with a huge supply of blood to quench his vampiric appetite during his stay. Dredd is not one to give up lightly, however, and he enforced quarantine regulations on Devlin's cat Grendel instead – meaning it either had to spend three weeks in quarantine or submit to castration before it could enter the city. Enraged at being caught out through this technicality, Devlin Waugh set off home, taking Grendel and his thirty-eight other prohibited items with him!

Judge Dredd the Megazine Volume 2: 1-9, 26

Judge Dredd Yearbook 1994

2000AD Graphic Novel: Swimming in Blood

Dimension Jump Globe

DEVICE: Dimensional transportation machine, Dimension Zinf 44/07

Brought to Deadworld by a group of travellers from a dimension they called Zinf 44/07, Dimension Jump Globes afforded Judge Death and his fellow Dark Judges a fantastic new opportunity to visit new worlds on which to dispense their own special brand of "jusssstice". Death alone was willing to use the technology at first and he employed one of the extremely compact hand-held Dimensional Jump Globes to travel to Mega-City One. The devices were studied by the top Mega-City Tek-Judges after this, but the technology baffled even them. Since completely empty dimensions outnumber functional ones by a ratio of several millions to one, the way in which a Dimension Jump Globe manages to select a viable destination each time it is used remains a mystery.

See also JUDGE DEATH, THE DARK JUDGES, DEADWORLD

Introduced: 2000AD Prog 228

Dink Jonson Jowett

CITIZEN: Juve, Mega-City One

When he found a way into the Fitzenheimer Garden, Dink Jowett thought that he had entered a whole new world. It was like nothing he had ever seen in Mega-City One and he was determined to keep the place a secret. This proved difficult, however, when he was picked up by Judge Dredd, who suspected him of a crime and Dink's "trespass" on the garden eventually came to light, but Martha Fitzenheimer had no wish to press charges against the Juve. However, Dredd charged him with other crimes and after a spell in the 'Cubes, Dink Jowett and his girlfriend Rosie became regular visitors to the garden, and they become firm friends with Martha Fitzenheimer. Disaster struck, though, when a vicious band of criminals led by Blender McCoy took refuge there and poor Dink lost his life protecting the garden against the criminal.

2000AD Progs 783, 784 (dies)

2000AD Sci-Fi Special 1986

Above: Dink Jowett in the "secret garden"

The Dinosaur Man

CITIZEN: Rex Peters, Mega-City One **CITIZEN: Airborne Passenger Vehicle**

Cyril J. Ratfinkle worked at a genetic research laboratory in Mega-City One which had access to some of the blood of the fearsome Tyrannosaurus Rex, Satanus, and he was keen to know what would happen is someone were to drink it. Consequently, he stole some of the blood and secretly slipped it into some wine drunk by one of his neighbours – Rex Peters – and then observed its effects. Poor unfortunate Rex soon found himself transformed into a Dinosaur Man and could not help himself from killing his own wife and then going out in search of flesh to eat. Ratfinkle was one of his first victims, so he was unable to see his little experiment through to the end, but the damage had been done. Judge Dredd was forced to kill Rex Peters, rather than allow him to continue with his unwitting rampage as Dinosaur Man, which came as a great relief to the man.

2000AD Progs 152-154

Dinosaur National Park

LOCATION: Recreational Park, Cursed Earth

One of America's most popular attractions, the Dinosaur National Park was founded in the middle of the 21st Century when cloning dinosaurs from ancient remains became a realistic scientific possibility. When the Atomic Wars of 2070 ripped a massive nuclear scar through the heart of the country, the Park was abandoned and the dinosaurs which survived were free to roam the Cursed Earth. The Tyrannosaurus Rex Satanus was the Park's star draw and he was among the survivors, free to wreak havoc among Cursed Earth communities for years after its closure.

See also SATANUS

Introduced: 2000AD Prog 73

Left: **Rex Peters becomes the Dinosaur Man**

Don Uggie Apelino

ANIMAL: Intelligence-enhanced ape, Mega-City One

Believing the operations of his gangster mob, the Ape Gang, to be legitimate, Don Uggie Apelino took the extraordinary step of petitioning the Judges to help them stop the rival East Side Mob from "muscling in" on their territory. Understandably the Judges took him none too seriously and refused to help, resulting in a brutal gang war erupting on Don Uggie's home turf, the area of Mega-City One known as "The Jungle". This led to the Judges quickly becoming involved and they soon put an end to the war by arresting virtually all the surviving participants. Don Uggie Apelino and his lieutenants, Fast Eeek and Joe Bananas, therefore found themselves doing time... in the Mega-City Zoo! The Don resented this treatment bitterly and when he got out, less than two years later, he put out a contract on Judge Dredd himself. Offering a one billion credit reward to anyone who could kill the Judge, Don Uggie set out to steal the money from the organisers of Mega-City One's annual lottery. He was apprehended doing this as the Judges were waiting for him to strike and he was soon on his way back to the Zoo. Poor Don Uggie actually had the winning lottery numbers, too, but Judge Dredd wouldn't let the criminal collect his rightful winnings and burnt his ticket instead!

The Mega-City Zoo was later wrecked during the Apocalypse War and Don Uggie Apelino and a few of his cohorts escaped. Unfortunately, they were exposed to a high level of radiation and soon regressed to a primitive state, forgetting who or what they had once been. The Don was still a natural leader, heading a large pack of apes which marauded through a nuclear-scarred Sector of the city, but Judge Dredd soon caught up with them and this time the sentence for their crimes was death.

See also APE GANG

2000AD Progs 39

2000AD Sci-Fi Special 1979

2000AD Annual 1983 (dies)

Below: **Don Uggie Apelino (front) with Fast Eeek and Joe Bananas**

Doomsayers

**GROUP: Quasi-religious cult,
Mega-City One**

When Sabbat came to Earth and prepared to raise the dead all over the world to assemble a fearsome zombie army, a new religious cult grew up in Mega-City One. Calling themselves the Doomsayers, they predicted impending doom for the planet and were very vocal in spreading the news that the end of the World was nigh. Unlike many similar cranks who preceded them, the Doomsayers actually seemed likely to win the argument when Sabbat's horrific plans were in full swing, but the group died away again fairly quickly when the Necromagus was finally defeated.

See SABBAT THE NECROMAGUS

2000AD Progs 789, 792, 798

Doomsday Dogs

**GROUP: Mutant terrorists,
Cursed Earth**

Followers of the near-mystical Father Earth, the Doomsday Dogs were his vicious advance guard. They invaded Mega-City One and planted explosives in the Power Tower, where heat from molten lava was used as an energy source. Although the Judges caught and arrested them, they only diffused one of the bombs they had planted. The other one would be activated by a huge power surge. Unfortunately, with the election for Mayor carried by individual push-button responses from citizens all over the city, that surge was imminent and Power Tower was doomed!

See also FATHER EARTH, POWER TOWER

2000AD Progs 122, 123

Drag Nets

**DEVICE: Net for capturing criminals,
Mega-City One Justice Department**

Especially useful for capturing criminals in aerial confrontations, these mechanised nets are very useful to the Judges. While they are used in Mega-City One itself, they have proved even more valuable to Judges using Hover Bikes in Luna-1, the city's moon colony.

Introduced: 2000AD Prog 48

Dream Palace

**BUILDING: Leisure Complex,
Mega-City One**

The Dream Palace offers the citizens of Mega-City One the opportunity to experience their wildest dreams. On payment of a reasonable fee, the Palace's customers are hooked up to sophisticated machinery that puts them into an extremely realistic virtual reality environment of their own making. Generally, this is a harmless enough pastime – although it is not unknown for criminals to use the "Dream Machines" to plot elaborate crimes!

Introduced: 2000AD Prog 26

Judge Joe Dredd
See page 51

The Dredd Act

LAW: Mega-City One

After an encounter with the evil Doctor Galt who was using animals in his research to develop a common cold culture, Judge Dredd was so moved by their plight – particularly that of a guinea pig called Monty who was badly mistreated by the Doctor and was due to be killed – that he instituted a change in the law to protect them. The Dredd Act was introduced in 2101 banning all experimentation on animals in Mega-City One and Monty became known as the "guinea pig who changed the law".

See also MONTY THE GUINEA PIG

Introduced: 2000AD Prog 126

The Dredd Syndrome

AFFLICTION: Psychosis, Mega-City One

In a city where the penalty for even the most minor misdemeanour can be extremely harsh, it is not uncommon for a citizen to develop a deep-rooted guilt complex after committing the most trivial of crimes. Occasionally this complex can become a full-blown psychosis, as the spectre of retribution from the Judges becomes too much for the sufferer to bear. The condition is a recognised one in Mega-City One and is referred to as the Dredd Syndrome Justice Department's Med-Judges, in deference to the most feared lawman of them all!

Introduced: 2000AD Prog 481

Dredd's Comportment

BOOK: Judges' Reference text, Mega-City One

When Cadet Judges are studying at the Academy of Law in Mega-City One, they tend to follow the text of a single reference work throughout their training. Several highly-respected Judges have contributed versions of this central guide, but the most popular by far is Dredd's Comportment. Outlining all the qualities required of an effective Judge and exploring the harsh but necessary forms of law enforcement in Mega-City One, Judge Dredd's book has provided the inspiration to many fine Judges who have benefited tremendously from the great lawman's experience and wisdom contained therein.

See also JUDGE DEKKER

Introduced: 2000AD Prog 373

Judge Joe Dredd

JUDGE: Mega-City One

Cloned from the DNA of the legendary Chief Judge Fargo, both Joe and Rico Dredd excelled at the Academy of Law and graduated with honour to become full Judges in 2079. Joe had always been the model Cadet, scoring superbly in every test and sticking so rigidly to the rules laid down by his Judge-Tutors that he was nicknamed "Old Stoney Face" by his fellow Cadets. Only Rico could beat him and invariably did, although his extra flair came with a fatal flaw in his personality. Joe had to arrest his own clone brother shortly after they hit the streets when Rico started up a protection racket, and it was only then that the Justice Department realised what a special Judge they had in Joe. Morphy, the Judge who passed him on his final street assessment, had recognised Joe Dredd's potential right away and they became firm friends over the years. In fact, Judge Morphy was almost like a father to Dredd and he was always there for him if he needed any advice. Judge Dredd spent the next twenty years on the streets of Mega-City One, gaining the experience and the reputation that made him the city's top lawman. The Judge's fears were realised when Call-me-Kenneth started the Robot Wars and thousands of Judges and citizens lost their lives before the robots were defeated. Dredd had been helped by Walter the Wobot during the conflict and

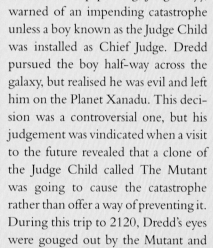

the Vending Droid soon moved into his apartment at Rowdy Yates Conapts, determined to serve the Judge – whether Dredd liked it or not! Shortly afterwards Rico returned, having served his full term on Titan for his crimes, and came looking for revenge on his brother. This time,

Joe was forced to kill him and this saddened him greatly, even after two decades of being toughened up on the streets.

A terrifyingly hectic period followed for Judge Dredd, as first he was appointed Judge-Marshal on Luna-1 for a six month term. Judges were not well respected there, but by the time he left, Dredd had reorganised the local Justice Department and the people there had learned to obey the law. Next, Judge Dredd was asked to lead an incredibly dangerous mission to carry vaccine across the Cursed Earth to the stricken Mega-City Two. When the Judge returned to Mega-City One, Cal became Chief Judge and Dredd had to marshal a ragged resistance force against the tyrant. Then Psi-Division's top pre-cog, Judge Feyy, warned of an impending catastrophe unless a boy known as the Judge Child was installed as Chief Judge. Dredd pursued the boy half-way across the galaxy, but realised he was evil and left him on the Planet Xanadu. This decision was a controversial one, but his judgement was vindicated when a visit to the future revealed that a clone of the Judge Child called The Mutant was going to cause the catastrophe rather than offer a way of preventing it. During this trip to 2120, Dredd's eyes were gouged out by the Mutant and

he had bionic replacements fitted before he and Psi-Judge Anderson eliminated the future threat by killing the infant clone in 2107. Before this, though, disaster had already overtaken Mega-City One in 2104, as East-Meg One launched a massive nuclear strike against them. Dredd was the American Judges' natural leader during the "Apocalypse War" and he was finally forced to take an elite squad of a Judges on a counter attack mission to destroy East-Meg One. Their success ended the war and the rebuilding of the nuclear scarred Mega-City One began in earnest.

In the years which followed, life became ever tougher in Mega-City One and, for the first time, Dredd began to have doubts about his role as a Judge. When he was asked to break up the Democratic Charter March in 2109, Dredd fulfilled Chief Judge Silver's orders to the letter, but he wasn't convinced that

his actions were justified. The attack of the Judda – warriors cloned from the finest genetic stock stolen from Mega-City One's own Genetic Control laboratory – was more of a pressing problem, however, and Dredd was forced to destroy them and their leader, Morton Judd – a renegade Judge himself – in order to save the city. Dredd's state of mind was not unknown to Chief Judge Silver, so he authorised the attempted rehabilitation of Kraken, one of the Judda who shared the bloodline of Fargo and Dredd. He hoped that Kraken could be re-educated and made to respect the law of Mega-City One, thus providing a possible replacement for the city's most potent symbol of Justice. Judge Dredd's doubts came to a head when he received an innocent letter from a boy who raised lots of questions about the Judges that he simply couldn't answer to his own satisfaction. As a result he submitted his resignation and his last act as a Judge was to fail Kraken after his final street assessment. Dredd's Long Walk into the Cursed Earth was kept a secret and Silver gave Judge Dredd's badge to Kraken, disregarding Dredd's final recommendation.

Joe Dredd patrolled the Cursed Earth for a hundred days, but then was attacked by the Sisters of Death and almost killed. Horribly disfigured and with no memory of who he was, he was discovered by young Yassa Povey who christened him the "Dead Man". When the Judge got his memory back he teamed up with ex-Chief Judge McGruder, who had taken the Long Walk before Dredd, and they investigated rumours of terrible happenings in Mega-City One. After several previous attempts to "judge" the city, Judge Death had finally seized control there in Dredd's absence and it took Mega-City One's top lawman to defeat him. Kraken had betrayed the city, so the real Dredd killed his impostor double and rejoined the Mega-City Judges. With the authority of the Justice Department in question, Judge Dredd insisted that a referendum be held on the issue of democracy and his gamble paid off as the Judges won out.

Dredd next saw off the threat of Sabbat the Necromagus, with the help of Hondo City's Judge Inspector Sadu and the mutant bounty hunter Johnny Alpha. Then he had to protect his own city from Judge Grice when the renegade escaped from Titan and sought revenge on the Mega-City One Judges. Grice unleashed the "Meat Virus" - a deadly alien plague – on Mega-City One, but he was finally killed by a weakened Dredd. Once the plague antidote had been distributed the city was safe once more, but recent crises meant there was a chronic shortage of Judges.

Chief Judge McGruder's solution was to set up the Mechanismo Project, in an effort to develop robot Judges. Ever distrustful of robots, Dredd opposed her plan bitterly and called on her to resign. He even went to the extreme of falsifying evidence to make the robots seem more unreliable than they really were. When this was discovered, McGruder had Dredd arrested and he was scheduled for transport to Titan for the second time in his career. An attempt on her life by one of the Mechanismo robots made the Chief Judge reconsider the situation, so Dredd was pardoned and McGruder duly resigned, announcing that her successor would be chosen by a ballot of all Senior Judges. Judge Dredd had already turned the job down more than once, so it was quite a surprise when he put his name forward for the election. In fact, he only did this to catch out someone who was trying to influence the contest unlawfully, but he stayed in the running rather than disrupt things by pulling out again. In the event, he polled just 130 votes to Hadrian Volt's 208, but he wasn't disappointed in the least, since he had voted for the new Chief Judge himself!

See also DEAD MAN, RICO DREDD, CHIEF JUDGE FARGO, JUDGE MORPHY, VIENNA DREDD

2000AD Sci-Fi Specials 1977-on; 2000AD Winter Specials 1988-on; Judge Dredd the Mega-Specials 1988-on; 2000AD Annuals 1978-1991; 2000AD Yearbooks 1992-on; Judge Dredd Annuals 1981-1991; Judge Dredd Yearbooks 1992-on; Dan Dare Annuals 1979, 1980; Judgement on Gotham 1-3; Judge Dredd #s 1-on; Legends of the Law #s 1-on

2000AD Graphic Novels: Mechanismo; Judgement on Gotham; Tales of the Damned; Top Dog; Babes in Arms; Book of the Dead; Democracy Now; Raptaur; Heavy Metal Dredd

East-Meg One

CITY: Largest City, Sov-Block

Following the Atomic Wars of 2070, the populations of Russia and many of its neighbouring States were concentrated into two vast cities in what became known as the Sov-Block. The first city, East-Meg One, was not only the largest, housing around half a billion people, but it also dominated its sister city, East-Meg Two, in political and economic terms – even though the two cities were nominally independent of each other. They each had their own Judge System, and East-Meg One was run by a Supreme Judge, who headed up their ruling Diktatorat. It was Supreme Judge Bulgarin who initiated the Apocalypse War against Mega-City One, after years of careful planning to ensure they couldn't lose. Unfortunately for Bulgarin, he reckoned without the ambition of his most trusted War-Marshal, "Mad Dog" Kazan, who had him killed during the war in order to succeed him as Supreme Judge. In turn, Kazan was to be disappointed, too, since Judge Dredd managed to end the war by wiping East-Meg One off the map by launching their own missiles at them! There are still a few survivors living in the radioactive environment of the wrecked Sov city, but to all intents and purposes East-Meg One no longer exists.

Introduced: 2000AD Prog 128

Destroyed: 2000AD Prog 267

East-Meg Two

CITY: Second City, Sov-Block

Founded after East-Meg One, the Sov-Block's second city was always dominated by its larger neighbour until that city was annihilated at the end of the Apocalypse War with Mega-City One. Understandably, anti-American feeling was prevalent in East-Meg Two for some time afterwards, but eventually the Judges there sought to build bridges with their Mega-City One counterparts. Supreme Judge Traktorfaktori of East-Meg Two made peace overtures to Chief Judge McGruder, with the full support of the city's Diktatorat, and relations between the cities have improved greatly in recent years – although Traktorfaktori's assassination in 2115 may have set the process back a bit.

Introduced: 2000AD Prog 270

Psi-Judge Ecks

JUDGE: Head of Psi-Division, Mega-City One

Judge Ecks enjoyed a long and distinguished career as Head of Psi-Division. His greatest interest was always in his pre-cogs and it was during his time that Judge Feyy made his famous prediction about impending doom for Mega-City One unless they could locate the mysterious "Judge Child". Ecks was extremely concerned when Judge Dredd returned from his quest to find the boy empty-handed. In the event, the Council endorsed Dredd's decision to abandon the boy and the Psi Chief was unable to pursue his investigations into the possible future catastrophe of 2120, since he was a victim of a more immediate one – Ecks was killed in the early days of the Apocalypse War.

2000AD Progs 182, 192, 197, 201, 217, 248 (reported dead)

Tek-Judge Eckson

JUDGE: Tek-Division, Mega-City One

Following the discredited work of Morton Judd, Tek-Judge Eckson was responsible for illegal research into developing a genetic virus strain that might produce completely passive citizens. Without seeking any kind of authorisation from the Chief Judge, he set up a test for the virus on some mutants in the Cursed Earth, but he miscalculated the dose and the contaminant proved fatal to the Brotherhood of Marshals. Seeking revenge, they sent a surviving Marshal to Mega-City One and he duly captured Eckson. Judge Dredd would not allow the Marshal to take the Tek-Judge off into the Cursed Earth for execution, however, and managed to save him from this fate – only to sentence Eckson to twenty years on Titan for his terrible crimes!

See also BROTHERHOOD OF MARSHALS, THE MARSHAL,

2000AD Progs 802, 803

Edwin "The Confessor" Parsey

CITIZEN: Mega-City One

Notorious at the Mega-City One Justice Department, Edwin Parsey was always confessing to crimes, yet he never committed any. When he confessed to being the mysterious "Invisible Man", who had been terrorising the city with a series of audacious robberies, Judge Dredd guessed that he knew more than he was actually saying. In fact, Edwin had discovered the true identity of the criminal and was watching him, looking for information to make his confession seem more authentic, so he unwittingly led the Judges to the real culprit. As a reward for his help, Judge Dredd sentenced Edwin to a month in the Iso-Cubes for giving false evidence – much to the delight of the man they called "The Confessor"!

See also INVISIBLE MAN

2000AD Prog 135

Cadet Judge Ekerson

JUDGE: Cadet, Mega-City One

One of the Cadet Judges who fought so bravely to defend Mega-City One against the twin onslaught of the Sisters of Death and the Dark Judges, Ekerson was particularly important to their efforts because of her psi powers. She was able to find the badly injured Psi-Judge Anderson, due to a psi link-up with her, and it was Anderson who was so important in breaking the Sisters' bridge to the city. Later, Cadet Judge Ekerson was in the thick of things again, when she took part in a Hotdog Run in the Cursed Earth as Sabbat unleashed his zombie attack on Mega-City One. Ekerson and her fellow Cadets only made it back to the city thanks to the supreme sacrifice of Judge Perrier who fought off the zombies as they broke through to safety.

2000AD Progs 687–695, 786–788

Eldster Ninja Mud-Wrestling Vigilantes

GROUP: Vigilantes, Mega-City One

Fed up with the all-too-common muggings carried out by Juves in Mega-City One, a group of Eldsters got together to form the Eldster Ninja Mud-Wrestling Vigilantes. So, dressed in specially modified pairs of pyjamas, they soon hit the streets, armed with a walking cane, an ear trumpet and several large buckets of mud! Wrestling their victims into submission, they were able to take out a gang of vicious Juves but Judge Dredd was quickly on the Eldsters' tail. He caught up with them easily and they responded by covering him in mud. The vigilantes thought they could take care of Dredd – using minimum force to avoid injuring him – but they reckoned without the lawman's prowess as a mud-wrestler. By the time he was finished with them, they were the Unconscious Eldster Ninja Mud-Wrestling Vigilantes.

2000AD Prog 601

Eleanor Groth

CITIZEN: Mega-City One

Unlucky enough to contract the extremely rare Arachnid Gene Virus, Eleanor Groth was horrified to find herself turning into a giant spider. First she noticed an excess of hair growing on her body – a problem she couldn't solve with depilatory creams or shaving. Then her hands began to resemble claws and she started to lose her normal brain functions. Her husband was determined to stick by her when the disease was diagnosed, but her affliction was too well advanced to be cured. The Judges then served her an exile order – since her genetic abnormality constituted a breach of the Mutant Segregation Act. Eleanor remained in the city as long as she could, but eventually the Judges insisted she go off into the Cursed Earth. Despite his earlier promises, her husband decided to stay behind with their children, rather than accompany her. Weeks later, the transformation into a mutant spider complete, Eleanor managed to get back into the city and she was killed by the Judges only after she had disposed of her spouse!

See also ARACHNID GENE VIRUS

2000AD Progs 603, 604, 612 (dies)

Elmort Devries

CITIZEN: Mega-City One

As Chairman of the Hunters Club, Elmort Devries had to be aware of security, since his organisation was responsible for so many murders that the Judges could have been onto them at almost any time. When one of their newest members lost his nerve, Devries moved their base completely to ensure that he couldn't possibly lead the law to them. The Judges were frustrated by their inability to track down the Hunters Club, but they knew it was only a matter of time. In the end, it was Elmort Devries' brainwave of "Death Aid" - a sponsored hunt for charity – that gave the Hunters Club away. The sheer volume of murders generated by them led the Judges to Devries and the Club's new base, but the killer was not for giving up. He tried to kill Dredd with a bazooka, but was ultimately shot dead himself. Elmort Devries almost had the last laugh, however, when a nuke he had activated just before his demise nearly upped his murder tally immeasurably – but Dredd was able to dump the device in the Black Atlantic in the nick of time.

See also DEATH AID, HUNTERS CLUB

2000AD Progs 408, 409, 711-715, 719, 720 (dies)

Above:
Elmort Devries picks on the wrong victim

Elvis the Killer Car

VEHICLE: Moon buggy, Luna-1

Keen to save some money on necessary repairs to his robotic car, Dave Paton decided to do the work himself. Unfortunately, he accidentally damaged the moon buggy's responsibility circuits in the process, causing it to strangle him and to run amok, attacking people on the streets of Luna-1. Elvis, as the car was known, soon attracted the attention of the Judges and had to seek refuge in a large parking lot. There, he set about removing other cars' responsibility circuits, in order to marshal an army to combat the Judges, who quickly reached the scene, brandishing powerful corrosive spray guns. These guns halted the crazed cars, but "The Killer Car" himself escaped via a back exit and hid out in a citizen's apartment. Elvis's greatest weakness was his mentality – that of a five year old –

and Judge Dredd was able to goad him out of hiding by claiming on Luna-1 television that he could easily outsmart the moon buggy. The car responded by ambushing Dredd in his own home and held him hostage inside his own locked car doors! Dredd did indeed outsmart him, though, when he activated an automatic safety device inside the car, ejecting him to safety as other Judges turned their corrosive guns on Elvis, rusting him out of existence.

Below:
Elvis commits his first murder and decides it's fun

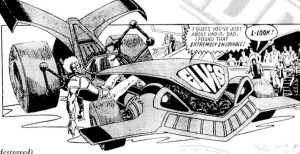

2000AD Progs 53-56 (destroyed)

Sov-Judge Nikita Engels
JUDGE: East-Meg One

Separated from his Unit in Mega-City One during the Apocalypse War, Sov-Judge Engels hid out in a maintenance loft for several weeks to avoid capture. He was extremely puzzled when he heard a radio broadcast which suggested that East-Meg One had been defeated and he was amazed at the lengths to which the enemy would go to suggest that they still controlled their city. Not at all sure what to do, the Sov-Judge decided to contact an Agony Aunt for advice, but he was taken for a harmless lunatic. Harmless Nikita Engels wasn't, and he soon proved it by restarting the war single-handedly, bombing various targets in the name of East-Meg One. Judge Dredd tracked him down quickly and he was forced to kill the Sov when he refused to surrender.

2000AD Progs 298, 299 (dies)

Executioner
CITIZEN: Vigilante, Mega-City One

Blanche Tatum exacts revenge on the men responsible for her husband's death

Young Blanche Kominsky was a 12th year Cadet at the Academy of Law when an unauthorised liaison with a male citizen, Nicholas Tatum, saw her expelled in 2093. She later married the man, becoming Blanche Tatum, and they went on to have two children. Tragically, her husband got in too deep with a loan operation and he found himself on the wrong side of a consortium of Mega-City One gangsters. When they got heavy with him, Nicholas Tatum couldn't handle it and he took his own life. Blanche Tatum was determined to have her revenge on the gangsters, so she used her Judge training to become an efficient killing machine and, posing as the "Executioner", she picked them off one by one. The Judges were keen to put a stop to this mysterious vigilante, but her methods seemed to identify her as a Judge, so they started by examining their own ranks. Naturally, this line of inquiry proved fruitless, but then Judge Dredd realised that the Executioner could just as easily be a former Cadet who never made it through to graduation. This line of investigation soon put Blanche Tatum in the frame and Dredd was on her tail immediately, but he was unable to stop her killing the last of the gangsters responsible for her husband's death. Judge Dredd tried to arrest her, but she wanted to die. Pointing a gun at the Judge, she gave him no option but to shoot her – even though her gun turned out not to be loaded.

2000AD Progs 291-294 (dies)

Exo-Men
GROUP: Criminal gang, Mega-City One

Hitting on the idea of using demolition workers' powerful exo-skeletons in the course of the crimes, the Exo-Men exploded into action by tearing apart a bank with what amounted to their suited "bare hands". They were unfortunate enough to find Judge Dredd on the scene very swiftly and their suits, built for power not speed, proved as much a hindrance as a boon in their attempt to escape. Three of the four Exo-Men were killed as they tried to avoid capture, but one of them escaped with a hostage when a misguided civil rights activist set him free. Ultimately, though, he was tracked down as well and he met his fate when a ricochet bullet hit the control panel on his exo-skeleton and it went berserk!

2000AD Progs 111, 112

Exploding Man
CITIZEN: Mega-City One

As the Apocalypse War begun, Ike Nobel was caught in one of the initial nuclear explosions. Instead of dying, however, his body became suffused with toxic chemicals and he found himself alive, but with every molecule of his body in the process of exploding. He staggered around through four years of (barely) living hell until he made it to a Justice Department Sector House, blowing it – and himself – up as retribution for all his suffering.

2000AD Prog 471 (dies)

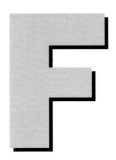

Fairly Hyperman

CITIZEN: Planet Kapok, Deep Space

Fairly Hyperman was the only survivor when his homeworld exploded and, upon his arrival on Earth, he found that its lower gravity gave him "new" powers, soon making him a hero. The Judges' policy on vigilantes was clear. Dredd took him out with green Kapokite bullets ending the career of a fairly unlikely hero!

2000AD Progs 529, 530

Fang Worms

ANIMAL: Genetically Engineered Worm, Mega-City One

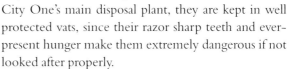

Fang Worms are not only extremely voracious and deadly, but they will eat almost anything if they get the opportunity. They were specially bred to consume all types of waste in an eco-friendly way. Housed at the Mega-City One's main disposal plant, they are kept in well protected vats, since their razor sharp teeth and ever-present hunger make them extremely dangerous if not looked after properly.

See also CHESTER WHUT

Introduced: 2000AD Prog 598

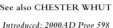

Left:
Fairly Hyperman demonstrates his fairly hyper powers

Chief Judge Eustace Fargo

JUDGE: Chief Judge, Mega-City One

Known as the "Father of Justice", Eustace Fargo was the city's first Chief Judge and he was responsible for the founding of the Judge system. He originally headed up the Judges as a glorified police force, with limited powers of instant sentencing and special training to help them contain crime in the newly built Mega-City in the middle of the 21st Century. Things changed in 2070, when President Booth initiated the Atomic Wars, forcing the Judges to depose him and take on the job of governing the Mega-Cities of America. Fargo therefore took charge of Mega-City One and he instituted the Council of Five to help him. It was to this body that Morton Judd, Head of Genetics in the Justice Department, proposed a radical plan to genetically engineer the citizens, making them easier to control. After all, they already produced Judges this way – Joe and Rico Dredd, for example, had been cloned from Judge Fargo's own DNA. The Chief Judge rejected the idea, pointing out that their primary task was to serve the citizens, not control them. Fargo had more immediate problems to consider, as he set about creating a new structure for government by the Judges.

See also MORTON JUDD

2000AD Prog 559 (flashback)

Judge Dredd #s 1-10

Father Earth

MUTANT: **Cult leader, Cursed Earth**

Half-man, half-plant, Father Earth was a bizarre mutant and prophet who believed that Mega-City One had to be destroyed to free the Earth of its tyranny of concrete and steel. He attracted thousands of mutant and outcast followers, combining his "oneness" with nature with an out and out ruthless streak against the city dwellers. A key group of his followers, The Doomsday Dogs, blew up Mega-City One's Power Tower and unleashed molten lava on its streets, which enabled Father Earth and his army to invade the city and attempt to overrun it. Although the threat of his artificially created "volcano" was soon ended, the mutant leader set free a host of deadly exhibits from the Mega-City Botanic Gardens and so he continued to prove a danger to the city. His kinship with the plants was tested to the limit, however, when he became entwined in a man-eating piece of vegetation he called the "God Plant". He was convinced that the plant would help him in his mission to destroy Mega-City One, but in fact it just ate him, leaving his followers to be rounded up by the Judges without difficulty!

See also DOOMSDAY DOGS, POWER TOWER

2000AD Progs 122-125

Judge Fear

JUDGE: Deadworld

One of Judge Death's three trusted lieutenants, Judge Fear has his own particular method of disposing of the living. Opening the grill on his helmet, he forces his victims to gaze into the face of Fear and they invariably die of sheer terror. Only one living being has ever survived his gaze – as he has proved on numerous occasions, Judge Dredd fears nothing at all!

See also DARK JUDGES

2000AD Progs 224-228, 416-424, 672, 684, 688-690, 694, 696-699, 734

Judge Dredd the Megazine Volume 1: 10-12

Judge Dredd the Megazine Volume 2: 45 (cameo), 50

Judge Dredd Annual 1983 (cameo)

Fergee

CITIZEN: **Citizen, Undercity – honorary Judge, Mega-City One**

Something of a misfit in Mega-City One, Fergee found himself on the wrong side of the law more than once and finally sought refuge from the Judges in the Undercity. He set up home in the dank and dangerous caverns around the highly polluted Ohio River – aka the Big Smelly – and soon proved himself the "top dog" amongst the mutants and weirdoes who lived there. When Judge Dredd and his anti-Cal rebel Judges crashed through city bottom and into the river in a roadliner fitted with highly effective crash-bags, Fergee was keen to deal with the intruders on his territory. Introducing himself as the "King of the Big Smelly", he took on Dredd in hand-to-club combat and lost! The Judge thereby won Fergee's respect and Dredd recognised that the brute could be a useful ally in the war against Cal.

When Fergee led his new friend back up to Mega-City One and helped him capture a Pat-Wagon, Dredd appointed him an honorary Judge. Warming to his new role, Fergee gleefully aided the Judge in dispatching a group of Kleggs who had taken over Dredd's apartment in Rowdy Yates Conapts, so that Walter the Wobot could be enlisted to try and steal one of Cal's Judge briefing tapes. Fergee enjoyed the status of honorary Judge and took his responsibilities more seriously than even Dredd could have dared hope during the final battle to depose Cal. With the mad Chief Judge determined to gas the entire city and about to press the fatal button at the top of the Statue of Judgement, Fergee charged into him and carried him off the top of the structure. He fell to his death along with Cal, but Judge Dredd ensured that Fergee's sacrifice would always be remembered in Mega-City One by erecting commemorative statues of the King of the Big Smelly all over the city.

2000AD Progs 100-104, 106-108 (dies), 118 (cameo), 134 (cameo)

Psi-Judge Feyy

JUDGE: Psi-Division, Mega-City One

Psi-Division's oldest pre-cog, Judge Feyy's visions of the future were known to be 88.8% accurate, so his dying prediction brought a chill to his colleagues. He foresaw a terrible war that would result in the destruction of Mega-City One in 2120, with foul creatures rising from the devastation to prey on the survivors. Feyy offered one hope for Mega-City One's salvation, however – he believed that a boy called Owen Krysler could guide the city through its hour of darkness and so inspired the quest for the "Judge Child".

See also JUDGE CHILD

2000AD Progs 156 (dies), 224 (cameo)

I HAVE ONLY A NAME – *OWEN KRYSLER* HE CAN GUIDE US THROUGH THE DARKNES FIND HIM –

FIND THE JUDGE CHILD!

Filmore Faro

CITIZEN: Cult leader, Cursed Earth

Believing himself to be descended from the Pharaohs of ancient Egypt, Filmore Faro dedicated his life to building impressive monuments to himself in the Cursed Earth. He liked to be known as the "Garbage God", but when he decided it was time to ascend to the spirit world, he organised a spectacular funeral parade and unveiled Faro's Tomb. He intended the Judge Child to die with him so that the boy could act as a guide for him on the other side, but he was abducted before Faro died at the hands of Judge Dredd.

See also BROTHERHOOD OF TRASH, JUDGE CHILD

2000AD Progs 157-159 (dies)

Fink Angel

CITIZEN: Mutant, Cursed Earth

Eldest son of Elmer "Pa" Angel, Fink was always a loner and at the age of seven went to live in a hole. As the years passed he became more estranged from his family until, finally, he left – taking his hole with him! He became a Cursed Earth desperado, using his encyclopaedic knowledge of poisons and his natural slyness to prosper. However, the radiation took its toll – turning him into a terrifying mutant. Fink befriended a mutant rat (Ratty) who became his constant companion.

When he heard that his family had been killed by the Judges, Fink came looking for revenge. He murdered Judge-Pilot Larter and captured Judge Hershey, only for Dredd to save her from a horrifying death on the Resyk conveyor belt. After a year in the 'Cubes, Fink escaped and retrieved Ratty from Resyk. Fink and Mean Machine then kidnapped Maria, Dredd's cleaning lady. The Judge managed rescue her, but almost found himself subjected to the Pa Angel Mark One Super-Scream Torture Machine. In fact, it was Fink who fell victim to the device when he was pushed onto it during his struggle against the Judge!

See also JUDGE CHILD, RATTY

2000AD Prog 193-196, 281-283, 285-288 (dies)

Judge Dredd Mega-Special: 2 (cameo)

Judge Dredd the Magazine Volume 2: 45 (cameo)

Judge Fire

JUDGE: Deadworld

The most dangerous of the four Dark Judges, Judge Fire can unleash deadly flames against his enemies and so is able to "Judge" victims in greater numbers than his colleagues. His fiery form also makes him the only Dark Judge whose physical form is impossible to trap in solid Boing. Unlike Death, Fear and Mortis, Judge Fire can simply burn his way out of such a trap!

See also DARK JUDGES, DEATHWORLD

2000AD Progs 224-228, 416-424, 672, 684, 688-690, 694, 696-699, 734

Judge Dredd the Magazine Volume 1: 10-12

Judge Dredd the Magazine Volume 2: 45 (cameo), 50

Judge Dredd Annual 1983 (cameo)

Deputy Chief Judge Fish

ANIMAL: Goldfish, Deputy Chief Judge, Mega-City One

Below:
Deputy Chief Judge Fish announces a new law

Appointed to the post of Deputy Chief Judge by the mad tyrant Cal, Fish was quite simply an ordinary goldfish made good. Despite his obvious lack of training for the job and the fact that he was physically unable to speak, Cal's former pet prospered in his new role and was even given the opportunity to announce his own law on live television. Cal pointed out that the penalty for breaking this new law was death, but no-one knew what it was that they weren't supposed to do, because all they heard was "BLOOP!" Deputy Chief Judge Fish's life came to a tragic and premature end when he was killed by Judge Slocum, who was desperate to manufacture a "sign", which would convince Chief Judge Cal to call off the mass execution of all the citizens in Mega-City One. Judge Fish was buried with all state honours, though much to Cal's annoyance, the people didn't turn out in their numbers for the funeral.

See also JUDGE SLOCUM

2000AD Progs 90-92, 94, 95 (dies)

Fisher Wildman

CITIZEN: Freehacker, Mega-City One

As a freelance reporter, Fisher Wildman was always on the lookout for a really big story, so he couldn't believe his luck when he stumbled across a fatal gassing accident. He soon discovered that the gas involved was used widely across Mega-City One by the Justice Department, since in very small quantities it was an effective but otherwise harmless tranquilliser and so made the citizens a little easier to control. Fisher took the story to the robotic editor of Newsmeg, but the Judges ensured that the reporter's exposé would never appear. Fearing widespread knowledge of this practice, Judge Dredd invoked the Security of the City act and Wildman was forced to undergo remedial brain surgery – so that he would remember only what the Justice Department wanted him to.

2000AD Progs 438, 439

Flying Squad

DIVISION: Justice Department, Mega-City One

A small, highly specially trained group of Judges in Mega-City One, the Flying Squad operate like regular Judges, except that they use "Zipper" Bikes – or sometimes Power Boards – rather than standard issue Lawmasters. The Zippers are highly manoeuvrable flying vehicles and enable Flying Squad Judges to make airborne patrols in areas ordinary Judges may find difficult to cover quickly in the multi-levelled city.

See also ZIPPER BIKE

Introduced: 2000AD Annual 1981

Deputy Chief Judge Fodder

JUDGE: Deputy Chief Judge, Mega-City One

Long-time second-in-command to Chief Judge Goodman, Fodder was far better respected as an administrator than as a man of action. His greatest achievement was the planning and equipping of the mission to cross the Cursed Earth to save Mega-City Two when it was stricken by the Virus Strain 2T(FRU)T. Sadly, this was also to prove his epitaph, as he was strangled by a victim of the plague and shoved through a food sterilisation chamber leading into the Quarantine Bubble occupied by his attacker.

2000AD Prog 61 (dies)

The Freedom League

ORGANISATION: Civil rights group, Mega-City One

One of Mega-City One's many democratic splinter groups, the Freedom League's leader was one of those discredited by the Judges before the ill-fated Democratic Charter March of 2109. The League was formally disbanded shortly afterwards, since most of its members had been arrested or discouraged by events during the march.

2000AD Progs 531-533

Professor E. Northcote Fribb

CITIZEN: Inventor, Mega-City One

After years of painstaking research, E. Northcote Fribb believed that he was ready to unravel the mystery of man's evolution. He had finally isolated an enzyme which could reverse the process of evolution, but he made the fatal error of sniffing it himself – one smell was too many and within minutes he grew hairy and turned into an ape! At the same time he lost interest in his enzyme and dropped it on the floor, inadvertently spreading the enzyme throughout the entire Charles Darwin City Block via its ventilation ducts. Chaos ensued as the Block quite literally went ape and the Judges had to burn the place down in the end to put a stop to the progress of the enzyme. By the time they had worked out that Fribb was responsible for the whole mess, he had regressed into a giant amoeba – but Judge Dredd arrested him anyway!

See also FRIBB ENZYME

2000AD Progs 184, 185

Fribb Enzyme

DRUG: Enzyme, Mega-City One

Professor E. Northcote Fribb's greatest discovery was an enzyme which actually reversed the process of evolution. Unfortunately for the Professor, it was also his last discovery, since he found himself regressing along with the other residents of the Charles Darwin Block after simply sniffing the stuff. So virulent was the Fribb Enzyme – as it came to be known – that Judge Dredd actually had to burn down the whole City Block to stop its effects spreading any further, although the survivors were first rounded up and taken to safety so that the Mega-City One scientists could try and re-evolve them!

Introduced: 2000AD Prog 183

Full Mental Jackets

GROUP: Juve gang, Mega-City One

One of Mega-City One's most feared criminal gangs, the Full Mental Jackets operated from Mac Murphy Block and were led by its "Warlord", Brian "Dog" Deever, until he was put in the Iso Cubes for three years by Judge Dredd. When the Dog got out he reclaimed his position in charge of the Jackets and involved his younger brother in their activities. Deever was finally stopped by his mother, who had already tipped off the Judges as to his whereabouts and shot him for introducing her other son to his nihilistic criminal lifestyle.

2000AD Prog 578-582

Futsie

TERM: Person suffering from 'Future Shock', Mega-City One

Life in a 22nd Century Mega-City can be very hard to cope with and a well-observed phenomenon is that of "Future Shock", a mental breakdown of epic proportions, often leading a "Futsie" to become violent and therefore a danger to other citizens as well as themselves. The Judges try hard to make allowances for this condition when they encounter it in the course of their duties and, wherever possible, they treat Futsies with a degree of compassion they would normally withhold from ordinary lawbreakers, as opposed to coming down hard on Futsies for their "crimes".

Introduced: 2000AD Prog 27

Below: **An unfortunate citizen goes into "Future Shock"**

G

Game Show Game

EVENT: Mock Game Show, Mega-City One

Barry Dreery had an overriding ambition all his life to become a game show host, but he was just too boring! When he actually got his chance to present a small-time quiz show, he proved extremely unpopular and the Association of Game Show Hosts wasted no time in throwing him out. The death of Barry's super-rich uncle during the Apocalypse War left him with an enormous inheritance, however, and he was ready to enact his revenge. He constructed the "Game Show Game" - a large and lethal assortment of Game Show style physical challenges designed with one purpose in mind... murder! No-one was terribly bothered when over four hundred Game Show hosts went missing in Mega-City One, but the Judges took an interest when several dozen of them turned up dead.

2000AD Prog 278, 279

Chief Judge Garcia

Below:
Chief Judge Garcia grows fat on the exploitation of his people

Cutting a gross and corrupt figure, the Pan Andes Conurb's Chief Judge Garcia sanctioned the illegal sugar trade to Mega-City One and grew fat on his share of the profits! He was finally exposed as a criminal – along with the majority of his fellow Judges - by Judge Dredd when he visited the city to investigate the source of the sugar supply. Garcia's life of luxury thus came to an end and he packed his bags ready for a trip to the Judges' Penal Colony on Titan.

2000AD Progs 876-878

Garfield Brose

CITIZEN: Mega-City One

Garfield Brose thought that his luck was in when he inherited a magic lamp from his uncle – with a real live Genie inside it! Unfortunately, his first wish for a billion credits gave the Judges cause to suspect him of some kind of criminal activity and his second wish – to get rid of Judge Dredd – piled up the trouble for poor Garfield. His final wish was even more disastrous, since in trying to escape the other Judges, he managed to transport himself to where Dredd was, far across the Universe. The Judge then demanded his three wishes from the Genie – threatening the mystical being with a Hi-Ex Shell if he didn't comply – and they all returned to Mega-City One. Garfield was despatched to an Iso-Cube with Dredd's second wish, while the Genie wound up in the adjoining 'Cube as a result of his third – proving that, in Mega-City One, even magic is no defence against the law!

2000AD Prog 514

Garrhounds

ALIEN RACE: Tracker Beasts, Planet Garlokk

Although not very intelligent, they have enabled the Garrs to rid the planet of their enemy the Nosferatus. Very efficient trackers, garrhounds have hounded the Nosferatus close to extinction.

2000AD Prog 433

Judge Dredd the Megazine Volume 1: 9

Geiger Wolves

ANIMALS: Mutant beasts, Cursed Earth

Horrific and deadly scavengers, these mutated animals are the Cursed Earth equivalent of hyenas. Geiger Wolves rarely attack live prey, preferring to rely on easier pickings, but they are capable of a vicious assault on anyone or anything who gets in between them and their next meal!

2000AD Progs 885

General Blood 'n' Guts

ROBOT: Commander, Legion of the Damned, Cursed Earth

The fanatical leader of an indefatigable army of robots, General Blood 'n' Guts had four bodies shot from under him before he was left severely disabled on the battlefield in Death Valley after the Battle of Armageddon in 2071. Still determined to fulfil his programming, he marshalled his forces one last time thirty years later when Judge Dredd and his fellow travellers passed through the valley on their way to deliver the 2T(FRU)T antidote to Mega-City Two.

See also BATTLE OF ARMAGEDDON,
LEGION OF THE DAMNED

2000AD Progs 83–85

Genetic Control

BUILDING: Section of Justice Department, Mega-City One

Cloning technology was perfected in Mega-City One in the second half of the 21st Century, but the details of the process were classified and the success of the project was virtually unheard of outside the Justice Department. The issue of cloning was considered to be a very delicate one, especially since Head of Genetics, Judge Morton Judd advocated the creation of a docile cloned citizenry for the city. Judd was overruled, but the techniques he had helped develop were regularly used to breed Judges from the quality genetic stock available from the Judges of the day. The Academy of Law's intake was therefore increased considerably thanks to the work carried out at Justice Department's Genetic Control laboratory.

See also JUDGE MORTON JUDD

Introduced: 2000AD Prog 30

Gestapo Bob Harris

CITIZEN: Mega-City One

The self-styled "Chief Judge" of Southside Sector 41, Bob was the leader of the Cosmic Punks, who declared themselves to be the law in the area after the overthrow of Judge Cal. When Judge Dredd reasserted the authority of the Justice Department in the Sector he banished Gestapo Bob Harris from the city for ten years, only for the punk to come back into the city when it was invaded by Father Earth and his mutant hordes. Bob was quickly apprehended and this time the sentence was life on a penal colony in space!

See also COSMIC PUNKS, FATHER EARTH

2000AD Progs 110, 124, 125

Cadet Judge Giant
See page 64

Judge Giant
See page 65

Gila-Munja

MUTANTS: Assassins, Cursed Earth

Part man, part beast and part ... well, something else entirely, the Gila-Munja are ideally suited to survival on the rough terrain of the Cursed Earth. Their cunning and poisonous claws make them very dangerous. Known as the "Tribe of the Assassins", the Gila-Munja consider death to be a matter of primitive honour and are willing to take on contract murders if a large enough fee is on offer. They move quickly and quietly, disappearing into the shadows as their skin changes colour to blend in with their surroundings.

2000AD Progs 231, 232, 235, 831

Judge Dredd the Megazine Volume 2: 50–53

Cadet Judge Giant

JUDGE: Cadet (now promoted to full Judge), Mega-City One

Young Giant lost his father, a distinguished Mega-City One Judge, when he was just a baby, so he formed an even closer attachment to his mother, Adele Dormer. Adele had been a rich and famous interior designer before the Apocalypse War, but she lost everything during the war and ended up in a displaced persons camp, begging for creds to stay alive. When she was murdered by a street gang some years later, her boy was left to fend for himself until he was picked up by the Judges. They took him into city care and only discovered the astonishing truth about his parentage when they carried out a routine genetic test on him. Although, young Giant was older than their regular intake, it was decided to induct him into the Academy of Law and the boy made excellent progress, like his father before him.

The anger within Cadet Giant was something his Judge-Tutors found hard to control, however, since the boy had witnessed his mother's murder and experienced the harshest side of life in Mega-City One before his training had even begun. He was assigned to Judge Dredd for some early street familiarisation in an effort to work out a degree of his aggression and, as luck would have it, the case they became involved with led them to Giant's mother's killer. Tracking down the producers of a number of Vi-Zines – magazines specialising in showing violent torture and real murders in graphic detail - they encountered the murderer and Giant desperately wanted to kill him. Dredd gave him the opportunity, but his gamble that the Cadet could control his emotions paid off. The boy simply arrested the maniac responsible his mother's death, realising that nothing was worth throwing away his future as a Judge for.

"SON."
"YOU'RE JOKING."
"THAT'S WHAT DREDD SAID."

Cadet Giant's attitude showed huge signs of improvement after this and, while he could never forget the scum who killed his mother in front of his eyes, he concentrated on pursuing justice in a fair and even-handed way. When the Sisters of Death turned Mega-City One into a Necropolis, Giant led a small group of Cadets who continued the battle against the Dark Judges when everything seemed lost. His actions, along with those of Judge Dredd, Chief Judge McGruder and Judge Anderson, ensured that the city was saved from the Sisters' evil influence, and the experience saw him grow in stature. Giant was in the thick of things once more when Sabbat launched his attack on Mega-City One - he was on a Hotdog Run in the Cursed Earth with Judges Dredd and Perrier when Sabbat's zombies began appearing. Cadet Giant only made it back to Mega-City One through the creatures when Perrier sacrificed her life to clear the way for them.

Following the defeat of Sabbat, Judge Grice and his fellow rogue Judges from Titan attacked Mega-City One. By the time Judge Dredd managed to stop them, they had further decimated the Justice Department and the city was in desperate need of new Judges. The accelerated graduation programme was begun at the Academy of Law and Cadet Giant was soon selected to become its youngest product. He was only fifteen when he was handed his half Eagle and his white Rookie's helmet in preparation for his final street assessment . Like his father before him, young Giant was assigned to Judge Dredd for the test and, despite some minor errors, he acquitted himself very well indeed. The Rookie helped Dredd take out a group of renegade robots led by none other than his former droid-servant, Walter the Wobot. The Senior Judge's irritation with the robot resulted in him making a few misjudgements of his own, but Giant covered his back well and duly graduated with honour from the Academy of Law – becoming the youngest ever wearer of the full Eagle and black helmet of a full Judge.

See also JUDGE GIANT

2000AD Progs 651-655, 687-695, 702, 703, 786, 788, 799

Judge Dredd the Megazine Volume 2: 50-52

Judge Giant

JUDGE: Mega-City One

Judge Giant was the only fully able-bodied Judge that Dredd could rely on, so his role in the ultimate defeat of Chief Judge Cal was vital.

Judge Giant distinguished himself during the course of the three years which followed, although he did allow one blemish on his character as a dedicated lawman when he fell in love with a citizen - top interior designer, Adele Dormer. Unknown to his Judge colleagues, he even fathered a son, but he didn't live to see the child grow up. Sadly, Judge Giant was killed by Orlok the Assassin, when he tried to apprehend the East-Meg Spy at a Water Purification Plant at the height of the Block Mania which afflicted Mega-City One prior to the Apocalypse War.

See also BLOCK MANIA, CADET JUDGE GIANT

2000AD Progs 27, 28, 38, 41, 87, 90-94, 97-102, 106-108, 182, 200, 233-235, 242 (dies)

Son of the famed Aeroball and Inferno star, John 'Giant' Clay, Judge Giant entered the Academy of Law at the age of 5 and began his training as Cadet. 15 years later he found himself as a Rookie Judge on his final street test under the supervision of none other than Judge Dredd. The test went rather badly for the Rookie, especially when he failed to capture a Futsie on a killing frenzy and then made a serious error in sentencing him after Dredd had made the arrest. But Giant redeemed himself when they were called to apprehend a kidnap gang, hiding out in an old Aeroball stadium, and he subsequently graduated to become a full Judge.

Judge Giant proved to be an excellent street Judge and was an extremely valuable ally for Judge Dredd when Cal took control of the city and ordered his death. By pretending to hate Dredd, Giant was able to volunteer for the job of executing him and thereby helped him escape. Because he had been on a month's leave, Giant had not been subject to Cal's brainwashing tapes during the Judges' Daily Crime Briefing sessions. Like Dredd, who had been in the Cursed Earth, and the Judge-Tutors who didn't attend the sessions, Giant was free of the new Chief Judge's control and, between them, they mounted a resistance effort against his rule.

Chief Judge Giza

JUDGE: Chief Judge, Luxor City

The long-serving and well-respected head of the Luxor Justice Department, Chief Judge Giza ensured that his city was a very safe place to live. The main reason for this was the strict code of punishment he enforced – law-breakers would not only serve their sentence imprisoned in the labyrinthine caverns beneath the Sphinx, but at the end of their sentence they would be summarily executed! Giza himself met a grisly fate at the hands of the ancient monster Ankhhor, who butchered him while he was answering a call of nature, and then fed on his Ka – the very essence of Giza's being – to build up his own supernatural strength.

See also ANKHHOR

2000AD Progs 860, 861 (dies)

"God-Judge"

MUTANT: Chief Judge, Las Vegas

After the Atomic Wars of 2070, law and order broke down right across the heart of America, with the whole area becoming a nuclear wasteland. In Las Vegas, where a small-scale Judge system had been in operation, the Mafia moved in and took over the local Hall of Justice. From then on, they were the law in Las Vegas and gambling became more than a leisure attraction, it become a way of life for every man, woman and child in the community. Lucky Mutiano was one in a long line of God-Judges who had presided over the city since the Mafia families had executed Abner Cobb, Civic Leader in Las Vegas at the time of the war. Unfortunately for Mutiano, the appointment to his position was made on an annual basis and every year he had to defend it by participating in a gang fight between all the rival Mafia families. When Judge Dredd visited Las Vegas on his way across the Cursed Earth, he used his status as a Judge to enter this fight and beat the gangsters to depose Mutiano and wrest control of the city back from the Mafia.

See also LEAGUE AGAINST GAMBLING

2000AD Progs 79, 80, 85 (cameo)

Chief Judge Goodman

JUDGE: Chief Judge, Mega-City One

No other Chief Judge before or since has served in the post longer than Clarence Goodman, but his reign finally came to an end when he was murdered on the orders of his own Deputy in 2101. Goodman succeeded Fargo as Chief Judge of Mega-City One shortly after the Atomic Wars of 2070 and, on the whole, he was well-liked by his people. The years that followed saw the establishment of firm but stable government, yet there were two major crises during his time in power. The first of these was the outbreak of civil war between Mega-Cities One and Three, when the third city declared full independence and renamed itself Texas City. With the Cursed Earth a near impenetrable barrier between the cities, Goodman eventually conceded that the civil war was futile and – in a move not entirely popular with all his colleagues – he recognised Texas City's independent status.

The second crisis came when the robots of Mega-City One rebelled against their masters and the Robot Wars claimed millions of lives. The Chief Judge had previously clashed with Judge Dredd on the issue of banning highly intelligent robots and when he refused to do this Dredd actually resigned. The advent of the robots' rebellion saw Goodman change his mind very fast and Judge Dredd took up his badge once more to put down the revolt. The Chief Judge knew just how much the city owed Dredd and how much it depended on him, so when he was forced to convict Judge Dredd of murder after he was framed by Deputy Chief Judge Cal, Goodman found it very hard to come to terms with his decision. Even after Judge Dredd had demonstrated his innocence, the Chief Judge was a broken man and Cal was free to plot his demise.

2000AD Progs 2, 11, 15, 17, 20, 21, 26, 28, 30, 34, 60, 86-89 (dies)

2000AD Sci-Fi Special 1979

2000AD Annual 1978

Dan Dare Annual 1979

Judge Goon

JUDGE: Mega-City One

While all Judges are required to bully citizens in certain circumstances, Judge Goon seems to take a special pleasure in this side of the job. His rough treatment of a perp, which looked likely to inspire a riot, seemed over the top to Psi-Judge Anderson when she witnessed it and she hauled Goon up before an adjudicator to account for himself. The brief hearing exonerated Judge Goon, much to Anderson's annoyance, since he was deemed to have used justifiable violence against the criminal. Later, when Goon was interrogating the Christian activist, Jon Baptiste, he clashed with Anderson again. She probed Baptiste's mind and was impressed by the purity of his belief, but Judge Goon was unsympathetic and accused her of being a "cruddy Judge". Anderson was therefore on a short fuse when Goon set about Jon Baptiste again and she stopped the bullying Judge by beating the tar out of him!

See also PSI-JUDGE ANDERSON, JON BAPTISTE

Judge Dredd the Magazine Volume 2: 11, 22–24, 52

Gort Hyman

CITIZEN: Civil rights activist, Mega-City One

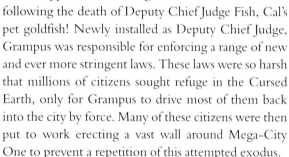

Gort Hyman was left to bring up his two children when his wife, Hester, was killed as the Judges regained control of the vid-station Channel 48 from Democratic Tendency. Until that moment, Gort had been unaware of his wife's political activities and was deeply shocked by her martyr's death. Slowly, he began to understand the reasons for her sacrifice and so he founded the Hester Hyman Trust to honour his wife's memories and her beliefs. Gort intended to help the Democratic Charter March of 2109 but the Judges were determined to prevent him from taking part. To their frustration, Gort Hyman had lived a blameless life and they were unable to discredit him, so they finally threatened to induct his two sons into the Academy of Law. Rather than see his boys become Judges, Gort withdrew from the March and even spoke out publicly against it.

See also DEMOCRATIC CHARTER GROUP,

HESTER HYMAN, HESTER HYMAN TRUST

2000AD Progs 460, 531–533

Deputy Chief Judge Grampus

ALIEN: Klegg Mercenary, Kara System; Deputy Chief Judge, Mega-City One

Brought to Earth by Chief Judge Cal, Grampus led his band of alien mercenaries on a last-ditch mission to quell the revolt against the insane ruler of Mega-City One. Judges Dredd, Griffin, Pepper and Giant and their fellow rebels were forced into retreat by the alien horde and so, thanks to Grampus, Cal found himself in command of the city once more. The alien's reward was an appointment to high office following the death of Deputy Chief Judge Fish, Cal's pet goldfish! Newly installed as Deputy Chief Judge, Grampus was responsible for enforcing a range of new and ever more stringent laws. These laws were so harsh that millions of citizens sought refuge in the Cursed Earth, only for Grampus to drive most of them back into the city by force. Many of these citizens were then put to work erecting a vast wall around Mega-City One to prevent a repetition of this attempted exodus.

However, the work was constantly disrupted by rebel raids and Chief Judge Cal knew that as long as Judge Dredd was alive, the citizens would have hope and would therefore resist him. Grampus duly took his Klegg Hounds out to track down Dredd by their sense of "taste" in an effort to finally eliminate Cal's main enemy. With frightening efficiency, the Hounds succeeded in their task and Grampus's mission certainly seemed to have ended in success when Dredd and the other key rebels' Roadliner vehicle ended up plummeting towards city bottom when they tried to escape. In fact, Dredd survived and Cal decided to nerve gas the entire population of Mega-City One shortly afterwards. Grampus and his fellow Kleggs understandably took this as their cue to depart Earth, but a desperate bid by the rebels to stop Cal saw the aliens' escape route blocked off. Grampus was killed in this final battle, as Judge Dredd and his resistance finally wrested control of their city back from the insane Chief Judge and his alien mercenary hench-beasts.

See also CHIEF JUDGE CAL, KLEGG HOUNDS

2000AD Prog 94–97, 99, 101, 104–107 (dies)

Above:
Grampus arrives in Mega-City One

Grand Hall of Justice

BUILDING: The Judges' headquarters in Mega-City One

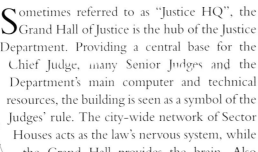

Sometimes referred to as "Justice HQ", the Grand Hall of Justice is the hub of the Justice Department. Providing a central base for the Chief Judge, many Senior Judges and the Department's main computer and technical resources, the building is seen as a symbol of the Judges' rule. The city-wide network of Sector Houses acts as the law's nervous system, while the Grand Hall provides the brain. Also contained within the building is the Hall of Heroes, the Justice Department's own tribute to fallen Judges, particularly those who have laid down their lives for the law. Meanwhile, temporary holding pens for recently arrested perps can be found underneath the headquarters.

The Grand Hall of Justice itself was built in the early days of the "Judge era", in the middle of the 21st Century, before the Judges actually took executive power over Mega-City One following the Atomic Wars of 2070. The first Chief Judge to preside there was Fargo, the much-lauded "Father of Justice" and founder of the Judges. He is commemorated by Judge Fargo's Sepulchre, a monument located in the Hall of Heroes, beneath which is located a top secret entrance to the building.

The Apocalypse War of 2104 saw the Grand Hall very heavily damaged when the East-Meg One invasion forces took over Mega-City One. It was rebuilt as a priority at the cessation of hostilities, but the new Grand Hall of Justice was also destroyed when a particularly over zealous practical joker calling himself the Prankster blew it up on the day of its opening! A second hasty rebuilding exercise was then embarked upon and this time the new new Grand Hall stood firm.

See also HALL OF HEROES, CHIEF JUDGE FARGO

Introduced: 2000AD Prog 2; Rebuilt (twice): 2000AD Prog 308

The Great Muldoon

CITIZEN: Showman, Mega-City One

An eccentric entertainer, the Great Muldoon was famous for his spectacular stunts, but everyone thought him insane when he came up with one which involved him diving through a solid steel plate into a tiny water barrel. He had somehow obtained a signed permit for the dive and insisted that he had a device which would convert his body molecules into hyperwaves capable of flowing through the metal and reforming on the other side. Even so, the Judges did everything they could to prevent him going ahead with the stunt, but by the time they could officially cancel his permit it was too late. The Great Muldoon had already begun his dive – juggling, reciting Hamlet and drinking a glass of water as he fell – only for the stunt to end with an almighty splat!

2000AD Prog 133

Tek-Judge Todd Greel
See opposite

Gribligs

ALIENS: Plexus, Deep Space

A semi-intelligent species from Plexus, Gribligs have a knack for survival and can breed like wildfire. Their cute appearance inspires a warm feeling in most people, but they are omnivorous and can be very dangerous when they attack in packs. When a Hudrick Priestly, a crew member of an interplanetary cargo ship, smuggled two Gribligs into Mega-City One, they soon multiplied. Although the Judges called in pest control, a few of them escaped by flushing themselves down the toilet! A month later, the first one was spotted loose on the city streets and it was clear that the Gribligs were in Mega-City One to stay!

2000AD Progs 464, 465

Tek-Judge Todd Greel

JUDGE: Head of Tek-Division, Mega-City One

As head of Mega-City One's Tek-Division Todd Greel set up the controversial Mechanismo Project. He brought in Tek-Judge Stich to create a number of prototype robot Judges and shared McGruder's disappointment when they went berserk on the streets. Greel personally oversaw the development of the Mark 2 robots and was highly suspicious when Judge Dredd reported a similar problem with them. The Mechanismo Project was officially suspended, but Greel was asked to continue the work in secret and create a Mark 2A model.

Tek-Judge Greel was determined to discover the truth about what had gone wrong with the "rogue" Mark 2 machine. Stich – who had been driven mad by the failure of the first wave of robots – had been the only witness to its "malfunction" apart from Judge Dredd, so Greel interrogated him until he remembered that Dredd had lied about the incident. The Tek Chief took this information to Chief Judge McGruder and she had Dredd arrested for falsifying evidence.

When the spacecraft carrying both Judge Dredd – on

route to Titan – and Chief Judge McGruder – on a sales trip – crashed on the Planet Hestia, it turned out that a Mark 2A robo had sabotaged the flight. The survivors of the crash eventually returned to Mega-City One, where Greel had been sitting in as acting Chief Judge, and the Mechanismo Project was closed down, while the Judges connected with it were investigated by the SJS. The saboteur was not found, but McGruder still didn't trust Greel, so her final act as Chief Judge was to demote him and transfer him to Traffic Control in the North-West Hab-Zone.

WE'RE GOING TO TRY SOMETHING A LITTLE MORE **POWERFUL** ON YOU THIS TIME.

See also MECHANISMO, TEK-JUDGE STICH

2000AD Progs 892-894, 910, 914, 915

Judge Dredd the Megazine Volume 2: 57

Judge Grice
See page 70

Chief Judge Griffin
See page 71

Grubb's Disease

AFFLICTION: Radiation-mutated disease, Mega-City One

Not quite the memorial Mayor Jim Grubb may have wished for, but the horrific disease which killed him – and almost caused a major epidemic in Mega-City One – was named after the unfortunate politician, so he attained a strange form of immortality thanks to the ghastly manner of his death. They also named the Jim Grubb Memorial Airport after him, but even that could never quite make people forget his fungus-covered face and the terrible disease he almost inflicted upon them.

See also MAYOR JIM GRUBB, MED-JUDGE KILDARE

Introduced: 2000AD Prog 275

Mayor Jim Grubb

CITIZEN: Mayor of Mega-City One

Although the position of Mayor in Mega-City One has never been more than a ceremonial post, Jim Grubb took his job very seriously indeed. It was his misfortune, then, that during his initial term of office Cal became Chief Judge. Publicly humiliated by being made to act like a chicken, Grubb somehow retained enough credibility to be returned for a second term. Tragically, his second period of office was cut short as Grubb went missing during the Apocalypse War and was presumed dead until he turned up in the ruined Sector 1. He was suffering from a highly contagious disease that caused his skin to become covered in fungus before killing him in a fit of delirium. Almost as if to underline the futility of his attempt to legitimise civilian politics in Mega-City One, Jim Grubb's final words were, "I am the Mushroom!" and he was promptly succeeded as Mayor by an orang-utan!

See also DAVE THE ORANG-UTAN, GRUBB'S DISEASE

2000AD Progs 92, 122, 206, 275, 276 (dies)

Judge Grice

After many years on the streets, Judge Grice was hardened to the task of maintaining law and order in Mega-City One, but nothing could prepare him for the onslaught of the Sisters of Death. Along with many of his colleagues, he was powerless to prevent them turning the city into a "necropolis" and became one of their unwitting pawns. When the evil Sisters were defeated, the Judges who failed to oppose them were shamed, but the depleted Justice Department couldn't do without them. Grice soon became a leading opposition voice to the newly re-installed Chief Judge McGruder, especially when she accepted Judge Dredd's proposal to hold a referendum on democracy. Judge Grice believed that the last thing Mega-City one needed was the possibility of a relaxation of its strict laws and he assembled a large group of supporters for that view. When it became clear that the referendum would proceed whatever he said, the embittered Judge did his best to sabotage the vote and to assassinate Judge Dredd. Grice's conspiracy was unsuccessful, however, and he soon found himself on a shuttle to the Titan Penal Colony with his fellow plotters.

Any vestige of Grice's sanity was quickly wiped out on Titan as he became the Penal Colony's most intransigent prisoner. Spending most of his time in solitary confinement, he saved up enough of his blood in small amounts to fake a suicide attempt. When the Titan-Judge Warders investigated his apparent demise, he took them unawares and effected an escape from his 'Cube. He then sparked off a riot and led a mass breakout from the Penal Colony, stopping only to personally dispose of Titan-Judge Khurtz, the brutal Judge-Governor, and to pick up the alien "Meat Virus", which was being studied in the Colony's Tek-Labs. Returning to Mega-City One, along with a vicious band of renegade Judges, Grice attacked the Grand Hall of Justice and took control of the place, after first exposing the whole city to the virus. His revenge would not be complete, however, until he had crushed Judge Dredd himself and this proved to be an impossible dream. Dredd – weakened by the Meat Virus – still outfought Grice in a final head-to-head confrontation and he then commanded his Lawmaster Bike to run the rogue Judge over repeatedly until he was dead! Grice's fellow renegades were soon rounded up after his death and they were put aboard a shuttle on its way back to Titan. Judge Dredd was willing to take no chances, though, so he blew up the shuttle once it cleared the Earth's atmosphere killing all on board!

See also MEAT VIRUS, SISTERS OF DEATH

2000AD Progs 706, 750, 752, 753, 834-841, 843-853 (dies)

Chief Judge Griffin

JUDGE: Chief Judge, Mega-City One

I TRUSTED HIS JUDGEMENT THEN — AND I TRUST IT NOW. THERE WILL **NOT** BE ANOTHER MISSION TO FIND THE **JUDGE CHILD**. I AM EXERCISING MY **VETO**!

PERHAPS WE COULD ALL DO WITH A LITTLE MORE OF WHAT DREDD'S GOT!

Fifth Chief Judge of Mega-City One, Griffin enjoyed a distinguished career as a Judge on the streets of Mega-City One before he was forced to stand down prematurely from active service due to injury. He opted to take a teaching post at the Academy of Law on his retirement and proved to be an effective and gifted Judge-Tutor, numbering Judge Dredd among his most successful students. Griffin eventually won promotion to the post of Principal of the Academy of Law, becoming responsible for the induction and training of all Judge Cadets.

In all likelihood, he would have been happy to see out his days at the Academy, but the ascension of Judge Cal to the position of Chief Judge changed all that. Cal's brainwashing of almost all the active Judges in Mega-City One meant that it fell to Griffin and a few other Judge-Tutors to help Judge Dredd in his resistance struggle against the tyrant. In the aftermath of Cal's defeat, Griffin was appointed as the new Chief Judge in recognition of his contribution to saving the city.

Sadly, his own reign as Chief Judge was to end in rather ignominious circumstances. During the Apocalypse War, Griffin was rocketed into Earth orbit so that he could direct Mega-City One's response to the East-Meg One invasion forces from a position of supposed safety. Unfortunately, the Sovs were able to track his spacecraft and they managed to capture him. Chief Judge Griffin was subsequently brainwashed on the orders of War Marshal Kazan and he was forced to denounce the Mega-City Judges on a live vid link-up, thus making him an (unwitting) traitor. With Griffin's broadcasts undermining the Judges' struggle to reclaim an already half destroyed Mega-City One, Judge Dredd was forced to execute his former teacher before he could further damage their morale.

See also THE ACADEMY OF LAW, CHIEF JUDGE CAL, WAR-MARSHAL "MAD DOG" KAZAN

2000AD Progs 27, 35, 91-102, 106-108 (becomes Chief Judge), 110, 111, 121, 122, 132, 139, 143, 145-148, 156, 182, 197, 200, 201204, 206, 207, 237, 240, 242, 244-249, 252, 260, 261 (dies)

Judge Dredd Annual 1981

CHIEF JUDGE GRIFFIN, I FIND YOU GUILTY OF **TREASON**! THE SENTENCE IS **DEATH**!

Grunwald

LOCATION: Robot Free-State, Planet Xanadu

Situated on "Open Planet" Xanadu, Grunwald offered sanctuary to robots from all over the galaxy. As a Robot Free-State – by order of its ruler, the Grunwalder – the volcanic Kingdom was a place where all kinds of robots could go to live without fear of persecution from their former human masters.

See also THE GRUNWALDER

Introduced: 2000AD Prog 179

The Grunwalder

ROBOT: Ruler, Planet Xanadu

The Grunwalder's name was legendary across the galaxy as he ruled the Robot Free-State of Grunwald on the Planet Xanadu. A robot himself, he offered a safe haven for any fellow droid, simply demanding their loyalty in return. When the Angel Gang arrived on Xanadu with the Judge Child, they sought refuge in Grunwald and the Grunwalder allowed them passage into his Kingdom. Judge Dredd was close behind, however, so the Angels didn't survive their visit to the Robot Free-State. Realising that the Judge Child was touched by a streak of evil, Dredd decided to abandon him there and the Grunwalder was more than pleased to accept him as a new slave. With the boy's help, the robot was able to gain control of the whole planet, so Xanadu was soon renamed "Grunwald's World" and declared a Robot Free-Planet. Owing a significant debt to the Judge Child, the Grunwalder helped him resurrect Mean Machine Angel when the boy sought revenge on Dredd for leaving him on Xanadu. Even though he was mostly immune to his slave's psychic powers, the robot was happy that he should vent his evil streak on someone else. The Judge Child's revenge mission failed and Dredd sent a spacecraft to destroy him. What Dredd didn't realise was that the Grunwalder had kept tissue

Below: Don't you just love being in control? The Grunwalder does!

samples from the boy and he soon began work on cloning him. Just as his work was coming to fruition, though, Judges Dredd and Anderson arrived to stop it. They had been alerted to his activities during a visit to a ghastly future Mega-City One, where a mutated Judge Child had taken over. They managed to kill the Mutant just after it had been "born". Grunwalder soon grasped the terrible implications of the Judges' visit and as they couldn't trust the robot they were forced to destroy him, too.

See also ANGEL GANG, JUDGE CHILD, GRUNWALD, THE MUTANT, XANADU

2000AD Progs 179-181, 282, 285, 288, 401, 406 (dies)

Guard-o-Ped

ORGANISATION: Bodyguards agency, Mega-City One

Are you tired of being mugged? Kent Fassbinder was convinced that the Mega-City One citizens were, so he founded the Guard-o-Ped Corporation, a Pedestrian Escort Agency providing protection on the streets. With a Guard-o-Ped "G-Man" at your side, you could feel safe even in the city's highest risk areas. The G-Men cost money, however, and their presence soon caused resentment. Soon it became the in-thing to mug a G-Man and the Fassbinder's Guard-o-Ped operation quickly fell apart. To cope with the ensuing chaos, Chief Judge McGruder legalised the dangerous but effective Anti-Mugging Suits and Guard-o-Ped went out of business. Kent Fassbinder was ruined and he turned to mugging himself, only to become one of the first fatalities of the Anti-Mugging Suits!

See also ANTI-MUGGING SUITS

2000AD Prog 354

H

H-Wagons

VEHICLE: Flying Transport, Mega-City One
Justice Department

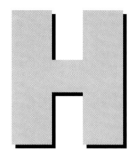

The Judges' most adapt-able and fastest mode of transport around Mega-City One and its outlying areas, Hover-Wagons – H-Wagons as they are popularly known – are well-armed saucer-shaped aircraft. Capable of vertical take off and landing, they are extremely fast and manoeu-vrable, making them perfect patrol vehicles in and around the city – although their range is fairly limited, so they are rarely used far out-side Mega-City One.

Introduced: 2000AD Prog 134

Haemophytes

PLANTS: Mutant parasites, Cursed Earth

Rooting themselves into their vic-tims' host bodies, Haemophytes take on human form and live in colonies, but need the blood of further victims for sustenance. One group, living in the Cursed Earth township of Slake City, used illegal quasi-religious broadcasts promising a better life there to attract victims from Mega-City One – until Judge Dredd tracked them down and exposed the awful truth about their cult.

2000AD Progs 895, 896

Hall of Heroes

LOCATION: Grand Hall of Justice,
Mega-City One

The Hall of Heroes commemorates those Judges who have contributed most to Mega-City One, either by individual acts of heroism or by a lifetime of dedication. The most famous exhibit there is Judge Fargo's Sepulchre, although Judge Anderson was a res-ident here for a while when she was encased in Boing along with the spirit form of Judge Death. At the time she was described as having made the ultimate sacrifice to save the city, but she was later freed unharmed when Death himself made his escape.

Introduced: 2000AD Prog 107

Heavy Metal Kids

ROBOTS: Massive Heavy-Duty Industrial
Robots, Mega-City One

Almost certainly the most powerful robots in com-mon use in Mega-City One, Heavy Metal Kids are huge industrial drones, possessing limited intelli-gence and rather suggestible personalities. They must therefore be strictly con-trolled and since a number of them formed a sizeable threat during the Robot Wars they have been equipped with super-rein-forced obedience circuits and behaviour inhibitors.

2000AD Progs 9, 12, 15, 16

*Judge Dredd the Megazine
Volume 2: 51*

Hellfire Club

GROUP: Criminals, Mega-City One

Anihilistic little grouping dedicated to causing death and destruction in order to relieve the boredom of life in Mega-City One, the Hellfire Club was a loose association of bloodthirsty juves. Murdering Judges was their ultimate goal, but three of their number – Boom, Zit and Nick – picked the wrong target when they killed Judge Harkness. Although highly irregular, she and fellow Judge Bryce had been lovers, and Bryce was gunning for revenge. In the end, the Hellfire Club members were captured, but not killed, thanks to the intervention of Judge Dredd, who was forced to kill Bryce rather than let him murder the juves in cold blood – and thereby break the law himself.

2000AD Prog 137

Helltrek

EVENT: Journey across the Cursed Earth

With life proving extremely tough for many citizens of Mega-City One, the prospect of leaving the city for the New Territories, deep into the Cursed Earth, has become increasingly attractive to the population of America's greatest megalopolis. Therefore regular "Helltreks" are organised by private citizens, involving convoys of vehicles taking on the highly dangerous journey to a new home. Survival chances on a Helltrek are not good in the radioactive wasteland, but there is no shortage of people willing to take the risk in the pursuit of a new life, free of the constraints of a Mega-City.

Introduced: 2000AD Prog 387

Henry Ford

ANIMAL: Mutant horse, Cursed Earth

Possessing remarkable intelligence and the ability to speak, Henry was no ordinary horse. He was in fact a mutant horse, belonging to Moze Bigleftear, the first resident of Atom Gulch to recognise the danger of the Black Plague – a massive swarm of mutant spiders heading for the town. Under protest Henry carried Moze to Mega-City One in search of help and then, after Judge Dredd had turned the spiders away from Atom Gulch and towards his city, the unfortunate horse was forced to make the journey again. This time he had to carry Dredd, since the Judge's Lawmaster Bike had been wrecked, so that he could warn the other Judges about the impending threat of the Black Plague. Poor Henry was bitten by the poisonous spiders on the way, but he survived and was fixed up by the Mega-City One medics, before being returned to Atom Gulch.

See also BLACK PLAGUE, MOZE BIGLEFTEAR

2000AD Progs 140-143

Judge Paul Herriman

JUDGE: Mega-City One

A well-respected and very experienced Senior Judge, Paul Herriman believed he was the ideal candidate for the job of Chief Judge when McGruder resigned the post in 2116. He was the first Judge to put himself forward for the job, citing his abilities as a conciliator able to heal the wounds in the Mega-City One Justice Department, but he failed in his bid since many of his colleagues thought him too keen to try and please everybody. They opted instead for the more hardline Hadrian Volt

2000AD Prog 916

Judge Dredd the Magazine Volume 2: 57

Judge Barbara Hershey

JUDGE: Mega-City One

Shortly after her graduation from the Academy of Law, Judge Hershey was the surprise choice to join the crew of the Justice 1 for the dangerous deep space mission to find the Judge Child. Working closely with Judge Dredd every step of the way, she came through the mission with great credit and was highly commended in his personal log. Hershey returned to the streets of Mega-City One a tougher and infinitely more experienced Judge, but she was ill-prepared for the attack of Fink Angel some months later, when he came seeking revenge on the Judges responsible for the deaths of his brothers and his Pa. The young Judge barely escaped, but she had already developed a knack for survival – a knack which came in useful during the Apocalypse War when Hershey was called upon again by Judge Dredd to join his Apocalypse Squad.

After the war, Hershey was promoted to Senior Judge and when Chief Judge McGruder resigned her position four years later, Hershey became the youngest ever member of the Council of Five. Her meteoric rise up the Justice Department's 'greasy pole' saw her hotly tipped to become Chief Judge in due course, but she denied any real ambitions in this direction. Even so, she soon experienced the power that goes with the office, since she was asked to sit in as acting-Chief Judge when McGruder – back for an unprecedented second term of office – attended a crisis meeting of Judges from all over the world to find a way to defeat Sabbat the Necromagus. Hershey was later part of the delegation of Senior Judges who tried to convince McGruder to reform the Council of Five – inactive since the Dark Judges had controlled Mega-City One – but the Chief Judge refused to comply, as she suspected Hershey was after her job. McGruder's judgement had definitely become questionable, but she insisted on remaining the only voice at the top of the

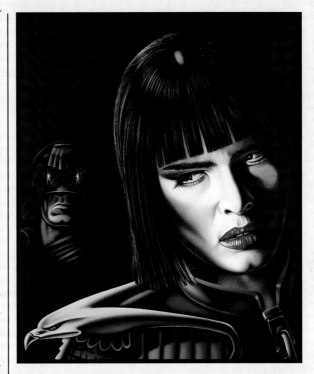

Justice Department until one of the Mechanismo robots she was so enthusiastic about tried to kill her. Realising her error at last, McGruder wasted no time in tendering her resignation and she entrusted Judge Hershey – along with SJS Chief Niles and Psi Chief Shenker – with the job of running the Justice Department until a new Chief Judge could be selected. Hershey was the only one of those three who actually put their name forward for the post, expressing her desire for more open government. Her views did not go down terribly well with her colleagues, however, and she received only 13 votes in the ballot among Senior Judges, while the new Chief Judge, Hadrian Volt, romped home with 208!

See also JUDGE CHILD, FINK ANGEL

2000AD Progs 162, 164, 167-170, 172-177, 181, 194-196, 263-266, 269, 270, 284, 300-303, 337, 338, 395, 396, 447, 530, 573, 623-625, 662, 706, 734, 735, 743-745, 754-756, 761, 789, 792, 796, 798, 806, 807, 826, 829, 845, 846, 848, 850-853, 866, 886-888, 891, 915-917

Judge Dredd the Megazine Volume 1: 1, 7; Volume 2: 7, 9, 12, 14-17, 25-30, 35-40, 57, 68

Judge Dredd Mega-Specials 1989, 1993

2000AD Winter Special 1993

Judge Dredd Annual 1988

Judge Dredd Yearbooks 1994, 1995

2000AD Yearbook 1995

Hester Hyman

CITIZEN: Civil rights activist, Mega-City One

Hester Hyman accepts her fate

Hester Hyman's life as a civil rights activist was a secret from her family and friends, but her belief in democracy was something she held very dear. Unable to face the prospect of her sons growing up in a city ruled through the kind of fear inspired by the Judges, she led the Democratic Tendency's take-over of Channel 48, when they presented their "Democratic Charter" live on air. Hester and her comrades died when the Judges recaptured the station, but she became a symbol for the democratic movement in the city. The Hester Hyman Trust was founded in her memory by her husband Gort with the intention of uniting the various civil rights groups in Mega-City One.

See also DEMOCRATIC TENDENCY, HESTER HYMAN TRUST

2000AD Prog 460 (dies)

Hester Hyman Trust

ORGANISATION: Civil rights group, Mega-City One

When Gort Hyman discovered that his wife had been a closet member of the Democratic Tendency- and that this had led to her death – he was horrified. But he soon began to understand her motivations and so founded the Hester Hyman Trust in her memory to try and achieve the dream of democracy for which she had given her life. The Trust was dedicated to arranging meetings between the leaders of the many democratic pressure groups in Mega-City One, until they were all in agreement and ready to unite under one banner and challenge the Judges as the Democratic Charter Group.

See also DEMOCRATIC CHARTER GROUP, GORT HYMAN

2000AD Progs 531–533

Holding Post

DEVICE: Temporary perp holding place, Mega-City One

Located all over Mega-City One, and over its moon colony, Luna-1, Holding Posts provide the Judges with a safe place to leave a criminal they have captured while they deal with another crime. Trapped by an advanced cuffing system, it is virtually impossible for the perp to escape from the Holding Post before he or she is picked by a Justice Department Pat-Wagon.

Introduced: 2000AD Prog 58

Highwaymen

GROUPS: Street pirates, Mega-City One

With thousands of Mo-Pads constantly on the move along the Mega-Ways of Mega-City One, there are rich pickings for Highwaymen – criminals who attack and rob them as they travel along. Because the scene of their crime is in perpetual motion, Highwaymen can be very hard to catch!

2000AD Prog 353

Hondo City

CITY: Japan

By the 22nd Century, Japan has become known as Hondo City and is policed by its Judge-Inspectors. Worshipped and feared like the Samurai Warlords of ancient Japan, these Judge-Inspectors proudly boast of a crime-free city. This is far from the truth, however, and Hondo City suffers from many of the same problems which beset its Western counterparts. Relations between Mega-City One and Hondo City are traditionally strained, but the world-wide menace of Sabbat the Necromagus saw an international council of Judges meeting in Hondo and links were strengthened.

Introduced: 2000AD Prog 608

Judge Honus

**JUDGE: Deputy Chief Judge,
Texas City**

Tough and uncompromising, Judge Honus delighted in his spell in charge of Texas City when its Chief Judge had to spend some time out of town. A great believer in the autonomy of his city, Honus was most uncooperative when Judge Dredd came to Texas City, looking to round up a large number of missing perps believed to be hiding out there. In fact, he put so many obstacles in the Judge's way that Dredd was forced to take on the role of an officially appointed debt collector in order to track down his perps without interference from the Texas City Justice Department!

Judge Dredd the Megazine Volume 2: 1, 2

Hounds of Klegg

**ALIEN RACE: Dull-witted servants
of the Kleggs, Kara System**

Hideous creatures who track their quarry using their ultra-sensitive sense of taste, the Hounds of Klegg provide an invaluable service to their alien masters. Their fearsome appearance inspires terror in their victims, though their low intelligence makes them less dangerous than they look.

See also KLEGGS

2000AD Progs 96–98

Hover-Bike

**VEHICLE: Judges' standard issue
'motorcycle', Luna-1**

The Hover Bikes used on the moon colony of Luna-1 are specially adapted versions of the Lawmaster Mk1, but are not really "Bikes" at all. Designed to operate in low gravity, complete with emergency life support equipment, they actually hover off the ground, making them the ideal mode of transport over the moon's rough terrain. Similar vehicles – Zipper Bikes – are sometimes used in Mega-City One by one of the Judges' special units, the Flying Squad.

See also LAWMASTER BIKE, ZIPPER BIKE

Introduced: 2000AD Prog 44

Howler

**ALIEN: Galactic Dominator,
origin and species unknown**

With his "Voice of Thunder", Howler could rightly refer to himself as a "Razer of Planets", but he wanted a quiet world to call home. He picked earth as a peaceful haven to return to in between his conquests, but he reckoned without Dredd. In Mega-City One, all Howler wanted was total subservience, a ready supply of cows, plus around twenty citizens to torture every day! Oddly enough, Dredd was unwilling to comply with his requests and, despite considerable injuries inflicted by the alien, he would not give in. Howler was a little peeved by the Judge's persistence and attempted to howl the city into oblivion. Unfortunately, he got a little too carried away and simply managed to shout himself to pieces!

Judge Dredd the Megazine Volume 2: 53–56 (dies)

Hunters Club

**ORGANISATION: Secret murderers club,
Mega-City One**

Run by the sinister Elmort Devries, the Hunters Club was a collection of killers who relieved the tedium of life by carrying out random murders. At each of their regular meetings one member was selected to be the hunter and their computer chose a victim. Their operation was disrupted when a new member got cold feet and had to be killed, but the Club simply changed its meeting place to avoid detection and continued with their business as usual. The Club was finally traced when Elmort Devries came up with "Death Aid' – a sponsored hunt. The mass slaughter which followed made the Hunters Club hideout easy to find and Dredd was able to put a stop to their murderous activities for good.

See also DEATH AID, ELMORT DEVRIES

2000AD Progs 407–411, 711–715, 719, 720

I

I-Block

BUILDING: Justice Department 'safe house', Mega-City One

Built to withstand anything short of a nuke, Isolation-Blocks are just about the most secure places in Mega-City One. Typically used to keep informants – and perps who have decided to turn 'Judges' Witness' – safe from attack by mob blitzers and the like, I-Blocks are equipped with high-powered lasers and have well-shielded sentry posts at the top which are continually manned.

Introduced: 2000AD Prog 231

Institute For Ethical Violence

BUILDING: Mega-City One

The forerunner to Mega-City One's Academy of Law, the Institute For Ethical Violence was founded by Eustace Fargo in 2010 as the first stage of his major judicial review. The Institute was to be the headquarters of and training establishment for Fargo's new Judges, who he planned would eventually take to the streets in order to dispense instant Justice to the citizens, ultimately replacing the old police force and court system.

See CHIEF JUDGE EUSTACE FARGO

Judge Dredd #s 1-6

Judge Inspector Aiko Inaba

JUDGE: Hondo City Justice Department

As a woman, Aiko Inaba is unique among the Judge Inspectors of Hondo City – sexism is so ingrained within their Justice Department that it is almost unthinkable that a woman should attain the post. In fact, when Inaba was assigned to Judge Inspector Shimura as a Cadet for a personal assessment it was assumed that he would fail her or direct her into a peripheral area of the Judges' operations, but instead he recommended her for promotion to full Judge Inspector. Despite pressure from Hondo's Chief Judge to reverse his decision, Shimura stuck by Inaba and she was duly promoted. When Shimura subsequently vanished and went 'ronin', the female Judge Inspector was put in charge of a squad to bring him in, dead or alive, but she ended up helping him against the Yakuza clans.

See also JUDGE INSPECTOR SHIMURA

Judge Dredd the Magazine Volume 2: 37-39, 50-55

The Invisible Man

CITIZEN: Criminal, Mega-City One

Benji Doonan was a cleaner, working for Inter-Time – a company that had developed an incredible time-warp device – when he got his hands on a prototype machine capable of stretching out a second into hours within a specified time field. Using the device to produce a time field around himself, he was able to carry out a series of audacious crimes, proclaiming himself to be the "Invisible Man". Of course, he was never invisible, he was simply moving at an incredible speed compared to everyone around him, so that no-one could actually see him carry out the robberies. Confident of his ability to confound the Judges, Doonan sent them regular warnings of his crimes, but Judge Dredd finally discovered his identity. Surprising him in his apartment, Dredd acted before Doonan could activate his time field and make his escape – shooting him as he hit the button on the time-warp device. Unfortunately for the criminal, he was wounded badly by the shot, but the Judge was unable to save his life, since hours passed for the dying Invisible Man – trapped inside the time field – while a mere second ticked by for Dredd.

See also EDWIN "THE CONFESSOR" PARSEY

2000AD Prog 135

Iso-Cubes

BUILDINGS: Prison cells, Mega-City One

Although a few older prisons still exist in Mega-City One, 99% of all perps find themselves doing time in the 'Cubes. These individual cells, housed in high-security prison blocks, serve to isolate prisoners for much of the period of their incarceration and they are constantly guarded by Judge-Warders, so escape from an Iso-Cube is virtually unheard of.

Introduced: 2000AD Prog 148

Sov-Judge Izaaks

JUDGE: East-Meg One

War Marshall "Mad Dog" Kazan's right hand man, Judge Izaaks was the Sov War Marshal's constant companion during the nuclear assault on Mega-City One. It was his job to keep Kazan fully informed as to the progress of the Apocalypse War, but Izaaks often found himself walking a dangerous tightrope. The "Mad Dog" did not take news of setbacks well and he blamed those around him, frequently consigning his own staff members to exile! When Judge Dredd escaped the clutches of a virtual army of Sov-Judges at the Grand Hall of Justice, the War Marshal exiled them all, but he was lenient on Izaaks and demoted him to the rank of Kadet. Kazan was in a considerably less generous mood when Judge Dredd went on to annihilate East-Meg One, however, and – unsure who to blame for this catastrophe – the "Mad Dog" concentrated his anger on the unfortunate Kadet. He made Izaaks play Russian Roulette with an antique revolver every day and generally made his life a misery until the former Judge could stand it no more. Realising that the war was lost, but that it would not be over until everyone was dead if Kazan got his way, Izaaks freed Judge Dredd and asked him to kill the War Marshal, since he could not bring himself to do the job. Dredd gladly obliged and the war was finally over as the Sovs surrendered to him unconditionally.

See also WAR MARSHAL "MAD DOG" KAZAN

2000AD Progs 250, 251, 256, 258-260, 262, 263, 267, 269, 270

J

J70 Stroke 13

ROBOT: General Purpose Droid, Mega-City One

During the Robot Wars most robots joined with Call-me-Kenneth in his bid to overthrow the "Fleshy Ones", but a few remained loyal to humankind. J70 Stroke 13 was one of the first to join Walter the Wobot in his opposition to the robot dictator and, for his part in the eventual victory of the Judges, he was rewarded with a pleasure circuit in a grand ceremony after the war.

2000AD Progs 15-17

Judge Jack

JUDGE: Mega-City One

A trusted colleague of Judge Dredd's, Judge Jack was part of the small but hand-picked team who accompanied him on his quest to cross the Cursed Earth by land to deliver the vital 2T(FRU)T plague vaccine to Mega-City Two. Jack played a major role in ensuring the success of the mission, but the horrors of the Cursed Earth took its toll on his sanity. Not many people could hang from the mouth of a slavering Tyrannosaurus Rex for three hours, but Jack survived with only minor physical injuries. Unfortunately, the mental scars from this experience were far more damaging and when the Judge faced the crazed robots of the "Legion of the Damned" in Death Valley, he finally cracked. Suddenly finding himself unable to act in a rational manner, Judge Jack became an easy target for the robots and he met his end, at least buying a little more time for his comrades to regroup and plan their next move against the Legion.

2000AD Progs 12, 62, 63, 65, 72-78, 83 (dies)

Doctor James Julius Gold

CITIZEN: Mega-City One

Proprietor of the Forever Towers Home for the Semi-dead, James Julius Gold made his living by keeping very rich clients in cryogenic suspension, so that they might spin out their last few hours of life into centuries. However, he became greedy when he found that his patients would tell him anything if he revived them just enough to make them capable of conscious thought. Using the information thus extracted, he blackmailed their living relatives through a third party, Jurgen Monks, who collected the money down at Ryker's Shuggy Hall. When one of the victims killed himself, his mother – a resident at Forever Towers – was able to finger Monks and the trail led Judge Dredd back to Dr Gold as the true mastermind behind the blackmailing. The doctor was prepared to kill Dredd rather than give up his scam, but instead took a homing bullet through the head. Before he died, though, Dredd was able to get him into the Justice Department's own Sus-An Chambers. James Julius Gold would be revived when his wounds could be healed, so that he could serve the full sentence for his crimes!

2000AD Prog 120

Right:
James Julius Gold tries to put Dredd on ice

Jeffrey Jacobi

CITIZEN: Hitman, Mega-City One

A pathological killer, Jeffrey Jacobi specialised in the "motiveless" murders of celebrities – he even put pictures of his many victims on his wall! He had planned to kill Mega-City One's Supersurf Champion Chopper when Judge Dredd brought him back from Oz, but the skysurfer escaped from the Judge and never returned. Jacobi blamed Dredd for this missed opportunity, so he decided to move the Judge to the top of his hit list. Having first blown him up, then taken him out  with a sniper bullet, the "Hitman" could hardly believe that the Judge had survived. Hospitalised – requiring a new lung and repairs to his damaged skull – Dredd appeared to be an easy target, but he kept his Lawgiver close to hand and, when Jacobi turned up to finish the job, the Judge blew him away!

2000AD Prog 571-573 (dies)

Psi-Judge Janus

JUDGE: Psi-Division, Mega-City One

Having just turned eighteen and received her full Eagle as a Mega-City One Psi-Judge, Janus's first real taste of action came when Grice and his fellow rogue Judges from Titan attacked the city and infected its citizens with the meat virus. She worked well with Bhaji, a Psi-Judge from Delhi-Cit, during the struggle to regain control of Mega-City One, and Janus acquitted herself well as the renegades were finally defeated.

See also JUDGE GRICE, PSI-JUDGE BHAJI

2000AD Prog 842-846, 848, 850-853

Jigsaw Disease

AFFLICTION: Wasting disease, Planet Ab

An unbelievable affliction, native to an unexplainably alien world, the Jigsaw Disease actually makes parts of its victims disappear piece by piece. Death is lingering, but certain, and there are few diseases more traumatic than one in which chunks of your own body keep on vanishing in front of your eyes – that's always assuming your eyes don't vanish first, of course, since the disease's effects are quite random!

Introduced: 2000AD Prog 172

Jimp

TERM: Judge Impersonator, Mega-City One

Being a Judge impersonator – or a Jimp – is a serious offence in Mega-City One, whether the faker is a criminal using the uniform to help in pulling off a crime, or an ordinary citizen dressing up for a costume party. Either way, Jimps are taking their lives in their hands, because if the Judges don't get you, the law-breakers probably will!

Introduced: 2000AD Prog 295

John "Giant" Clay

CITIZEN: Mega-City One

World-famous Aeroball and Inferno sports star in his youth, John Clay had seen a great deal of tragedy in his life and wanted his son to be able to look after himself and have a worthwhile career. So he enrolled him at the Academy of Law and the boy began training as a Judge under the name of Cadet Giant.

See also JUDGE GIANT

2000AD Prog 28

John Kilroy Henders

CITIZEN: Mega-City One

In a city with 87% unemployment, having more than one job is a serious offence, but Citizen Henders loved working so much that he managed to land no less than three jobs! The Judges were alerted when they realised he was pulling in 12 thousand credits a year but was spending 30 thousand. The only question remaining is when did he find the time to spend his cash?

2000AD Prog 342

Johnny Alpha

MUTANT: Earth, 2176 A.D.

A mutant bounty from Earth's future, Johnny Alpha – real name John Kreelman – came to Mega-City One with his partner Wulf in search of two mass murderers with large prices on their heads. His accreditation as a Search and Destroy Agent – or "Strontium Dog' - meant nothing to Judge Dredd, however, and he was about to arrest the mutant when Wulf Sternhammer surprised the Judge and knocked him unconscious. The bounty hunters then managed to escape back to their own time.

Johnny Alpha showed up again two years later in Hondo City, on the trail of Sabbat the Necromagus. Alpha was alone this time and he soon clashed with Hondo's top lawman, Judge-Inspector Sadu. The battle was short-lived, as the Hondo Judges were fast becoming preoccupied with Sabbat's zombie hordes and it was obvious that Johnny Alpha could help. When Judges from all over the world launched their final assault against Sabbat, Judge Dredd strongly opposed the inclusion of the renegade mutant on the mission, but Alpha secretly took Judge-Sergeant Joyce's place. In the event, the bounty hunter's mutant powers proved crucial, and thanks to his contribution to the defeat of Sabbat he was granted a judicial pardon for his "crimes". With the Necromagus safely on ice, Johnny Alpha and Dredd parted on respectful if not friendly terms and the mutant returned to his own time.

See also SABBAT THE NECROMAGUS

2000AD Prog 793-796, 798, 799

Judge Dredd the Megazine Volume 2: 4-7, 9, 45

Judge Dredd Annual 1991

2000AD Graphic Novel: Top Dog

Johnny Teardrop

CITIZEN: Game show presenter, Mega-City One

Presenting one of the most popular vid-shows ever made Johnny Teardrop one of the city's best-paid entertainers. His ability for wringing out the maximum human interest in the pathetic plight of his contestants was legendary, but he ran into trouble when 41 of them were murdered after having their addresses broadcast on his show. Although Dredd caught the criminals responsible, Johnny had to face up to the prospect of massive lawsuits from the dead contestants' relatives and so the final sob story on Sob Story was his own!

2000AD Progs 131, 132

Jon Baptiste

CITIZEN: Religious Leader, Mega-City One

When Jon Baptiste's Christian rallies began to attract large numbers of citizens, the Judges became very interested. Some Justice Department hard-liners suspected the preacher of a hidden anti-social agenda, but he only ever advocated love and peace, urging his followers to reject aggression in favour of compassion and understanding. He was brought in for interrogation by Judges Goon and Anderson, so that the nature of his "threat" could be determined. Goon came down hard on the Christian, but Anderson tried a psi-scan on him. Overwhelmed by the purity of Baptiste's faith and his innate "goodness", she became angry when Goon tried to bully him further, and a fight followed. Anderson found herself questioning her role as a Judge, so when her colleagues faked a confession and then staged his "suicide", her doubts were magnified a thousandfold.

See also JUDGE GOON, PSI-JUDGE ANDERSON

Judge Dredd the Megazine Volume 2: 22-24 (dies)

Jonni Kiss

CITIZEN: French Quarter, Euro-Cit

An international hitman of renown, Jonni Kiss had a large number of Judge killings to his credit when he was asked to assassinate East-Meg Two's Supreme Judge Traktorfaktori. The job was passed onto him by an anonymous client and he accomplished it with ease, only to discover that Traktorfaktori had just been a decoy. Jonni's real target was to be Judge Dredd and the contract on the Mega-City Judge remains outstanding, as the assassin awaits his moment to strike.

2000AD Prog 830

Judge-Sergeant Joyce

JUDGE: Emerald Isle

One of Murphyville's best-respected and well-liked Judge-Sergeants, Charlie Joyce got the opportunity to work alongside Judge Dredd when the famous lawman visited the Emerald Isle looking for former mob blitzer Bonny Staples. Joyce's drinking and womanising came as a shock to Dredd, but codes of conduct for a Murphyville Judge-Sergeant are quite different to those for Judges. Dredd livened things up for Joyce during his stay – between them they virtually wiped out the Sons of Erin liberation group and saw off the

Mega-City hitman. Their paths crossed again in graver circumstances, when Sabbat almost killed everyone on Earth with his zombie army. Joyce was part of the group selected to take the battle to Sabbat and was mightily relieved to see the Necromagus defeated. A short while after this, Joyce visited the Big Meg on the trail of a group of bank robbers, but he wasn't made welcome and he didn't enjoy his stay at all.

See also BONNY STAPLES, SONS OF ERIN

2000AD Progs 728-732, 793, 794, 796, 798, 799, 804-807

Judge Dredd the Megazine Volume 2: 5, 8

Judge Dredd Yearbook 1993

Left: Jon Baptiste preaches to the unconverted

Judge Morton Judd

JUDGE: Renegade, Mega-City One

As Head of Genetics and a prominent member of the Council of Five, Morton Judd was a powerful voice in the Justice Department after the Atomic Wars. At Genetic Control, his Tek-Judges had perfected cloning with a number of successes – most notably Judge Joe Dredd, who had been cloned from the DNA of Chief Judge Fargo. With Meg One in turmoil following the war, Judd proposed a radical solution to the problem of policing an overcrowded city, packed with 400 million potential perps. He wanted to clone the citizenry as well as the Judges and so create a docile and obedient population. Morton Judd's views found an echo among many of his colleagues, but Chief Judge Fargo overruled him, pointing out that the Judges' first duty was to serve, not control. The Head of Genetics refused to accept and tried to assassinate him, only to be outwitted. Judd and a number of his followers were scheduled for execution for their betrayal, but they were rescued at the last moment and managed to flee Mega-City One with a batch of genetic material.

In the difficult days which followed, the apprehension of Morton Judd was given a very low priority and he was presumed dead until he reappeared almost forty years later. Having built a secret base inside the caves of Ayers Rock in the Radback of Oz, Judd started to breed his own army of "Judges" called the Judda from the DNA stock he had taken from the Justice Department. He despatched a group of them via sophisticated teleportation devices to Mega-City One to kill several key Judges. One of the invaders was captured, and Dredd was able to use his teleport machine to return to Judd's base. This intrusion forced Morton Judd to accelerate his mass assault on the Grand Hall of Justice, but the Judge took Judd's own teleport device and got back there first. Forewarned, the Judges were ready for the onslaught and Dredd teleported an armed nuke back to Ayers Rock, ending Morton Judd's dream and his life in massive conflagration.

See also THE JUDDA

2000AD Progs 559-563 (dies), 676 (cameo)

The Judda

ORGANISATION: Morton Judd's personal army, Ayers Rock

Below:
The Judda invade Mega-City One

Cloned from genetic material stolen from the Justice Department's Genetic Control by renegade Tek-Judges working with Morton Judd, the "Judda" were based in a secret hideout inside Ayers Rock in the Oz Radback. In the space of forty years, the caves there had been transformed into the "Halls of Judd", a mockery of the Grand Hall of Justice in Mega-City One. The Judda wore uniforms loosely styled on those of the Judges of that city and in different circumstances they would have almost certainly grown up in the Academy of Law. Having been cloned from the DNA of distinguished Judges, the Judda were conditioned from birth to obey Morton Judd.

Their number grew throughout the years until Judd was ready to seek revenge on Mega-City One and, with the use of personal teleport devices, an advance guard went there to kill certain key Judges, the only survivor among whom was Dredd. When Dredd primed a nuke with a ten second fuse and teleported it back to Ayers Rock, Morton Judd and hundreds of his followers were killed instantly, while the surviving Judda were rounded up. Only a few of them were taken alive – among them Kraken, who shared his bloodline with Judge Dredd and was later inducted into the Academy of Law as Dredd's possible future replacement. Kraken was the only member of the Judda who was allowed to live – his "brothers" were all executed for their crimes against the city.

See also MORTON JUDD, JUDGE KRAKEN

Introduced: 2000AD Prog 551

The Judge Child

CITIZEN: Juve, Mega-City One

Owen Krysler was born in Mega-City One, but his parents moved out to a settlement in the Cursed Earth when he was still quite young. There were two distinguishing things about Owen – first, he bore a remarkable birthmark on his forehead in the shape of the Eagle of Justice and, second, he possessed incredibly powerful psi-powers.

When Psi-Judge Feyy made his dying prediction in 2102 about impending doom for Mega-City One in 2120, he warned that the city would not survive unless they could find the "Judge Child" and install him as Chief Judge to guide them through the catastrophe. Psi-Division soon identified Owen as this Judge Child and Judge Dredd was sent into the Cursed Earth to locate the Kryslers. Unfortunately, he found Owen's parents dead, murdered by mutant slavers, and discovered that the boy had been sold into slavery.

Judge Dredd tracked the Judge Child to the Brotherhood of Trash, but just when he thought he had the boy in his grasp, one of the Brothers escaped with him. Brother Bunsen took him to Texas City, where Owen fell into the hands of the Angel Gang. They soon realised how valuable the Judge Child could be to them, so the Angels commandeered a spacecraft and took refuge in deep space. Judge Dredd led a mission to find them, but it was a long while before he caught up with the desperadoes on the Planet Xanadu. The Angels sought refuge in Grunwald, a Kingdom run by a mysterious and powerful robot, but Dredd wiped out the entire criminal family anyway. The "Grunwalder" himself chose not to intervene in events and it was an unexpected bonus for him when the Judge decided to leave the Judge Child with him, since Dredd was convinced the boy was evil.

Owen Krysler stayed with the Grunwalder and used his power to help him gain control of Xanadu, but he remained bitter at his rejection by Dredd. Seeking revenge on him, the Judge Child reanimated Mean Machine Angel using a mystical potion obtained for him by the Grunwalder. He then employed his powers to free Fink Angel from a Mega-City One Iso-Cube in order that the Angels could kill the Judge for him. Ultimately, they failed and Owen Krysler's execution was ordered by Chief Judge McGruder. While the Grunwalder was sorry to lose his most useful slave, he made no effort to shield him and the Judge Child was killed by a missile fired from a Mega-City One spacecraft manned by robots immune to his psi-power. However, unknown to the Judges, the Grunwalder did keep some tissue samples from the boy, just in case he ever felt the need to clone him ...

See also ANGEL GANG, GRUNWALDER, MUTANT

2000AD Progs 156, 160, 173, 176, 177, 179-181, 281-286, 288 (dies)

"Judge Dredd"

MUTANT: Radburg, Cursed Earth

When a deranged mutant breezed into town, the citizens of Radburg guessed that trouble was brewing, but when he found a magazine featuring the adventures of Judge Dredd, all hell broke loose. The mutant fashioned a special uniform and set himself up as the local lawman - "Judge Dredd"! Unfortunately, his laws were insane and all punishable by death, as such things as the wearing of brown shoes and coughing in the courthouse became capital crimes. When the real Judge Dredd happened upon his namesake, he decided to execute the mad mutant, but "Judge Dredd" had other ideas. Disillusioned with his hero, the "lawman" tried to burn him at the stake, but the Mega-City One Judge escaped the fire and took out the mutant and his deputies – helped by the fact that "Judge Dredd" tried to use Judge Dredd's Lawgiver Gun and it exploded when it refused to acknowledge the mutant as the genuine article!

2000AD Progs 474, 475 (dies)

Judge Dredd Robot

ROBOT: Simulacrum, Mega-City One

Specially built by the robotics genius Chick Parker, of Moderna Robots, this robot was remarkably lifelike and, programmed with every piece of information possible on Judge Dredd, it was almost identical to the original. This information was supplied from classified computer files by Deputy Chief Judge Cal, who had ordered the machine to be built and then used it to frame Dredd for murder. While he was resting after his arduous journey across the Cursed Earth to Mega-City Two, his robot double disrupted a newspaper office and killed two reporters. Lots of witnesses identified him, so Judge Dredd was arrested by the Special Judicial Squad in the morning and he was subsequently convicted of murder and sentenced to twenty years on Titan. Refusing to accept that he could have committed the crime without realising it, Dredd escaped from the spacecraft carrying him to the Penal Colony and hunted down the robot – destroying it, but leaving just enough of it intact to prove his innocence.

2000AD Progs 86-88 (destroyed)

Judge Dredd Zombie

Mega-City One

When Judges Dredd and Anderson were sent forward in time to the Mega-City One of 2120 to investigate the disaster predicted by Judge Feyy back in 2102, they encountered many horrors in a city run by the hideously disfigured Mutant. None of them was quite as disturbing as the Judge Dredd Zombie, however, since the creature was the reanimated body of the hastily murdered Judge Dredd of that time. The Mutant regretted killing Dredd in a fit of anger and was delighted with the opportunity to make him suffer properly when the time travelling Judges turned up and he was able to pitch the Dredd Zombie against them. As in life, Dredd proved an indefatigable opponent as a zombie and he pursued Dredd and Anderson all the way back to their time machine. Only when they left 2120 did the creature drop to the ground lifeless, as its link with the Mutant was broken. The Judge Dredd Zombie was declared harmless when they arrived back in their own time and it was put on display in the Justice Department's Black Museum, where it remains – despite the fact that the future which spawned it has supposedly been eliminated.

See also MUTANT

2000AD Progs 402-406

Judgement of Solomon

EVENT: Legal Judgement, American Mega-Cities

The crimes of Robert L. Booth, the last President of the United States, were so terrible that his punishment had to be severe. He was responsible for the outbreak of the devastating Atomic Wars in 2070, which saw billions of casualties world-wide, yet the execution of North America's last President was not an option for the judicial system of the time. One of the most respected lawmen of his day, Judge Solomon, therefore made a unique judgement – condemning President Booth to a "living death" by sentencing him to 100 years in suspended animation in a specially built "tomb" underneath Fort Knox!

See also PRESIDENT ROBERT L. BOOTH

2000AD Prog 68

Judge-Tutor

SOCIAL CATEGORY: Justice Department, Mega-City One

Fulfilling one of the most important roles in the Mega-City One Justice Department, Judge-Tutors run the Academy of Law and supervise every aspect of their Cadets' lives. Most Judge-Tutors are retired or badly injured street Judges who opted to teach at the Academy rather than take the Long Walk into the Cursed Earth, so they bring a lifetime of experience to the job and they are each asked to specialise in a certain aspect of a Judge's training.

See also ACADEMY OF LAW

Introduced: 2000AD Prog 35

Judge Tyrannosaur

ANIMAL: Tyrannosaurus Rex, Cursed Earth

When a stray dinosaur inadvertently saved the life of Mega-City One's oldest woman from a vicious mutant criminal in the Cursed Earth, it became a folk hero of sorts in the city. Over a million citizens signed a petition calling on the Justice Department to make the beast a Judge and they even made a giant badge for it to wear. At a special ceremony arranged by these citizens to present it to the Tyrannosaur, however, the creature stomped on some of his fans and Judge Dredd was forced to take the monster out with a Hi-Ex shell!

2000AD Prog 855 (dies)

Jug McKenzie

CITIZEN: Professional Skysurfer, Sydney-Melbourne Conurb

Three times Supersurf Champion, Jug McKenzie's most spectacular victory was his third in Supersurf 10 when he had to beat off the challenge of Mega-City One's former Champion, the fugitive Chopper. After a thrilling race, the "Wizard of Oz" pipped his rival by the merest of margins and was lauded as the greatest skysurfer of all time by his adoring fans in Oz. Chopper had certainly won his respect, though, and Jug was willing to take a big risk when it appeared that the Mega-City One skysurfer was likely to get shot by Judge Dredd, as he tried to escape following the race. Jug bumped his Power Board into the Judge as he took aim with his Lawgiver and Chopper got away, but the Oz-Judges refused to take any action against their most popular sportsman, much to Dredd's annoyance.

An unofficial rematch between the skysurfers went the other way, when Jug McKenzie and Chopper met a few months later, but the real contest was coming a year later in Supersurf 11. Unfortunately, the race was bought out by the shady businessman Stig, who moved it to Mega-City Two and introduced various extra dangers into it – such as snipers along its route! Sensibly, Jug refused to compete in what looked like becoming a bloodbath, although he almost entered at the last minute to prove he wasn't chicken. Since he had been drinking heavily, Jug's girlfriend and Chopper – who had become a great friend of the Wizard of Oz – stopped him by locking him in a cupboard! Jug's absence from Supersurf 11 signalled the end of his career, but he had got out at the top and, in truth, he was burnt out as a serious athlete by then anyway.

See also CHOPPER

2000AD Progs 545, 553, 554, 557, 564-570, 588, 591, 595-597, 655-659

Judge Dredd the Megazine Volume 1: 1-5

Left:
Victory for Jug McKenzie at Supersurf 10

Junior Angel

CITIZEN: Cursed Earth

Elmer "Pa" Angel's favourite son, Junior was the youngest member of the infamous Angel Gang and delighted in torturing and maiming people, following closely in his father's footsteps.

See also ANGEL GANG

2000AD Progs 160, 161, 173, 176, 177, 179-181 (dies), 195 (flashback)

Judge Annual 1983 (cameo)

Justice 1, 2, 3 & 4

SPACECRAFT: Mega-City One
Justice Department

Justice 1 is a deep-space cruiser designed for a small crew of Judges and a large robotic back-up to perform most essential tasks during interplanetary flight.

Justice 2 is a compact space shuttle, normally located on a secret launchpad beneath Mega-City One, and used for orbital flights in times of extreme emergency. During the Apocalypse War, Chief Judge Griffin was despatched into orbit for his own safety.

Justice 3 is a very large Earth orbiter and is kept in permanent geo-stationary orbit. Acting like a space station, it is used by the Judges as a base for maintaining law and order on their many orbiting space colonies.

Far smaller than the similar Justice 1, the Justice 4 is a cruiser designed to carry a small crew and is regularly used for inter-continental transport by the Judges

Introduced: 2000AD Prog 162 (Justice 1); 252 (Justice 2); 319 (Justice 3); 623 (Justice 4)

Justice Department

ORGANISATION: Ruling Administration, Mega-City One

The Justice Department is both the main administration centre of government in Mega-City One and the group of people who run that administration. The Grand Hall of Justice, The Academy of Law and the Iso-Blocks are all part of the Department's buildings and the many Sector Houses around the city are in regular contact with this central control complex, via M.A.C., the Judges' Computer Database. As a body, the Justice Department not only runs all Judge operations, but is also responsible for the governing of Mega-City One in all other respects, headed up as it is by the Chief Judge.

Introduced: 2000AD Prog 2

Juve Cube

BUILDING: Young offenders prison, Mega-City One

Similar institutions to Mega-City One's Iso-Cubes, these provide prison accommodation for young perps and therefore greater attention is paid to the possibilities of rehabilitating their occupants.

Introduced: 2000AD Prog 207 (term), 598 (visual)

K

K2000 Samurai Attack Suit

WEAPON: Battle suit, Hondo City

Combining the qualities of a state-of-the-art armoured suit with a range of the most powerful weapons ever to be devised by the Hondo City Tek-Judges, the K2000 Samurai Attack Suit is the ultimate in personal combat equipment. When Judges from all over the World united to make their final assault on Sabbat the Necromagus, they made use of these Attack Suits to give them a vital edge against his zombie hordes.

Introduced: 2000AD Prog 794

Karl Raider

CITIZEN: Former Judge, Mega-City One

Having studied at the Academy of Law alongside Joe Dredd himself, Karl Raider graduated with the Class of '79. He enjoyed twenty years as an effective street Judge before he met and fell in love with an ordinary citizen called Carol. Raider gave up his career as a Judge in order to live with her, but she was killed during the Apocalypse War. The former Judge never fully recovered from the shock of her death and years later – seeking some kind of meaning to his life – he went on a vigilante killing spree. Judge Dredd tracked him down with the help of Wally Squad Judge Lola Palmtree and was forced to kill his former friend.

See also MURK DERRYSON

2000AD Progs 810-814 (dies)

Judge Kamun

JUDGE: Luxor City

Part of one of the toughest Judge Systems on Earth, Kamun was a highly respected Senior Judge in Luxor, but he harboured a dark secret. He was a believer in the ancient beast-faced Gods and, along with a strong like-minded Cadre of his fellow Judges, he served the dreadful supernatural being, Ankhhor. Kamun arranged for a number of Luxor's finest Judges to be consumed by Ankhhor, in order for the undead creature to build its strength, and finally sought to serve up Judge Dredd to his master. Dredd proved to be a tougher meal to prepare than Kamun had expected, however, and the Mega-City One Judge killed the Egyptian before he could deliver him to Ankhhor.

See also ANKHHOR

2000AD Progs 859-863 (dies)

Left:
Senior Judge Kamun, a tough lawman from the ancient city of Luxor

Psi-Judge Karyn

JUDGE: Psi-Division, Mega-City One

Although Karyn has a range of psi powers – mind-reading, empathic abilities and so on – her speciality is in the area of precognition. Her talent had manifested itself at an early age and she was inducted into the Justice Department's Psi School. Karyn graduated as a star pupil, deemed more than ready to hit the streets of Mega-City One as a Psi-Judge. Her first major case saw Karyn aid Judge Dredd in tracking down the alien Raptaur – a creature which could make itself appear invisible by creating a psi-fog – and she has been kept very busy since then. With Mega-City One always short of Judges, Psi-Judge Karyn has made quite a name for herself in the Justice Department.

See also RAPTAUR

Judge Dredd the Magazine Volume 1: 14–17; Judge Dredd the Magazine Volume 2: 57–61

Judge Dredd Mega-Special 1994

Judge Dredd Yearbook 1994

2000AD Graphic Novel: Raptaur

Ex-Judge Kaufmann

JUDGE: Renegade, Mega-City One

Having spent almost ten years on the Titan Penal Colony, Kaufmann was due to become eligible to regain his badge – albeit as a Titan-Judge – when renegade Judge Grice led a mass breakout from the place. With Kaufmann having been violently abused by the Titan-Judges, few of his fellow prisoners suspected he would betray them during the escape attempt, but he caught them by surprise and very nearly thwarted Grice's plans. A decade on Titan had softened Kaufmann up, though, and Grice – driven by his desire for revenge on Mega-City One and Judge Dredd in particular – managed to overpower and kill him with ease.

See also JUDGE GRICE

2000AD Progs 834–840 (dies)

War-Marshall "Mad Dog" Kazan
See opposite

Kenny Who?

CITIZEN: Artist, Cal Hab Zone

A country boy from the wilds of the Caledonian Hab Zone, Kenny Who? was desperate to draw comic strips for the Mega-City One trashzine company, Big 1 Publishing. He travelled to the big city, but was told that everything was drawn by computers. Kenny went off to drown his sorrows, but was outraged when the publisher announced the discovery of a fantastic new artist, Jimmy Who?. Big 1 had scanned his artwork into their system, so Jimmy Who? was actually a computer capable of drawing in his style. Kenny responded by attacking the Senior Editor responsible for "stealing" his art style and smashing the computer – actions which earned him five years in the Mega-City One Iso-Cubes. Three years later, Kenny's wife and children turned up looking for him and persuaded Judge Dredd to waive the remainder of his sentence in favour of deporting him.

2000AD Progs 477–479

Judge Dredd the Magazine Volume 1: 1–3

War-Marshal "Mad Dog" Kazan

JUDGE: War-Marshal, East-Meg One

East-Meg One's most feared Judge, War Marshal Kazan was often known by his nickname "Mad Dog" – a label of which he was quite proud. Kazan was the commander of ground forces during the Sov attack on Mega-City One that came to be known as the Apocalypse War, and he saw his hugely superior invaders quickly take control of the city. Pleased with his progress, the "Mad Dog" opened a second front of his own in the war when he arranged for Sov-Judges loyal to him to murder the members of the East-Meg One Diktatorat. Declaring himself the new Supreme Judge, Kazan continued to oversee the war against Mega-City One, but was annoyed by his enemy's refusal to give up. Led by Judge Dredd, the Mega-City Judges fought a determined guerrilla war until Chief Judge Griffin was captured and brainwashed by the Sovs. The War-Marshal set up a vid-broadcast featuring the Chief Judge and had him betray his own side live on-air to try and sap the will of the resistance. Although Judge Dredd limited the damage by killing Griffin during his fateful interview, drastic action was required by the Mega-City One Judges. To this end, Dredd formed the Apocalypse Squad and – to the horror of Kazan and his invading forces – was successful in carrying out a desperate raid which resulted in the annihilation of East-Meg One. Most of the Sov invaders lost heart in the wake of this action, but Kazan would not contemplate surrender and was determined to fight on until his last man fell. He was finally betrayed by his own second-in-command, Sov-Judge Izaaks, who recognised that all was lost and allowed Judge Dredd the opportunity to kill the War-Marshal. Defiant to the end, the "Mad Dog" made no apology for his actions as Dredd executed him for his crimes against Mega-City One.

See also APOCALYPSE SQUAD, CHIEF JUDGE GRIFFIN, SOV-JUDGE IZAAKS, MICHAEL PARKINOV

2000AD Prog 250, 251, 253, 255, 256, 258–260, 262, 263, 267, 269, 270 (dies)

Kenzal Davitchek

CITIZEN: Civil rights activist,
Mega-City One

YOU AND I ARE THE ONLY LEADERS LEFT NOW. CAN YOU WALK, KENZAL? WE NEED YOU IN THE MARCH.

I...I'LL TRY.

Democrats Blondel Dupré and Kenzal Davitchek prepare to march

As the leader of the Sons of the Constitution, one of the groups united by the Democratic Charter, Kenzal Davitchek was expected to be a prominent figure on the Democratic Charter March. So when he dropped out of it well before the end, it was seen as a snub to the movement. In fact, the Judges had picked him up the day before and kept him on his feet all night without food or water. Being an older man, Kenzal was unable to stand up to this kind of treatment and when it came to leading the march he was barely fit to walk. Following the violent break up of the Democratic Charter March, Kenzal attempted to hold together his dwindling group of supporters, but he was finished as a serious political spokesman in Mega-City One.

See also DEMOCRATIC CHARTER GROUP, SONS OF THE CONSTITUTION

2000AD Progs 531-533

Kevin O'Neill

CITIZEN: Curator of the Special Effects Museum, Mega-City One

The decline in popularity of his robot monsters led Kevin O'Neill to seek revenge on the company who made the Dream Projection machines he believed were responsible. He argued that Sensor-Round's equipment, which provided a sophisticated form of holographic projection, had replaced the "real thing" at the Special Effects Museum. O'Neill's solution was to systematically murder all the top executives of Sensor-Round using his robots. When Judge Dredd investigated the deaths, the mad curator set Krong, a mighty robot ape on the lawman, only for O'Neill himself to be crushed by the enormous ape in the battle which followed!

2000AD Prog 5 (dies)

Judge-Governor Khurtz

JUDGE: Governor, Titan Penal Colony

The toughest form of punishment in Mega-City One is reserved for Judges who have gone bad – a twenty stretch on Titan. The Penal Colony there is run by specially appointed Titan-Judges, who are led by a Judge-Governor. Shortly after joining their number, Titan-Judge Khurtz acquired a reputation as the most cruel and violent Judge on the force, and this enhanced his prospects of promotion no end. Khurtz soon became Judge-Governor of Titan and delighted in the barbaric nature of his duties – specialising as he did in devising new and more horrifying forms of torture, using his prisoners as test subjects! Under orders from Chief Judge McGruder, Khurtz was also responsible for trying to develop the alien "Meat Virus" as an ultimate deterrent for Mega-City One. The Judge-Governor was killed, however, when his most intransigent prisoner – the renegade Judge Grice – effected a mass breakout from the Penal Colony and dropped him into a vat of molten slag.

See also JUDGE GRICE, MEAT VIRUS

2000AD Progs 834-841 (dies)

Med-Judge Kildare

JUDGE: Med-Division, Mega-City One

When a mutated fungus disease afflicted Mega-City One in the wake of the Apocalypse War, Med-Judge Kildare was asked to isolate a cure. Subjecting himself to the disease, he knew his chances of survival were slim, but he needed a guinea pig and he was the best man for the job. Although the brave Med-Judge failed to find a cure for the deadly virus, his unorthodox method of studying it yielded vital information regarding its reproduction cycle and ideas on how to prevent it spreading. Through his own death, Kildare ensured that millions of potential victims of the disease in Mega-City One would live.

See also GRUBB'S DISEASE

2000AD Progs 275-277 (dies)

Kleggs

ALIEN RACE: Space Mercenaries, Kara System

The Kleggs are space nomads, having long since been driven from the Kara System, a sector of space they once ruled. They are brutal mercenaries, fighting for the joy of killing and taking their payment in the one currency they trust... meat! When they were called into Mega-City One by the mad Chief Judge Cal to help him maintain control of the city against Judge Dredd's rebels, the Kleggs' fondest wish was to be given license to eat the citizens, though negotiations for their services never quite reached that stage. Following their hasty retreat back into space on the tyrant Cal's downfall, Kleggs are understandably banned from setting foot in Mega-City One on pain of immediate execution.

See also CHIEF JUDGE CAL, HOUNDS OF KLEGG

Introduced: 2000AD Prog 94

Komputel

BUILDING: Hotel, Mega-City One

THE ELEVATOR TOOK DREDD TO THE CENTRAL COMPUTER COMPLEX...

YOU'VE MADE A BIG MISTAKE YOU BUNCH OF OVERLOADED TRANSISTORS! ANYTHING TO SAY BEFORE I BLOW YOU APART?

YOU WILL NOT DESTROY ME, HUMAN. YOUR REASONING IS INCORRECT - YOU ARE INEFFICIENT, LIKE ALL OTHER HUMANS - THAT'S WHY I KILL THEM - WE MUST STAMP OUT INEFFICIENCY!

Opened amidst much pomp and ceremony, Mega-City One's first fully-automated hotel proved to be the kind of scientific advance the city could have done without. Within minutes of its activation, Komputel malfunctioned and began killing its guests. Fortunately, Judge Dredd was assigned to police the grand opening and he was able to shut down the hotel by destroying its computer brain, so at least some of its guests survived.

2000AD Prog 32

Judge Korkoran

JUDGE: Mega-CIty One

When Mega-City One was infiltrated by were-wolves from the Undercity, Korkoran was unfortunate enough to be bitten by one of the creatures and thus was infected with the "werewolf disease". He became a werewolf himself, but fortunately was brought into a Justice Department Med-Lab in time to have the condition controlled. Under the care of Med-Judge Cassidy, who managed to isolate the cause of his affliction. He was soon cured and subsequently made a full recovery.

See also MED-JUDGE CASSIDY

2000AD Progs 322-325, 328

GRAAH! RIPPPP! DROKK HE'S LOOSE!

Judge Kraken

JUDGE: Mega-City One

Cloned from the bloodline of Chief Judge Fargo by the renegade Mega-City One Judge, Morton Judd, Kraken shared his heritage with none other than Judge Dredd. He was brought up to despise the Judges of Dredd's city, however, and when Judd launched a massive revenge attack, Kraken was amongst those chosen to teleport directly into the heart of the Mega-City. Judge Dredd put paid to Morton Judd's threat by nuking his Ayers Rock base out of existence, but a number of his "Judda" were left in Mega-City One. They were all quickly rounded up or killed and only Kraken was spared execution for his crimes against the city. He was secretly transferred to the Academy of Law by Chief Judge Silver and placed under the personal tutelage of Judge-Tutor Odell.

Kraken's conditioning by Judd was hard to break and the unlikely Cadet learnt to play along with his tutor – trying to convince him that he was being won over – and, very slowly, the Judda inside him began to diminish. Kraken started to realise that his place might be on the streets of Mega-City One. When Odell was sure that he had expunged Judd's teachings from his pupil, Kraken was declared ready to take his final assessment.

Chief Judge Silver decided to assign Judge Dredd to supervise the assessment, hoping that their shared bloodline would enable the older man to make an accurate judgement on his fitness to become a full Judge. Kraken performed admirably during the test, but his manner and a few ill-chosen words gave Dredd cause to doubt him, so he failed the Rookie. Silver knew he couldn't turn the former Judda out onto the streets as a civilian, so he reimposed the death sentence on him. Kraken was understandably aggrieved by Dredd's decision, but he demonstrated the fact that he was a loyal Judge by making no attempt to escape his own death – and actually administering his own "lethal injection"!

Chief Judge Silver had arranged Kraken's "execution" as the ultimate test and the lethal drug was in fact only a powerful anaesthetic. Silver needed Judge Kraken, since Dredd himself had just resigned and had opted to take the Long Walk, but the event had been kept very under wraps. A replacement "Dredd" was required and the former Judda was the only man available with the right bloodline. So, not only was Kraken awarded his full eagle on his revival, but he actually became Judge Dredd.

The new Judge Dredd's actions on the streets were exemplary and he was deliberately kept out of contact with his fellow Judges as much as possible to disguise the fact that he was a far younger man. Unfortunately for Kraken, when the Sisters of Death first made their presence felt in Mega-City One, they seized upon the turmoil that still existed in his mind and used the image of Morton Judd to help them manipulate his actions. Unwittingly, Kraken kidnapped Psi-Judge Agee so that the Sisters could use her mind as a bridge to her city, then he released Judge Death and the other Dark Judges from their imprisonment in limbo.

Judge Death transformed him into a kind of semi-zombie, so that he could take his place as a fifth Dark Judge, but when the monsters were finally defeated, Kraken was genuinely ashamed and utterly appalled by his involvement in their crimes. He turned himself over to the real Judge Dredd – who had come back to save his city, along with former Chief Judge McGruder – and the Dark Judges' unwilling puppet was duly executed for his part in the catalogue of horror. In spite of his background and the deep suspicion with which he was viewed by Judge Dredd, Kraken was massively disappointed by his tragic failure and welcomed this belated release from his unbearable guilt.

See also JUDDA, JUDGE-TUTOR ODELL

2000AD Prog 583, 584, 650, 662-671, 674-685, 698 (dies), 734 (flashback)

Krilz

CITIZEN: Dealer in stolen vehicles, Mega-City One

Antique "petrol burners" are the cream of the used car market in Mega-City One, with rich "art" collectors willing to pay awesome sums for such rare items. Krilz was a supplier of such vehicles, usually stolen, until he was put out of business permanently by Judge Dredd.

2000AD Prog 8

Krong

ROBOT: Giant animatronic ape, Mega-City One Special Effects Museum

When the Curator of the Mega-City One Special Effects Museum went crazy, murdering the people he blamed for the decline in trade at the Museum, Judge Dredd soon came knocking at the door. Krong was then pitched into battle against him, but – having been designed more for film special effects than for combat – the robot ape was no match for a heavily armed Judge.

See also KEVIN O'NEILL

2000AD Prog 5 (destroyed)

Judge Barry Kurten

JUDGE: Renegade, Mega-City One

Barimore Kurten's parents were gunned down in front of him when he was just four and a half, and the trauma of the event left an indelible impression on the young boy. He scored well in aptitude tests, though, so it was decided to induct him into the Academy of Law, where he progressed well and duly graduated as a Judge fifteen years later. Barry Kurten warmed to his task on the Mega-City One streets well, but he often felt the urge to be tougher on the perps than normal procedure allowed. The scars of his childhood experience had far from healed and he soon found himself accompanied by a strange blue creature called "Mo" who urged him to

flout regulations and get as tough as he liked! Mo had been Kurten's childhood nickname and this manifestation represented his own repressed feelings of bitterness and revenge for the killing of his parents. Judge Dredd spotted the instability in his colleague, but it took a while before the Justice Department shrinks could be convinced to pull Judge Kurten off street duties.

By the time they did, Barry – and Mo! – had realised he was under investigation, so he took ten million credits from drug dealer and headed for Banana City. He bought into the Justice Department there and soon became known as Judge Diablo. Kurten reckoned without word getting back to Judge Dredd that he was in town, however, and it was just a matter of time before the seriously deranged Judge was found. Going undercover to Banana City, Dredd had orders to either apprehend or terminate Kurten and the rogue Judge's refusal to surrender ensured that he was forced to take the latter option.

2000AD Progs 615-618, 624, 625 (dies)

Ladonna

CITIZEN: Pop Star, Mega-City One

When former Munce taster Esther Gilroy married a plastic surgeon he transformed her with a full body job – including face change, liposuction and silicone implants – and she began a whole new career. Esther became Ladonna, Mega-City One's sexiest singing sensation and Judge Dredd was convinced that the mania surrounding her concert tour was a threat to the city. He ordered her arrest for public indecency, but her fans went berserk all over Mega-City One and Chief Judge McGruder decided that an early release would be prudent. Unfortunately for Ladonna, she had to serve her 30 year sentence in a time stretcher before they let her go later that day – and this time not even her talented husband could restore her youthful allure!

Judge Dredd the Megazine Volume 2: 30

Judge Otis Landslide

JUDGE: Wally Squad, Mega-CIty One

A highly skilled undercover Judge, Otis Landslide operated from an apartment in Laurence Harvey Block and had successfully established himself as an ordinary citizen. When he received an order from Wally Squad Control to assassinate Chief Judge McGruder he was shocked, but pursued the task with his customary dedication. Landslide infiltrated the Academy of Law as the Chief Judge was due to speak to a new crop of Rookie Judges and he took a shot at her. Luckily for McGruder, Judge Dredd managed to save her, but the undercover Judge escaped. Dredd tracked him down quickly, though he was forced to kill him when Landslide refused to surrender.

2000AD Progs 881-883 (dies)

Land Race

EVENT: Method used to allot land in Luna-1

Whenever a newly-domed territory is opened in Luna-1, the plots of land made available are allotted to citizens and corporations on the basis of a Land Race. This usually turns out to be a mad scramble involving all manner of vehicles and the Judges have to keep a close eye on events to ensure fair play. In fact, the biggest problems associated with the Land Race tend to come afterwards when territorial disputes generally emerge – either because there are rival claims for one plot, or because an individual or a company wished to tie up a large area, but missed out on a key plot of land.

Introduced: 2000AD Prog 47

Judge-Pilot Larter

JUDGE: Spacecraft Pilot, Mega-City One

Hand-picked as Judge-Pilot on the quest to find the Judge Child, Larter was one of the three survivors of the mission, along with Judges Dredd and Hershey. Unfortunately, after returning to Mega-City One, the pilot was murdered by Fink Angel, who was seeking revenge for the deaths of his family at the hands of Judge Dredd. Poor Larter's death was particularly gruesome, since Fink paralysed him, then set hundreds of rats on him and he was eaten alive by the hungry beasts.

See also FINK ANGEL

2000AD Progs 162, 166, 170, 174, 175, 181, 193 (dies)

Laser Defence System

**DEVICE: Defensive laser network,
American Mega-Cities**

Still in its experimental stages in 2070, America's laser defence system was unable to prevent the mass destruction of nuclear war across the whole of the country, but its three Mega-Cities were afforded limited protection from the deadly missiles raining down upon them. Thus, these major conurbations were the only areas in the United States to avoid being turned into an atomic wasteland by the war. Subsequent work on the laser network saw it being perfected by the close of the 21st Century, though it failed to save most of Mega-City One when it was attacked by East-Meg One forces in 2104. The Sovs themselves employed a far more effective form of defence against Mega-City One's retaliation – the remarkable Apocalypse Warp, which quite literaly "warped" oncoming missiles into another dimension.

Introduced: 2000AD Prog 128

The Lawgiver

CITIZEN: Cursed Earth

Despotic ruler of the Cursed Earth town of Deliverance, the Lawgiver was fond of meting out a particularly gruesome brand of punishment to anyone who violated his harsh laws. The town was regularly overrun with mutant rats – or the "Devil's Lapdogs" as they were termed by the local townsfolk – and lawbreakers were tied up and left in the open when the creatures approached. With this fate a deterrent few would defy the Lawgiver, but Judge Dredd was intent on putting a stop to the practice when he passed through Deliverance on his mission to cross the Cursed Earth and reach Mega-City Two with the 2T(FRUT)T plague virus. Realising that the rats were attracted by the town's siren, Dredd was able to lure them away from Deliverance using the siren on his Quasar Bike, thus preventing an horrific double execution. The Lawgiver, furious that the death sentence on two of his townsfolk had been thwarted by Dredd's actions, left his shelter a little too early and fell victim himself to the last few remaining rats in the town before they were all lured away by the siren.

2000AD Progs 63, 64 (dies) 85 (cameo)

Lawgiver Gun

**WEAPON: Judges' standard issue hand-gun,
Mega-CIty One**

The Judges' Lawgiver is a deadly multi-faceted weapon, featuring manual and automatic focusing and targeting, plus an in-built computer capable of controlling its operation. It can, however, only be operated by its designated Judge owner, whose palm print is programmed into the gun's computer memory. Should an attempt be made by any unrecognised user to fire a Lawgiver, it is programmed to blow up in that person's hand!

The gun has a maximum range of up to three miles and has six distinct settings: HEAT SEEKER – a general purpose shell, propelled by the unstable element, 'Argon 886'; RICOCHET – a rubber missile, intended for human targets; INCENDIARY; ARMOUR-PIERCING; GRENADE; and HIGH EXPLOSIVE – even more powerful than the Grenade setting.

Introduced: 2000AD Prog 2 (concept), 12 (term)

Lawmaster Bike

**VEHICLE: Judges' standard issue motorcycle,
Mega-City One**

Very high-powered, fast and manoeuvrable, the Lawmaster Bike provides the Judges of Mega-CIty One with an efficient and adaptable method of transport, as well as a mobile stockpile of equipment and weaponry. It comes with a Synitron audio on-board computer, a Cyclops Phylon TX laser cannon, an ammunition and stores pod and a personal scatter gun, kept in an in-built holster. The Bike is tremendously powerful, boasting a Notron 4000cc engine, and it also benefits from having bullet-proof, all-weather tyres.  Although the Lawmaster Mk1 has proved a great success on the streets of Mega-City One, the improved Mk2 version – sometimes referred to as a Quasar Bike – has become standard issue to Judges in recent years.

See also QUASAR BIKE

Introduced: 2000AD Prog 2 (concept), 3 (term)

Lawrod Rifle

WEAPON: Judges' standard issue rifle, Mega-City One

A more powerful rifle version of a Judge's Lawgiver Gun, the Lawrod is used far more rarely, specifically in tactical or combat situations, rather than during a Judges regular patrols on the streets of Mega-City One.

Introduced: 2000AD Prog 7 (concept), 21 (term)

Above: The Lawrod Rifle in action

League of Fatties

ORGANISATION: Excessively fat group, Mega-City One

With food shortages a major problem in Mega-City One following the Apocalypse War, tight rationing was introduced. A number of the city's excessively fat citizens were angry about these restrictions and would do almost anything to beg, borrow or steal more food! They formed the League of Fatties and carried out scores of "food crimes" - hijacking supplies on their way from Texas City in an audacious raid amongst other things. The common factor in most of their crimes was a singular lack of success, however, since Fatties were just not cut out for crime! The Judges finally put an end to the chaos caused by the desperate porkers when they opened four Segregation Blocks and forced anyone over 300 kilos in Mega-City One to live in them.

2000AD Progs 273, 274

League Against Gambling

ORGANISATION: Anti-Mafia Group, Las Vegas

The League Against Gambling based their doctrine on the writings of Abner Cobb, the Civic Leader of Las Vegas executed by the Mafia when the Syndicate took control of the city. While opposing the mob's rule, the League found themselves powerless to prevent gambling from taking over every aspect their lives and they pinned their hopes on the coming of a saviour from the East – a man clad in black, as foretold by Cobb before his death. When Judge Dredd arrived he seemed to fit the bill and, sure enough, he defeated the Mafia Judges, inspiring the League Against Gambling to rise up and reclaim their city from the villains. The fact that Dredd left them, instead of staying around for one score years and four, didn't quite square up with Abner Cobb's predictions, but the newly free citizens of Las Vegas didn't really mind!

See also "GOD-JUDGE"

2000AD Progs 79, 80

Legion

MUTANT: Mega-City One

The rogue result of one in a billion DNA, Legion was a super mutant – a remarkable freak of nature. Held in Mega-City One, Legion defied all attempts to analyse, control or even execute it. Three Psi-Judges died having delved into its mind and it soon proved impossible to contain safely. The Judges decided to ship Legion off to the Luna-1 maximum security prison, but the spacecraft carrying it crash-landed in the Cursed Earth and Legion was the only survivor.

The super mutant amused himself in the badlands outside Texas City for a while, killing the locals and cultivating a small army of gila-munja, mutants and zombies. Then he came to the attention of Preacher Cain – the Missionary Man – who set about exorcising Legion, seeing him as some kind of "anti-Christ". The monster proved a tough opponent, but silver bullets fired from Cain's powerful shotgun slowed him down and Legion was finally killed when he was thrown into a volcanic pit by the Preacher!

Judge Dredd the Megazine Volume 2: 50-55 (dies)

Legion of the Damned

ROBOTS: Presidential Guard, Cursed Earth

When Robert L. Booth, the last President of the United States, was deposed, his fiercely loyal and extremely savage robotic army fought on. They were programmed to fight on for all eternity against the Judges and it wasn't until the Battle of Armageddon of 2071 that their threat was effectively ended. Thirty years later, however, the surviving robots mustered enough strength to stand in the way of Judge Dredd's mission to deliver plague vaccine to Mega-City Two. Judge Jack and Spikes "Harvey" Rotten both fell to the robots, but they would not give way until all the Judges were dead. Realising that he had to make them believe he was dead, Dredd dressed up the deceased Spikes as a Judge and sent him into the line of fire on the back of a Quasar Bike. Having eliminated this target, the Legion of the Damned's leader, General Blood 'n' Guts ordered his troops to stand down — satisfied that their mission was accomplished for the time being — and they returned to their dormant state once more.

See also BATTLE OF ARMAGEDDON, PRESIDENT BOOTH

2000AD Progs 83-85

Lesser Lingo

WORLD: Epsilon System, Deep Space

Colonised by Earth people in 2055, Lesser Lingo was already populated by a strange alien race called just "the aliens" who had a wacky outlook on life and rarely told the truth. Some of these aliens were only too happy to serve the humans and consented to having their wings amputated, but other so-called "wild aliens" resented the fact that the intruders would not share the secret of their Biochips with them. These Biochips allowed people to borrow each others' bodies and so live on after death. When the wild aliens kidnapped the human President's Biochip he found that their power of flight excited him, so after he was rescued by Judge Dredd who was visiting Lesser Lingo during his quest to find the Judge Child he granted the creatures equality. This meant that they were given their own Biochips and he was able to borrow the body of a wild alien whenever he wanted!

See also BIOCHIP

Introduced: 2000AD Prog 164

Link Angel

CITIZEN: Texas City Badlands, Cursed Earth

Second son of the infamous Elmer "Pa" Angel, Link was a mean critter in the true tradition of his family. Fiercely loyal to his Pa, he was always at the older man's side and helped him kidnap the Judge Child. Having stolen a spacecraft and head off with into space with the boy, Link and the rest of his family finally ended up on Xanadu and decided to hide out there. When Judge Dredd finally tracked them to the planet, Link and Mean Machine teamed up to deal with him, but Mean's dial got stuck on four and a half in the struggle. He went berserk and unwittingly killed Link with an almighty super-mean head butt!

See also ANGEL GANG, XANADU

2000AD Progs 160, 161, 173, 176-178 (dies), 195 (flashback)

The Long Walk

EVENT: Judge retirement ceremony, Mega-City One

When a Judge is either too badly injured or too old to effectively police the streets of Mega-City One, or should their mental attitude become incompatible with their normal duties, they have a limited number of choices. They may elect to take an administrative role in the Justice Department or even a teaching post at the Academy of Law, but most Judges choose to take "The Long Walk" on retirement. A far tougher option, this involves taking the law to the lawless, either in the Cursed Earth or in the vast Undercity beneath Mega-City One. Judges are allowed to keep their standard issue equipment – on the strict understanding that they will not allow their Lawmaster Bike or Lawgiver Gun to fall into the wrong hands – when they run a gauntlet of honour as they leave the city. Few are ever heard of again, as they face the only challenge greater than policing a Mega-City – that of trying to uphold the law in the atomic wasteland outside it.

Introduced: 2000AD Prog 147

Judge Minty takes the Long Walk

OPEN THE GATES!

WHEN A JUDGE'S USEFUL LIFE WAS FINISHED, HE COULD CHOOSE TO TAKE THE LONG WALK INTO MUTIELAND –

Tek-Judge Lopez

JUDGE: Tek-Division, Mega-City One

A hot-shot engineer specialising in spacecraft design and maintenance, Judge Lopez was the ideal choice to accompany Judge Dredd on his mission to find the Judge Child in deep space. If anyone could ensure that the Justice 1 would stay in good shape throughout their quest it was Lopez, but Judge Dredd was never too impressed by his facial hair! In fact, he made life very difficult for Judge Lopez because he refused to shave off his moustache and in the end Dredd chose him as the "volunteer" to use the dangerous precognitive drug, Oracle Spice in an effort to discover where the Angel Gang had taken the Judge Child. Dredd got his information, but the unfortunate Tek-Judge paid for it with his life.

2000AD Prog 162, 164, 166, 167, 172, 173 (dies)

Lopez and Dredd discuss a hairy topic

Judge Luciano

JUDGE: Mega-City One

Formerly a Wally Squad Judge, Luciano lost his nerve on an undercover operation and was brought up before Chief Judge McGruder in 2105. He was returned to uniform and seconded to clerical duties at the West Wall until the Dark Judges and the Sisters of Death took control of Mega-City One seven years later. Having been stationed at the Wall, Judge Luciano was able to flee the city in order to escape the Necropolis and he found his way to a refugee camp a short way into the Cursed Earth. There, he used his status as a Judge to bully the ragged group of citizens living in the camp into giving him food and drink, but he reckoned without the arrival of Judge Dredd in the guise of the "Dead Man". Dredd was incensed by Luciano's actions, so he stripped the coward of his uniform and took his Lawmaster, sending the disgraced Judge off into the radioactive wasteland of the Cursed Earth without transport or any supplies! Judge Dredd was then able to don Luciano's helmet and so rejoin the Mega-City One Judges before returning to the city to face the Sisters of Death once more.

See also DEAD MAN, SISTERS OF DEATH

2000AD Prog 686

Luna-1

CITY: Moon Colony belonging to the American Mega-Cities

In the middle of the 21st Century a new "space race" saw the three American Mega-Cities strive to establish a base on the moon, and in 2061 they claimed an area of one million square miles as their own. To the citizens of Mega-City One, Luna-1 represented a wild, new frontier – full of new opportunities, but also laced with danger. To maintain law and order there, each of the American Cities would take turns to nominate a Judge to become Judge-Marshal of Luna-1 for a period of six months. This arrangement was only partially successful and it came to an end following Judge Dredd's term of office, when he recommended his trusted deputy, Judge Tex, for the post on a permanent basis.

Introduced: 2000AD Prog 42

Lunar Olympics

EVENT: Sporting Competition, Luna-1

Earth records mean nothing to athletes on the moon and during the first ever Lunar Olympics, held in 2100 in Luna-1, new standards were set in almost every event! Spectacular records have continued to be set in subsequent games, but they have also been beset by political recriminations typical of these kind of events.

Introduced: 2000AD Prog 50

Lurker

CITIZEN: Mega-City One

Lurking in the shadows of Mega-City One, the Lurker specialised in robbing dead bodies or the unconscious victims of other crimes or accidents. He would sneak around the back alleys of the city and scavenge for such "left-overs", but he made a big mistake when he got hold of a secure lead-lined case. From its owner's dying words to him, the sneak thief believed the case contained ten million credits – in fact, it contained radioactive isotopes emitting around ten million rads and he was burned to a crisp when he managed to get it open!

2000AD Prog 449 (dies)

M

M. A. C.

COMPUTER: Justice Department's Central Database

The Judges' Macro-Analysis Computer – or M.A.C. as it is more commonly known – is to all intents and purposes the "brain" of Mega-City One. It is programmed with a mass of data relating to the City and is hooked up to monitors of all kinds across the megalopolis. M.A.C. can therefore analyse situations in which a crime has been committed – or is likely to be committed! - and give the Judges vital aid in the detection of its probable perpetrators.

Introduced: 2000AD Prog 24

Manta Prowl Tank

VEHICLE: Riot Control Tank, Mega-City One Justice Department

Designed by one of Mega-City One's leading Teks, former Council of Five member Judge Brufen, Manta Prowl Tanks could be described as mobile Sector Houses. With a crew of 18 Judges, it has its own Med-Bay and Holding Pens, all within one formidable vehicle, created for riot control. Equipped with lasers, stumm gas, riot foam, searchlights, spotlights and radar, the Manta Prowl Tank is the ultimate deterrent against crime in Mega-City One.

Introduced: 2000AD Prog 343

Judge Ed MacBrayne

JUDGE: Calhab

Like all of Calhab's Judges, Ed MacBrayne has a genetically-enhanced resistance to radioactivity, an attribute which is extremely valuable in the nuclear and toxic waste dumping ground that is Scotland in the early years of the 22nd Century. MacBrayne is a violent man, but he is ever mindful of how tough life can be in Calhab. The radiation-soaked atmosphere there has created a weird and unruly populace, while the criminals of the territory have formed themselves into well-armed whisky clans. MacBrayne was tragically affected by their activities when his partner, Judge Murdo, was killed in a battle with them, and he went on to work with Judge Buchan. Ed MacBrayne struggles on in a dispirited department, although even his resolve was tested to its limits when catastrophe overcame Calhab in 2116 when the the Song-in-the-Sky satellite which kept the people there under control was destroyed.

Judge Dredd the Megazine Volume 2: 10-13, 18, 31-33, 46-49, 63-70

Manuel Girsheeft

CITIZEN: Pan Andes Conurb

To all appearances, Manuel Girsheeft was an ordinary, if overweight, tourist wishing to spend some time in Mega-City One. He was unlucky enough to find Judge Dredd on Customs Detail in his usual thorough mood and the Judge had a hunch that he was a smuggler. It was soon clear that the Andean wasn't carrying sugar, drugs, tobacco, or even coffee. X-rays and an intimate body search seemed to come up clean, but Dredd wasn't satisfied as there was something suspicious about the fat tourist. Finally, the Judge ordered an exploratory operation to find out what Girsheeft had to hide and it turned out to be two extra hearts, six extra kidneys, three surplus livers, two extra sets of lungs, a spare windpipe, two extra spleens and twenty eight metres of borrowed large intestine. The creep was a walking organ bank, carrying a hundred thousand creds worth of spare parts in his bulky frame – though he'd lost some weight by the time Dredd had finished with him!

2000AD Progs 595

Maria

CITIZEN: Housekeeper, Mega-City One

Maria and Walter the Wobot get an unwelcome visitor

As the housekeeper employed to clean and tidy several of the apartments in Rowdy Yates Conapts, Maria had the singular honour of being Judge Dredd's housekeeper. This was something the cleaner was fiercely proud of and she often fretted over the Judge's well-being, concerned about his hectic and dangerous lifestyle! Being of Italian origin, she frequently prepared pasta-based meals for Dredd to ensure that he was eating properly and the lawman was quite embarrassed by her fussing. Nonetheless, he appreciated her efforts and was just as concerned about her welfare, as she was his. Despite her wiry frame, Maria knew how to look after herself in a scrap and when Block Mania broke out in Mega-City One she became heavily involved in the fighting. During the Sov invasion which followed, she had to be kept under control by Walter the Wobot, since she was the last remaining citizen left suffering from the viral agent which caused the Mania.

Over the years, the housekeeper's proximity to Dredd led her into some very dangerous situations and this eventually wore down her enthusiasm for serving the Judge. When she was captured by the Fink and Mean Machine Angel – who believed that she was Dredd's wife! - the experience was too much for her already fragile nerves to bear. Even though the Judge rescued her unharmed, Maria decided that she had had enough and so resigned her position as his housekeeper.

Life didn't treat her well after this incident and Maria wound up living in a Cardboard City near Edmundo Ross Block. She had suffered a serious bout of post-traumatic stress and become addicted to synthi-ale to solve her problems. This made her unreliable and cleaning work became hard to find. Begging to stay alive, she soon realised how tough life is, living on the streets of Mega-City One. Judge Dredd bumped into her almost seven years later and was saddened to see her this way. He tried to convince her to sign up for a rehab programme, but Maria wouldn't listen, because she blamed the Judge for her predicament. When she sorted out a gang of killers from the nearby City Block, beating them into submission, Dredd was glad of the assist and asked her about the rehab again, but she refused to take any notice of him. The Judge had no choice then, but to arrest her – due to the city's strict anti-vigilante laws – and he sentenced Maria to a spell on a rehab programme!

See also FINK ANGEL, MEAN MACHINE ANGEL, WALTER THE WOBOT

2000AD Progs 5, 12, 17, 18, 26, 30, 34, 59, 86, 87, 93, 114, 252, 253, 255, 256, 259, 262, 263, 285–288, 643–645

The Marshal

CITIZEN: Lawman, Cursed Earth

A member of the Brotherhood of Marshals, The Marshal was one of only a few survivors of a genetic virus which was unleashed upon his fellows by a Mega-City One Judge. Tek-Judge Eckson had secretly developed the virus, but miscalculated the amount he used in their water supply and so it proved fatal. The Marshal came to Mega-City One looking for justice and soon discovered that Eckson was the guilty party. He captured the Judge and tried to take him back to the Cursed Earth for an execution, but Judge Dredd stopped the Marshal and was forced to kill him to prevent him from getting away.

See also BROTHERHOOD OF MARSHALS,
TEK-JUDGE ECKSON

2000AD Progs 800-803 (dies)

2000AD Graphic Novel: Tales of the Damned

The Maze

BUILDING: Housing Scheme, Mega-City One

The F. Loyd Mazny Housing Scheme was the most complex development ever built in Mega-City One and soon became known as the "Maze". Initially housing two million people, every single sign inside the place had been vandalised within three weeks. The result was disaster, as Maze residents wandered around the complex, unable to find their homes. More than 150 starved to death, just looking for the way out! The place was closed down, but it was over a year before the last of the residents found the exit. By then, the scheme's architect had wisely emigrated and the Maze had become the haunt of derelicts and other lost souls.

Introduced: 2000AD Prog 190

Max Normal

CITIZEN: Nark, Mega-City One

In a city populated by all kinds of weirdoes, punks and kneepad-obsessed fashion victims, Max Normal cuts a remarkable figure in his smart businessman's suit and bowler hat. The "Pinstripe Freak", as he likes to be known, operates on the seedier side of life in Mega-City One and for many years he was Judge Dredd's best informer. His many contacts in the city's underworld kept him in touch with the word on the street and his value to the Justice Department ensured that he was afforded some leeway in his sometimes shady activities. Certainly, Max accumulated a great deal of wealth in a short time – far outstripping the amounts Judge Dredd ever gave him for information – although he always claimed that his prowess as a Shuggy player was the main contributory factor to his earnings.

Max's trademark style of dress was both an asset and a liability when it came to being a nark, however, and he soon became a marked man. Wisely, he retired before things became too hot for him and Judge Dredd lost one of his most useful pairs of eyes on the streets. Unfortunately for the Pinstripe Freak, he had already become identified with the Judge and his retirement was disrupted a number of times by perps who were out to get back at Dredd. Streetwise enough to look after himself most of the time, Max Normal has been kidnapped more than once and used as a lure to trap Judge Dredd. Unwilling to risk his life any more than he strictly has to, the former informant keeps a lower profile than ever and his pinstripe suit is rarely seen in public these days.

2000AD Progs 20, 88, 238, 240, 490, 599, 763, 764

2000AD Sci-Fi Special 1981

Judge Dredd Annuals 1981-1984, 1987

Chief Judge McGruder

JUDGE: Chief Judge, Mega-City One

Called upon to rebuild the discredited SJS in the wake of the tyrant Cal's demise, Judge McGruder made it a formidable – and incorruptible – force once more. As a Council of Five member, McGruder soon became one of the Justice Department's most prominent figures and when Judge Dredd returned from his mission to find the Judge Child, she criticised his decision to leave the boy behind. During the Apocalypse War, McGruder went missing and was presumed dead, but she turned up

suffering from terrible injuries and led the clean-up operation to expel the last Sovs from Mega-City One. As the only Council member to survive the war, McGruder became Chief Judge and set about rebuilding her shattered city. After three years, McGruder began to have doubts about her own judgement and when one of her mistakes cost the life of Psi Chief Omar, she resigned and took the Long Walk.

Her exile had a profound effect and when she met Dredd years later he hardly recognised her. Wizened and stooped, she had developed an odd multiple personality and had even grown a beard! The former Chief Judge was still able to play a key role in the defeat of the Sisters of Death who had taken over Mega-City One and, in the aftermath of the crisis, McGruder elected herself Chief Judge again. She then set about reasserting the authority of the Judges and, at Dredd's insistence, presided over the Democratic Referendum which finally saw democracy rejected by the city's citizens. Shortly afterwards, McGruder met with other Chief Judges from all over the world in Hondo City in an effort to find a way to

combat Sabbat. Then the renegade Judge Grice escaped from Titan and led a devastating attack on Mega-City One, during which Grice threw McGruder off the top of the West Wall. She should have been killed by the eighty foot drop, but once again proved resilient to major injury and made a spectacular recovery.

With the Judges' ranks severely depleted, McGruder sanctioned the Mechanismo Project, in an attempt to create effective robot Judges. When her judgement in this was questioned, McGruder became convinced there was a conspiracy against her and she used the opportunity to expose Dredd's attempts to discredit her robots. His arrest deflected attention from McGruder's problems and she was able to proceed with her plan to use the Mechanismo robots, and even to sell them to the city's space colonies. The Chief Judge finally realised her mistake when one of the robots tried to kill her, so she pardoned Dredd, cancelled the Mechanismo Project and resigned for a second time. In her leaving speech, she announced a world lecture tour to promote her memoirs, "McGruder: The Justice Years", but she promised to turn up occasionally and stick her nose into Justice Department business whenshe felt like it!

See also MECHANISMO, SPECIAL JUDICIAL SQUAD

2000AD Progs 182, 195, 197, 200, 201, 269-271, 273, 274, 277, 278, 280, 284, 285, 287, 290, 300, 306, 308, 309, 311, 313, 314, 325, 337, 350, 354, 355, 364, 367, 368, 374, 377, 388, 442, 451-455, 457, 685-687, 690-696, 702, 706, 713, 715, 719, 727, 733-735, 743-745, 754- 756, 761, 789, 790, 792-794, 796, 798, 799, 801, 802, 816, 826, 829, 835, 842- 846, 854, 855, 868-871, 873, 876, 881- 883, 886, 887, 891, 904, 905, 907, 909, 912-915

Judge Dredd the Megazine Volume 2: 10, 17, 22, 25, 26, 30, 35, 37, 39-43, 45-63

2000AD Winter Special 1993

Judge Dredd Annuals 1984, 1985

Judge Dredd Yearbook 1995

2000AD Yearbook 1993

Mean Machine Angel

CITIZEN: Texas City Badlands, Cursed Earth

Young Mean was the white sheep of the Angel family, because as a boy he wasn't bad at all. Delighting in the wonders of nature, he loved flowers, birds and butterflies and even kept a pet bunny rabbit. While Mean was quite used to relentless bullying, the worst moment of his childhood was when his brother Link butchered his rabbit for fun. Even this couldn't whip up any honest hatred within the boy and Pa Angel decided enough was enough, so he kidnapped a Texas City surgeon to put things right. Poor Mean was horrified as he was prepared for an operation in which his right arm was replaced with a mechanical claw and a special numbered dial was fixed to his forehead. This dial was linked directly to Mean's brain and kept him in a constant state of aggression, which could be varied, dependent on the number selected on his head. No. 1 was surly, 2 was mean, 3 was vicious and 4 was brutal – although Mean Machine, as he came to be known, was to prove most dangerous on those rare occasions when his dial setting got stuck on 4½!

Mean quickly acquired a reputation as one of the most dangerous criminals in the Cursed Earth – as well as one of the most stupid! It was love at first sight, though, when he met Seven Pound Sadie Suggs – named after the 7lb hammer she used when perpetrating her crimes. Mean Machine almost married Sadie, but she ran off with the wedding presents! Soon after, the Angels kidnapped the Judge Child and took him to the Planet Xanadu, where Dredd caught up with them and killed Mean along with the rest of his family.

Mean Machine was resurrected by the Judge Child, however, and he was sent back to Earth to kill Dredd. Teaming up with his brother Fink, Mean almost succeeded, but he wound up doing time in aPsycho Cube instead. Since then, Mean has been held in captivity almost continuously, give or take the odd short-lived escape, and has defied all attempts to rehabilitate him, including hypnotism and extensive brain surgery. During the maniac's most recent escape, he discovered that he had a son – the result of his brief encounter with Sadie Suggs – but the boy suffered from the same affliction as Mean before his operation, he wasn't bad at all!

See also ANGEL GANG, JUDGE CHILD

2000AD Progs 160, 161, 173, 176, 177, 178, 195, 281, 282, 284–288, 377–383, 450, 730–736

Judge Dredd the Megazine Volume 2: 45, 47, 63–70

Judge Dredd Annual 1983 (cameo)

Judge Dredd Yearbooks 1994, 1995

Judgement on Gotham 1

2000AD Graphic Novel: Mechanismo

Meat Virus

AFFLICTION: Killer plague, Titan

A strange alien bomb discovered on Titan contained an extremely virulent and deadly plague. The fall-out from the alien device seeped through the flesh of anyone who came into contact with it, making their skin sick and killing them within two weeks. Chief Judge McGruder authorised research into the so-called "Meat Virus", but her city was infected with it when Judge Grice escaped from the Titan Penal Colony and brought it toearth. Only after Grice was defeated were the Judges able to administer the antidote city-wide.

See also JUDGE GRICE

Introduced: 2000AD Prog 838

Mechanismo

ROBOTS: Robotic Judge Project, Mega-City One

In the wake of Sabbat's zombie assault on Mega-City One, the Judge force was left severely depleted. so Chief Judge McGruder authorised a major new project code named "Mechanismo". The Project was set up in top secret circumstances by the Chief Tek, Judge Greel, and he appointed robotics expert Tek-Judge Desmon Stich to head it up. Stich developed a series of Robot Judge prototypes, until he had a fully working Mark 1 machine ready to test on the streets. With a reinforced armour shell, capable of withstanding laser strikes, the Mechanismo robot was well-protected and carried a very powerful multi-purpose sidearm. Its infra-red and image intensification sensors gave it excellent vision in all circumstances and it enjoyed constant contact with the Justice Department mainframe, giving it instant access to information on any perp it recognised.

The robot's initial exposure to the city's streets went fairly smoothly, so the Chief Judge gave the go-ahead for an extensive trial. Thus, ten Mechanismo robots were sent into action, but they malfunctioned and six innocent citizens were murdered before the robots could be deactivated and takenback to the Justice Department for repair. Dredd was insistent that the project should be closed down, especially when one machine – Number 5 – became active again and escaped. The rogue robot went on a rampage of death and destruction that was only ended when it got lost in the city sewer system. Despite this, McGruder ordered a Mark 2 version to be developed and these second wave robots were rushed onto the streets when Number 5 reappeared almost a year later. One of the Mark 2s managed to terminate the rogue Mark 1 machine, but Judge Dredd destroyed it in turn. He then made it look like Number 5 had got the better of the Mark 2 in order to convince the Chief Judge to close down the project.

McGruder reluctantly agreed, but she arranged for the Mechanismo Project to continue secretly and modifications were made to the Mark 2s. This time Chief Tek-Judge Greel took personal control of the project, ensuring that no other Senior Judges knew anything about it. Finally, the existence of the Mark 2A Robot Judges came to light and a number of Judges – including Dredd – called on the Chief Judge to resign. McGruder refused and presented evidence of Judge Dredd's previous deception to discredit him and put him under arrest. She then announced her intention to place the new robots on the streets in force and even to sell them to help the Mega-City One economy.

Her attempt to market the robots ended in disaster, however, when she took them to the Mega-City One colony on Hestia and one of the machines sabotaged her spacecraft, causing it to crash in the Wilderlands of the planet. The Chief Judge was badly injured, but when she finally returned to the city, she was forced to close down the Mechanismo project for good.

See also TEK-JUDGE GREEL, TEK-JUDGE STICH

Introduced: Judge Dredd the Megazine Volume 2: 12

2000AD Graphic Novel: Mechanismo

Mega-City 5000

EVENT: Illegal Motorbike Race, Mega-City One

Every year the Bike Gangs of Mega-City One get together to compete in the Mega-City 5000 – a vicious anarchic motorcycle challenge between 5000 contestants from the many gangs. The race is run across the city, bringing death and destruction in its wake, so the Judges battle the bikers each year to try and stop it.

Introduced: 2000AD Prog 40

Mega-City One

CITY: Eastern Seaboard, former U.S.A.

As the problems of overpopulation and pollution became chronic in 21st Century America, a radical solution was proposed. A vast "Mega-City" was built on the Eastern Seaboard – right on top of the old cities below, which were mostly concreted over. The new city was designed to accommodate the most awesome crowding of people the world had ever seen, but it also proved to be a breeding ground for crime on an unprecedented scale. For this reason, the Judges were needed to mete out instant justice in the regular course of their duties, and Mega-City One soon became a model for two further American cities, as well as for countless similar megalopolises all over the world.

Even though the first Mega-City has had to survive two nuclear conflicts and numerous other crises, it remains an incredibly complex city, with over 1000 million miles of roadway in constant use. Its population peaked at around 800 million at the start of the 22nd Century, but subsequent catastrophes have left it with something like half that number of citizens.

Introduced: 2000AD Prog 2

Mega-City Two

CITY: West Coast, former U.S.A.

Covering five thousand square miles of the Californian West Coast, Mega-City Two became America's second city after the Atomic Wars of 2070. Although allied with Mega-City One and Texas City, it was independently governed by its own Justice Department and, on one famous occasion, they displayed a remarkable degree of neutrality when they refused to intervene in the so-called "Apocalypse War" between its sister city and East-Meg One. This was despite the fact that Mega-City Two owed its very survival to a mission of mercy carried out by the Judges of Mega-City One when the second city was afflicted with the deadly Virus Strain 2T(FRU)T in 2100.

Twelve years later, however, Mega-City Two was completely overrun by zombies unleashed by the evil Necromagus, Sabbat. With the city beyond hope of rescue, the place was nuked out of existence on the orders of a council of Judges from all over the world.

Introduced: 2000AD Prog 42

Destroyed: Judge Dredd the Megazine Volume 2: 7

Megaman

CITIZEN: Mega-City One

Ogden Schlep was one of Mega-City One's weediest citizens – until he splashed out on a powerful exo-skeleton and a jet-pack to became Megaman! Schlep fought crime in his heroic guise, but the Judges were not impressed with his vigilante actions, so they quickly identified him and Judge Dredd was despatched to his apartment to arrest him. The hapless hero tried to explain the he was on the side of the good guys, but Dredd was having none of it and Megaman proved decidedly less than "mega" in a straight fight. The unfortunate Schlep was still a novice when it came to manoeuvring his jet pack in a confined space and the device blew up after bouncing him around the apartment for a while!

2000AD Prog 442 (dies)

Meka-City

BUILDING: South Sector 555, Mega-City One

The robot stronghold of Meka-City

Built amid the ruins of South Sector 555 by renegade robots in just two days, Meka-City housed thousands of droids dispossessed during the Apocalypse War. They were led by the powerful wrestling robot, Precious Leglock, who ruled his city with a literal grip of iron until Judge Dredd managed to defeat him in the ring. The city was then dismantled even more rapidly by order of the Justice Department!

See also PRECIOUS LEGLOCK

Introduced: 2000AD Prog 271

Mikhael Parkinov

CITIZEN: Vid-star, East-Meg One

The Sov-Blok's most popular Chat Show Host, Mikhael Parkinov was called in by War-Marshal Kazan when he wanted to put Mega-City One's Chief Judge Griffin on the spot during the Apocalypse War. Needing a major propaganda coup to put an end to the Mega-City's resistance, he had arranged for the Chief Judge to be kidnapped and brainwashed – making him a very amenable guest for Mikhael to interview. Even under the lightest of pressure from the Chat Show Host during a specially arranged show, staged in Mega-City One's own Grand Hall of Justice, Griffin was happy to concede the war to the Sovs and readily betray his own city with a happy smile on his face!

2000AD Prog 261

Milton D. Frankenstein

CITIZEN: Mega-City One

Formerly a professor at the Mega-City Tech, Milton D. Frankenstein left under a cloud due to his interest in the banned area of DNA cloning. Advances in this field by the Judges had long been kept secret, so Frankenstein believed he was breaking new ground. He was so determined to perfect the techniques of cloning that he set up his own illegal laboratory and enlisted the help of one of his former pupils, Charles Beaker, to try and create fully grown humans by using his own DNA! His first "success" was Dennis, the DNA Man, but his assistant saw the folly in Frankenstein's work and tried to stop it. Under orders, Dennis killed Beaker and when his body was later found by the Judges, suspicion fell upon the Professor. By the time they caught up with him, Frankenstein had created a small army of DNA Men, each less perfect than the last, and the Judges were forced to destroy them all. The Professor, realising that his only chance of continuing his experiments was to leave the city, took Dennis and fled. The Judges were too late to prevent him from escaping their jurisdiction, but his own creation turned on him at the end – so Dennis and the Professor died together just outside Mega-City One.

See also DENNIS THE DNA MAN

2000AD Progs 113-115

Ministry of Fear

ORGANISATION: Mega-City One

Set up under top secret circumstances by the mysterious "Overseer", the Ministry of Fear wore similar costumes to the Judges of Mega-City One and contributed to the chaos in the city streets when every Judge apart from Dredd himself was dismissed by Chief Justice Fargo in 2045. The "Ministry" was led by the dedicated Minister Synn and they proved to be a powerful terrorist force, with their main attention going towards wiping out the city's corrupt police. Dredd eventually discovered that the Overseer was in fact Fargo himself and that the Ministry of Fear was part of his overall plan to ensure that the Judges would ultimately gain control of the Mega-City.

See also CHIEF JUDGE EUSTACE FARGO

Introduced: Judge Dredd # 5

Judge Minty

JUDGE: Retired, Mega-City One

While taking on the Kovaks Mob alongside Judge Dredd, Judge Minty's reactions and judgement proved inadequate and he found himself in a hospital bed after Dredd had made the arrests. Admitting that he had begun to entertain thoughts of treating the citizens with kindness, rather than enforcing the usual brand of harsh laws, Minty knew his time to quit had come. Retiring with honour, he chose the Long Walk into the Cursed Earth instead.

2000AD Prog 147

Missionary Man

JUDGE: Outlands Marshal, Texas City Badlands

The Cursed Earth is home to all sorts of mutants, monsters and murderers, so a special kind of lawkeeper is needed to maintain order there. Unfortunately, such stout-hearted protectors of the innocent are few and far between in most areas of the radioactive wasteland, but at least the Badlands just south of Texas City are patrolled by a small number of Outlands Marshals. The most famous of these is Preacher Cain, the "Missionary Man" - although some doubt exists as to whether the Marshal's badge he wears is really his own. In fact, little is known about Cain's background and not even his deputy, Resurrection Joe, knows who he really is. One thing is certain, though – you don't mess with the Missionary Man. With a bible in one hand and a gun in the other, Preacher Cain generally delivers a few words from the good book to the bad guys – before he blows them away!

See also LEGION

Judge Dredd the Megazine Volume 2: 29, 30, 43, 50-59, 63-66

Judge Dredd Mega-Special 1994

Judge Dredd Yearbook 1995

Mister Buzzz

MUTANT: Cursed Earth origin, operating in Mega-City One

Before the vast wall was erected around Mega-City One, mutants from the Cursed Earth found it much easier to enter the city undetected. Mister Buzzz not only defied Mega-City One's strict anti-mutant laws by going there, he had no qualms about flouting many other Mega-City laws, too. He soon found himself the leader of a feared "Murder Gang", despite the fact that he was completely blind - "seeing" by listening for the echoes from the BZZZ noises he would make in much the way a bat might navigate in the dark.

2000AD Prog 22

Mock Chocs

FOODSTUFF: Candy, Mega-City One

With sugar illegal in Mega-City One, most sweet products share the same fate. There is still a thriving candy market, however, as manufacturers compete to make different types of "Mock Chocs", which not only attract customers because they are delicious, but also conform to the strict legal guidelines!

Introduced: 2000AD Prog 614

Modular Fighting Unit

VEHICLE: Ground combat unit, Mega-City One Justice Department

Actually two extremely powerful vehicles that join together to form one mighty battle tank, the Modular Fighting Unit was used by Judge Dredd when he made his historic crossing of the Cursed Earth to deliver plague vaccine to Mega-City Two. The two specific parts are the K2001 Land Raider – a passenger carrier equipped with four-wheel drive, a thermo-nuclear engine, flame-thrower, machine guns and a special cargo bay – and the Killdozer – a nuclear blast-proof mobile fighting machine armed with Nemesis rockets, laser guns and cannons.

Introduced: 2000AD Prog 62

Sov-Judge Molotov

JUDGE: East-Meg One

Commander of a Sov-Block Anti-Pollution ship operating in the Black Atlantic, Judge Molotov's true mission was to run spying missions in Mega-City One. When Judge Dredd uncovered a plot to steal the plans for his city's Laser Defences, he tracked the operation back to the ship and – though it was outside the 40 mile limit of his jurisdiction – he was still determined to arrest everyone on board. Molotov was in no mood to surrender and instead tried to kill Dredd, who found himself plunged into the polluted water. The Mega-City One Judge made it on board and survived only thanks to the urgent attention of the ship's medic, Dr Rodnina – much to the annoyance of Judge Molotov. With Dredd in his power, the Sov-Judge ordered his death, but his enemy proved more resourceful than expected and managed to escape. Dredd seized his opportunity to arrest Molotov at gunpoint and, with him as a hostage, took the whole Sov-Block ship into the Mega-City One harbour under arrest!

2000AD Progs 128, 129

Monsteroso

ROBOT: Construction Droid, Mega-City One

As part of the "Big M" series, Monsteroso was one of the largest construction robots in Mega-City One, so it was pretty bad news when he went haywire and began a rampage through the city! Monsteroso was responsible for untold damage as he stomped around looking for a fight, but he wasn't tough enough to take on Judge Dredd. Having jumped onto the robot's giant head from a nearby flyover, Dredd was able to shoot out his control circuits and Monsteroso responded by decapitating himself!

2000AD Prog 412

Monty the Guinea Pig

ANIMAL: Guinea pig, Mega-City One

When Judge Dredd was approached for help by a talking cat, he was surprised to say the least. The fact that the cat was asking him to help a doomed guinea pig was all the more bizarre. Dredd followed up the lead and discovered Doctor Galt experimenting on various animals in his dingy laboratory. Under Mega-City One law, his activities were legal, but Judge Dredd could smell a rat (as well as a guinea pig, presumably). In fact, Galt had developed a common cold culture, with which he intended to blackmail the city. Poor Monty had been lined up for the doctor's final test of the culture, but Dredd stepped in just in time to save him and the only victim of it turned out to be Galt – the first (fatal) victim of a cold for almost 100 years!

See also THE DREDD ACT

2000AD Prog 126

Mo-Pad

VEHICLE: Mobile Home, Mega-City One

Despite the enormous amount of accommodation offered its citizens by the vast City Blocks, Mega-City One still has a severe housing shortage. With Displaced Persons Camps a very unattractive option, those able to afford it can invest in a Mo-Pad. Sometimes quite luxurious, these provide homes for at least eighteen million citizens, but they are far from ideal places to live. Permanently on the move along more than 1000 million miles of roadway around the city, living in a Mo-Pad is not easy, even though they almost all have an automatic mode, so that their owner is not forever preoccupied by driving the vehicle.

Introduced: 2000AD Prog 131

Mophioso

ALIENS: Gangsters, Planet Mophio

Using their natural electrical powers, the Mophioso believed that they would find it an easy task to muscle in on Mega-City One's "mega-rackets" and take over from all the local gangsters. Judge Dredd soon caught on to the aliens' intentions, but rather than deport them immediately, he allowed them to initiate a mob war. The Mega-City's racketeers found it hard to resist the Mophioso and their own activities suffered as result. Once the aliens had driven a wedge through the gangsters' organisations, Dredd was ready to pick up the pieces and impound then deport the Mophioso before they were able to establish themselves in the Mega-City One underworld.

2000AD Progs 222, 223

Mori Colon

CITIZEN: Unemployed Pollster, Mega-City One

When he lost his job as a professional Pollster, Mori Colon found it impossible to kick the habit. In everything he did, he just couldn't help himself asking people to specify one of three possible options: A, B or C. His obsession with polling his friends continually, soon left him without any, so he sought a new way of meeting people and decided to become a serial killer. Mori found polling his victims on murder-related issues a satisfying way of passing the time until he took on an entire "research group". By holding up the local Morons Club he attracted the attention of the Judges and soon found himself either (A) going free, (B) getting away with a 5 cred fine, or (C) doing time in the Psycho-Cubes for multiple homicide!

2000AD Prog 824

Judge Morphy

JUDGE: Mega-City One

As a Senior Judge, Morphy supervised many Rookies' final street assessments in his time, but none more significant than when he passed Joe Dredd and recommended him for his full Eagle. Dredd always looked up to Morphy and consulted him for advice whenever he had a problem. Although Dredd's "clone father" was former Chief Judge Fargo himself, Judge Morphy was the nearest he had to a real father and they were close friends. When Dredd first had doubts about his judgement many years later, he expressed his concerns to Morphy. The older man knew exactly what his Rookie was going through and assured him that every Judge has doubts from time to time. His advice was for Dredd to start wearing tight boots,

Above: **Judge Morphy goes about his business!**

as it had worked for him years before. Morphy insisted that he was so busy cursing the boots that his other worries went right out of his mind! Dredd thought the suggestion was a joke at first, but he traded his own pair for a size smaller and it really did help. Judge Morphy served on the streets of Mega-City One for more than forty years and had been offered a teaching post at the Academy of Law when he was gunned down by a gang of Stookie dealers. The loss of his mentor was deeply upsetting to Judge Dredd, especially as he was having even more fundamental doubts about his own role as a Judge at the time.

2000AD Progs 387, 664-667 (dies), 775 (flashback)

Morton Phillips

CITIZEN: Civil rights activist, Mega-City One

As the leader of the Freedom League, Morton Phillips was one of key figures due to join the Democratic Charter March, but through a combination of innuendo and false evidence, the Judges discredited him as a Sov collaborator during the Apocalypse War. Nothing could be proved, but Morton's political credibility was destroyed.

See also **FREEDOM LEAGUE**

2000AD Progs 531-533

Moze Bigleftear

MUTANT: Atom Gulch, Cursed Earth

An obvious physical deformity gave Moze his second name, but he never let his mutation or the fact that he could barely scrape a living from the radioactive wasteland of the Cursed Earth get him down. At least not until his home town of Atom Gulch looked like being overrun by a massive swarm of poisonous mutated spiders anyway. The so-called "Black Plague" of spiders gave him some cause for concern and he decided to ride his mutant horse, Henry Ford, to Mega-City One in search of help. Judge Dredd listened to Moze Bigleftear and decided to investigate his problem. Dredd had the citizens of Atom Gulch dig a trench around their town which they could then turn into a flaming barrier against the spiders. Although some of the creatures made it into his town, Moze was delighted to see that through his and the Judge's efforts they were finally warded off.

See also BLACK PLAGUE, HENRY FORD

2000AD Progs 140-142

Mr Moonie

Mr Moonie plots Judge Dredd's downfall

CITIZEN: Explorer and businessman, Luna-1

When the Luna-1 colony was established on the moon, explorer and entrepreneur C. W. Moonie was naturally drawn there. He arrived determined to find evidence of life on the moon and, tragically, his quest was successful. He discovered a deadly bacteria that afflicted him – disfiguring his face and body, and affecting his mind. Moonie became a recluse after this and as time passed he became more and more embittered by his plight. Turning his talents to running a criminal syndicate, masquerading as a legitimate business concern, he soon became one of the most powerful men in Luna-1. When Judge Dredd became Judge-Marshal of the city, Mr Moonie recognised the threat he posed and made numerous attempts to kill him. This was to prove the former explorer's undoing, since it led Dredd right to him and ultimately the Judge saw to it that he would spend his final days locked up in the Luna-1 Iso-Cubes.

2000AD Progs 45, 46

Mrs Gunderson

CITIZEN: Landlady, Mega-City One

When Judge Death finally vacated an apartment rented out to him by Mrs Gunderson, the Judges were puzzled by the fact that he had left her unharmed. Having captured him some time later, they brought the two together again to discover that he couldn't kill her because she was the only truly innocent living creature he had ever encountered!

Judge Dredd the Megazine Volume 1: 1–12 Volume 2: 15

Murd the Oppressor

ALIEN: Necromancer, Planet Necros

Supremely evil ruler of the Planet Necros, Murd had lived for thousands of years, using the mysterious substance Oracle Spice to further his influence. Along with his "familiar", a giant toad, and his evil helpers, the Watchers, he brought misery to the planet until Judges Dredd and Hershey arrived in search of the spice. Murd actually killed Judge Dredd, but used his mystical powers to revive him because he wanted to feed the Judge alive to Sagbelly the Toad. Ultimately, he regretted this, since Dredd turned the tables on him and it was Murd who found himself swallowed by the Toad!

See also ORACLE SPICE, SAGBELLY THE TOAD, WATCHERS

2000AD Progs 170-171 (dies), 172 (cameo), 797 (cameo)

Judge Annual 1983 (cameo)

Murk Derryson

CITIZEN: Gangster, Mega-City One

Specialising in "Chump Dumping" - offering better lives on new planets to downtrodden mutants and then dumping them in space after accepting their fee – Murk Derryson built a small but lucrative criminal organisation in Mega-City One, always staying just out of the reach of the Judges. Things went badly wrong for Murk, though, when former Judge Karl Raider decided to wreck his business in a completely unsanctioned vigilante action. Raider invaded his hideout and chopped his hands off in retribution for a similar act perpetrated by the gangster and the resulting vendetta saw Derryson - "Stumpy" to his friends! - exposed to the Judges and he was finally killed in a confrontation with Judge Dredd.

See also KARL RAIDER

2000AD Progs 810-814 (dies)

The Mutant

MUTANT: Clone of the Judge Child, Mega-City One 2120

Disappointed at the loss of his most valued slave – when Chief Judge McGruder ordered the execution of the Judge Child – the Grunwalder set about trying to clone the boy from some tissue samples he had secretly kept. The product of his experiments, however, was a hideously deformed clone with awesome mental powers, which dwarfed those of the Judge Child. "The Mutant", as it soon became known, also had a lust for revenge on Judge Dredd and the whole of Mega-City One, following their treatment of his former self. To this end, he spent years gathering his power until he was ready to crush the city. In 2120, the Mutant took over Mega-City One, killed most of the Judges, including Dredd, and turned the rest of them into "Blues" - vampire creatures more interested in the blood of their citizens than the law! These events fulfilled Psi-Judge Feyy's famous dying prediction, but it had turned out that the Judge Child was the threat rather than their salvation.

Only when Judges Dredd and Anderson turned up in 2120, having travelled forward from the year 2107, did the Mutant's plans start to go astray. At first, he was delighted to have another chance to torment Dredd, who he regretted having killed so quickly the first time. He gouged out the Judge's eyes, then he reanimated the body of the Dredd he'd already killed and sent it after him and Anderson. The Mutant enjoyed the chase until he realised that the Judges were going to make it back to their time machine and then the full consequences of their escape began to dawn on him. Back in 2107, Dredd used the information the Mutant himself had given him about his origins to formulate a plan to defeat him. Once he'd had some new robotic eyes implanted, Dredd set off for Xanadu, along with Anderson. Once there, they put a stop to the Grunwalder's experiments and they killed the newly-born mutant before its power could grow strong enough to prevent them. They also terminated the Grunwalder himself, just in case he began his experiments again, and the future they had recently visited appeared to be clear of the catastrophe they had witnessed. Only time would tell for sure.

See also GRUNWALDER, JUDGE CHILD

2000AD Progs 393-406 (dies)

Mutie the Pig

JUDGE: Renegade, Mega-City One

One of Judge Dredd's closest friends at the Academy of Law was Judge Gibson, so it came as a shock for Dredd to discover that some twenty years after their graduation his friend had turned to a life of crime. Adopting the guise of Mutie the Pig, Gibson had secretly become an armed robber, while maintaining his public identity as a Judge. Realising Dredd was close to exposing him, Gibson tried to kill him and believed he had been successful when the Justice Department announced Dredd's demise. However, Dredd's "death" was a ruse to trap the rogue Judge and he was able to apprehend his former class-mate during Mutie the Pig's next armed robbery. Unmasked at last, Judge Gibson invoked "Cadet's Rights" and so, following a frantic duel through the mock-Mega-City One streets, Dredd had no choice but to shoot the rogue Judge.

2000AD Progs 34, 35

N

The Neon Knights

ORGANISATION: Vigilantes, Mega-City One

IN THE NAME OF ALL HUMANS, I-GRAND MASTER OF THE NEON KNIGHTS- DO ORDER THE EXECUTION OF THIS MACHINE.

Fuelled by the bitterness after the Robot Wars of 2099, a number of secretive vigilante klans were formed with the aim of destroying robots. The Neon Knights were one of the most visible of these groups, but they made a big mistake when they captured Walter the Wobot. Because Walter was officially classified as a free citizen of Mega-City One, the Judges had to take his kidnap more seriously than they might have if he were an ordinary robot, so Judge Dredd infiltrated the hooded vigilantes organisation to help him. As he set about arresting the whole group, Dredd unmasked their leader, revealing him to be a cyborg! Stunned by this fact, the rest of the vigilantes gave up quietly and the Neon Knights were officially closed down.

2000AD Prog 29

Neutron Flats

LOCATION: Town, Cursed Earth

One of the busiest and most prosperous towns in the Cursed Earth, the local economy in Neutron Flats was based almost entirely on slave trading. Although no genuine authority operated there, the extremely wealthy Brotherhood of Trash was the dominant force in the local community, under the leadership of the quite insane Filmore Faro – now deceased.

See also BROTHERHOOD OF TRASH, FILMORE FARO

Introduced: 2000AD Prog 157

"New You" Face Change Parlour

BUILDING: Commercial Face Change Boutique, Mega-City One

Offering the ultimate in "cosmetic surgery", New You is popular with citizens who really want a change of image. Their instant Face Change machines allow their customers to completely change their appearance to order – a service which has often been of interest to Mega-City criminals! Although portable face change machines have since come onto the market, "New You" retains its reputation for professionalism in this area and many citizens wouldn't go anywhere else.

Introduced: 2000AD Prog 3

Nightmare Gun

WEAPON: Nightmare-inducing Gun, Planet Grall

When a Grall Wipe-out Squad came to Mega-City One brandishing one of their most weapons – a Nightmare Gun – they reckoned without the mental strength of Judge Dredd, who proved impervious to it. They were captured, as was their gun, which fired an invisible beam that would inspire terrible fear in its victim, often causing death. When the Justice Department's Tek-Division got their hands on the gun, they developed the technology to create their own Fear Amplification Beam (FAB), a milder version of the original which they could use on any citizen they had particular reason to intimidate!

See also GRALL WIPE-OUT SQUAD

Introduced: 2000AD Prog 190

SJS Judge Rog Niles

JUDGE: Head of Special Judicial Squad, Mega-City One

Having come through the ranks of the Mega-City One Justice Department and passed some of the toughest vetting procedures imaginable, Rog Niles was selected for the Judges' most sensitive and, many would argue, most powerful position short of Chief Judge itself – head of the feared SJS. The Special Judicial Squad are empowered to investigate the Judges themselves, so their leader must be of the purest character or the consequences could be dire. One of Niles's predecessors, Judge Cal, showed just how effectively the position could be abused when he used the SJS as his own personal army to seize control of the Justice Department and murder Chief Judge Goodman in 2101. Judge Niles's character was therefore deemed beyond reproach before he was appointed SJS head and he has since demonstrated his aptitude for the role. He was asked to run Mega-City One along with Judges Hershey and Shenker for an interim period when Chief Judge McGruder resigned in 2116. As preparations were made to vote on her successor, Niles was encouraged to put himself forward, but he showed his commitment to the SJS by declining to stand.

2000AD Prog 706, 914, 915-918

Judge Dredd the Megazine Volume 2: 57, 68

Nobby Klunk

CITIZEN: Simp, Mega-City One

Frustrated by the insignificance of his existence, Nobby Klunk discovered the wonders of "Simping" on his wedding day. Turning up for the ceremony wearing a canoe, a top hat with flowers in and a carrot on his nose, amongst other things, Nobby certainly made an impression, but his wife to be was not pleased. It was only after a farcical series of accidents saw him injured that his beloved Clovis agreed to go through with their marriage. Unfortunately, Nobby's constant Simping put a considerable strain on their relationship and eventually, Dredd had them divorced.

2000AD Prog 527, 574

Nosferatus

ALIEN RACE: Shape-shifters, Planet Garlokk

The Nosferatus have been hunted almost to extinction by the Garrs, the predominant species on their home planet, but the survivors of the race still represent a terrifying threat to the rest of the Galaxy. Feeding by injecting digestive protozymes into their victims to liquidise their insides, making them ready to be sucked out, Nosferatus are extremely dangerous predators and, because they are capable of changing their appearance at will, they can surprise their victims with ease.

2000AD Prog 430-433

Judge Dredd the Megazine Volume 1: 7, 8

Novar

MUTANT: Citizen, Cursed Earth

Born of parents mutated by the radiation fall-out from the Atomic Wars, Novar was possessed of tremendous psionic talents. He was able to read minds, as well as to manipulate things through telekinesis, but used his powers to worthy ends. In fact, he helped Judge Dredd to defeat the fanatical Brotherhood of Darkness, during the lawman's quest to cross the Cursed Earth in order to deliver the antidote to the plague afflicting Mega-City Two.

2000AD Prog 66

Above: A Nosferatu picks over the bones of its many victims

Left: Nobby Klunk's marriage ceremony

O

Judge Ocks

JUDGE: Mega-City One

Having been selected to join Judge Dredd's Apocalypse Squad, Ocks was one of Mega-City One's saviours when they successfully destroyed East-Meg One, thereby ending the Apocalypse War. A bond was formed between the brave Judges on that mission and Dredd called on Judge Ocks once more, when he was asked to clean up the crime-ridden Shanty Town on the edge of Mega-City One, housing thousands of its displaced citizens. More or less single-handedly, Ocks was responsible for ensuring that lawbreakers were turned away from the settlement and into the Cursed Earth!

See also APOCALYPSE SQUAD

2000AD Progs 263-267, 269, 270, 301-303

Judge-Tutor Odell

JUDGE: Academy of Law, Mega-City One

One of the Academy of Law's most experienced Judge-Tutors, Odell was entrusted with a very special Cadet following the defeat of the Judda. On the orders of Chief Judge Silver, one of their group who shared the bloodline of Judges Dredd and Fargo was spared execution. Odell's mission was turn this enemy into a possible replacement for its greatest hero – Judge Dredd! Kraken proved a difficult pupil but Odell was determined to succeed. Slowly but surely, he broke down Kraken's Judda training and instilled a dedication to Mega-City One law. The Cadet's early rebelliousness was eventually replaced by an eagerness to serve on the streets of the city he had been brought up to hate and Odell was at last convinced that Kraken was ready. The test was supervised by Judge Dredd himself and Odell was horrified when Dredd failed him, despite an apparently immaculate performance.

The Judge-Tutor believed in Kraken and was bitter at Dredd's decision, for it meant the death sentence outstanding on his pupil would certainly be carried out. He was willing to risk his own life, then, when the Chief Judge proposed one last gamble. Odell accompanied the failed Judge when he was transported to Resyk to be terminated by lethal injection, knowing full well that if any Judda remained within the young man, he would kill him and try to escape. Odell played his part well, but was delighted when Kraken went to his "death" quietly – since the whole thing was faked.

Kraken was given Dredd's badge, since the older man had chosen to retire, and the Judge-Tutor proudly observed his career develop until the Sisters of Death arrived. When they took over and perverted Kraken's mind, the Judge-Tutor felt so guilty over his part in putting the former Judda on the streets, that he took his own life .

See also JUDGE KRAKEN

2000AD Progs 583, 584, 650, 662, 663, 667-670, 681, 734 (reported dead)

Old Joe Blind

CITIZEN: Planet Xanadu,

One of many independent prospectors on the open planet Xanadu, Old Joe was unfortunate enough to have a run-in with the Angel Gang shortly after they arrived there. For his crime of "lookin' at us", Junior saw that he got a good lesson in manners – he tortured Joe, blinding him and his horse. Many would have died as a result of the wounds but hatred kept "Old Joe Blind" going. He developed a sixth sense which helped Judge Dredd locate the Angels. Along the way, though, Joe was ambushed and tortured further by Link Angel and then Junior Angel. Mean Machine even butted his horse to death! Old Joe finally allowed his battered body to rest when he had seen – or rather heard! – Judge Dredd kill all four members of the Angel Gang.

2000AD Progs 177-180 (dies)

Oracle Spice

DRUG: Dangerous hallucinogenic, Planet Necros

Secreted from a wart on the hindquarters of the vile Sagbelly the Toad, this powerful substance gives its users erratic visions of the future. It takes 10,000 years to understand and the only creature who had mastery over it was Murd the Oppressor, who used it to help him control Necros. The supply of the spice was cut off when Sagbelly died during Judge Dredd's visit to the planet in search of the Judge Child.

See also MURD THE OPPRESSOR, SAGBELLY THE TOAD

Introduced: 2000AD Prog 164

Psi-Judge Omar

JUDGE: Chief of Psi-Division, Mega-City One

Powerful natural Psis rarely exhibit the kind of leadership potential required to head up one of the most important Divisions in the Justice Department, but Judge Omar was as strong in will and courage as he was in mind. He was a popular choice to become Psi-Division Chief. During the investigation of the "haunting" of Sector House 9, he was forced to battle mind-to-mind with Leroy Tamerlain – a dying psi-criminal, who was using a psionic amplifier to boost his own abilities a thousandfold. Omar barely survived the encounter, but he eventually overcame the criminal. Less than two years later, Omar had to use a psionic amplifier himself, sacrificing himself for the city.

See also SHOJAN

2000AD Progs 361-363, 452-455 (dies)

Orlok the Assassin

JUDGE: Spy, East-Meg One

Hand-picked to begin the assault on Mega-City One prior to the Apocalypse War, Orlok was given the job of spreading Block Mania there. Orlok was responsible for the deaths of several Judges, including Judge Giant, but he was finally captured and remained in custody throughout the war and after East-Meg One's unexpected defeat he burned with rage. A group of East-Meg One survivors succeeded in freeing him and Orlok returned to his city to plot revenge .

He tried channelling latent hatred through the psi-power of children in Mega-City One and caused thousands of deaths before being thwarted by Psi-Judge Anderson. Shortly after this, however, Orlok was declared "stateless" as relations between the Sov Block and Mega-City One thawed. He headed for Mars , and was forced to team up with Anderson. After an incredible revelation created a bond between them, they parted on equal terms. The experience certainly had a profound effect on Orlok. After a lifetime as an assassin, he had decided it was time to help the kind of people he might previously have despised.

See also PSI-JUDGE ANDERSON, BLOCK MANIA

2000AD Progs 241-245, 528, 529, 531, 641, 643, 644

Judge Dredd the Megazine Volume 2: 30-34, 54-56

2000AD Graphic Novel: Childhood's End

Above:
Prospector Old Joe Blind

Far left:
Orlok the Assassin

Otto Sump

CITIZEN: Mega-City One

The biggest hard luck case in Mega-City One, poor Otto was so ugly that the only job he could ever get was as a rat scarer. Even then, animal rights activists got him the sack because they claimed it was unfair on the rats! Otto Sump's luck changed, though, when he appeared on the vid-show Sob Story. Every week unfortunate citizens appeared on the show and begged for money, but many of the most successful contestants were later murdered for the money they had been sent by sympathetic viewers. Judge Dredd arranged for Sump to make an appearance in the knowledge that he would be one of the biggest "winners" ever and so would attract the attention of the murderers. The plan worked well. Dredd caught the killers, and even better for Sump, he became a billionaire!

UGLY ? DON'T TELL ME ABOUT UGLY! I GOT UGLY COMIN' OUTA MY EARS!

Otto's attempts to invest his money and build a business empire were less successful, however, as each one seemed to be doomed for one reason or another.

First he bought a chain of beauty clinics, but insisted on carrying out treatments himself and he regularly made a mess of things. This led to the salons being remarketed as "Ugly Clinics" and the Ugly look caught on for a while in Mega-City One. The Judges' hefty Ugly Tax put paid to the mass "Ugly" market, so Otto turned his attention to creating a new foodstuff called "Gunge". After the Apocalypse War food was scarce, so by putting all sorts of bugs and other unpleasant things into a can, Otto Sump was sure he was onto a tasty nutritious winner! Unfortunately, Moral Health campaigners got it banned and the Judges commandeered his operation to transform Gunge into a Justice Department approved foodstuff in generic packaging. Next, the irrepressible billionaire hit on the idea of producing "smart sweets". His advertising suggested that these made people clever, but he made no specific claims and the sweets were in fact placebos – legal but harmless tablets. Unfortunately, some very stupid criminals started taking them to help them plan robberies and Judge Dredd convinced Otto to take early retirement – by offering him five years in the 'Cubes if he didn't stop making smart sweets!

See also UGLY CLINICS

2000AD Progs 132, 186-188, 280, 436

Judge Dredd the Megazine Volume 2: 45 (cameo)

Oxygen Board

COMPANY: Luna-1

All of Luna-1's oxygen is controlled by the Oxygen Board and this includes private supplies to the air-locked apartments in the city. Supply is maintained on a continuous basis via ducts leading into each dwelling, but citizens are expected to keep up regular payments to pay for it. Should these payments fail to be made, the Oxygen Board are empowered to cut off the supply, making an apartment uninhabitable. This practice is frowned upon in some circles, however, since it is not unknown for citizens to become trapped inside an apartment when it is evacuated of breathable air, thus making them pay the ultimate price for an unpaid bill!

Introduced: 2000AD Prog 57

Oz

COUNTRY: Australia

The Sydney-Melbourne Conurb houses the majority of the population in Oz and life is a lot more free and easy there than it is in Mega-City One, although the people of the city face many of the same problems due to crime and the conseqeunces of past nuclear conflicts. Oz-Judges, too, are considerably more laid back than their counterparts – allowing themselves a sense of humour when necessary! Great believers in sport, the Oz authorities were the first to sanction a legal staging of the World Skysurfing Championship – Supersurf 8 in 2107 – and it was held there for three years running.

Introduced: 2000AD Prog 545

P

Judge Lola Palmtree

JUDGE: **Wally Squad, Mega-City One**

One of Mega-City One's most effective undercover Judges, Lola Palmtree has a particular talent for blending in with the citizens and she has had a number of notable successes in infiltrating major criminal operations. She was also used to gain the confidence of Karl Raider, a former Judge on a vigilante mission, before he was finally tracked down and killed by Judge Dredd.

2000AD Progs 741, 811-813

Elmer "Pa" Angel

CITIZEN: **Criminal, Texas City Badlands**

Elmer Angel acquired a reputation as Texas City's baddest man at a surprisingly early age and did everything possible during his life to prove that the title was well-deserved. His band of outlaws – the Angel Gang – was known for its viciousness, but Elmer could never quite find confederates who would live up to his own evil standards, so in the end he was forced to turn the Angel Gang into a strictly family affair. He married and produced four sons, three of whom turned out to be suitably nasty by nature, while young "Mean"

needed some drastic corrective surgery to transform him into the kind of maniac Elmer was proud to call his son. "Pa" Angel's wife died due to complications during the birth of Junior – probably the most despicable of all the Angel progeny – but the old man's grief was short-lived. He had too many foul deeds to perpetrate with his boys to waste time on sentimentality and these occupied his time.

Junior was definitely his Pa's favourite son, especially after Fink – the oldest of the four – left home, although Elmer was proud of his whole family. The Angel Gang operated successfully out of the Texas City Badlands, bringing terror and mayhem to everyone they met until they stumbled across a boy from Mega-City One who could see the future and who was being tracked by Judge Dredd. Owen Krysler – or the Judge Child – was believed to be the city's only hope during some coming catastrophe, so Dredd was understandably desperate to find the boy. Pa seized his chance and kidnapped Krysler, taking him off into space in order to escape the Judge's clutches. Certain that the Judge Child was a

resource of incalculable value, the Angel Gang finally reached the Planet Xanadu and attempted to do a deal with the mysterious Grunwalder – android ruler of a huge Robot Free-State there. Unfortunately for Pa and his boys, Judge Dredd managed to find them on Xanadu and, one by one, he killed the young Angels. With his sons all dead and already badly wounded himself, Elmer "Pa" Angel was a broken man and finally fell to his own death in a volcanic ravine – with a little help from the twisted mind powers of Owen Krysler himself!

See also JUDGE CHILD, MEAN MACHINE ANGEL, JUNIOR ANGEL, LINK ANGEL, GRUNWALDER

2000AD Progs 160, 161, 173, 176, 177, 179-181 (dies), 195 (flashback)

Judge Dredd Annual 1983 (cameo)

Elmer Angel, "Pa" to the entire angel gang

Pan Andes Conurb

CITY: Northern Mexico

Just across the old United States border is Mexico's surviving population centre, the Pan Andes Conurb. The city supplies most of the sugar brought into Mega-City One and illegally sold on the black market – a trade which the local Judges have traditionally turned a blind eye to, or indeed have played an active role in perpetuating! When Judge Dredd was sent to the city to investigate the source of one batch of sugar he actually ended up arresting well over half of the Pan Andes Conurb Judges for corruption – including the Chief Judge – and was forced to take charge of street policing there for a while, until the few honest Judges left could reorganise themselves into a group capable of maintaining law and order in their city.

See also CHIEF JUDGE GARCIA

Introduced: 2000AD Prog 873

The Pat-Wagons on patrol during Cal's reign of terror

Pat-Wagon

VEHICLE: Standard Patrol Vehicle, Mega-City One Justice Department

The Judges' Pat-Wagon is a formidable vehicle and provides street Judges with an excellent alternative to their usual Lawmaster Bikes on regular patrols in Mega-City One. Normally manned by two Judges, Pat-Wagons are heavily armed and also boast powerful spotlights, making them especially useful in riot situations or in encounters with extremely well-armed perps. Fast and manoeuvrable, both on the clogged Mega-Ways and the alleys of the city, Pat-Wagons can be used as fast-response units as well as regular patrol vehicles. It is also possible to use them to pick up lawbreakers and transport them to the Iso-Cubes, whereas Judges on their Lawmasters often have to rely on perps being collected by an H-Wagon – or indeed a Pat-Wagon – later.

Introduced: 2000AD Prog 102

Peepers

TERM: Illegal observers of citizens, Mega-City One

Becoming a Peeper in Mega-City One is not a simple task, since to observe the goings-on in an apartment in a neighbouring City Block requires some specialist equipment. High-intensity binoculars with night-vision lenses are a must, but the next most important asset a Peeper can have is patience. Clever Peepers can avoid detection by the Justice Department for years, but the penalty for invading the privacy of other citizens is severe. Occasionally, though, exceptionally accomplished Peepers are given an alternative to the Iso-Cubes – they are forced to peep for the City and the information they can glean can be extremely valuable to the Judges in stamping on crime!

Introduced: 2000AD Prog 491

Deputy Chief Judge Pepper

JUDGE: Deputy Chief Judge, Mega-City One

Following a distinguished career as a street Judge, Pepper retired and took a teaching post at the Academy of Law. He soon became one of the most respected Judge-Tutors there and numbered Judge Dredd amongst his most successful pupils. When one of his less celebrated pupils – Judge Cal – seized control of the Justice Department, however, Judge Pepper came out of retirement to aid the rebel cause against the tyrant. Joining up with Judge Dredd's small group, he played a vital role in the resistance against Cal, most notably when he employed his technical knowledge to construct a briefing tape which could be used to break the Chief Judge's influence on the Mega-City One Judges. Following Cal's death, Pepper was asked to take on the position of Deputy Chief Judge, serving under the newly appointed Chief Judge Griffin. Sadly, less than two years later, Pepper was brutally gunned down by a madman who believed that such a crime would guarantee him a winning run on the popular vid-show "Any Confessions?" – although it actually got him killed when Judge Dredd shot him as he tried to escape!

2000AD Progs 92-94, 97, 98, 100-102, 106-108, 110, 122, 145, 182, 197, 200, 201 (dies)

Judge Percy

JUDGE: Special Judicial Squad, Mega-City One

One of Chief Judge Cal's key men in the early days, Judge Percy made a disastrous mistake when he allowed Judge Dredd to escape his custody with the help of Judge Giant. Cal would have executed him for his error, but Judge Slocum instructed Percy to put on a frilly dress and managed to convince Cal that Deputy Chief Judge Fish had pronounced sentence on him. If Judge Percy was going to act like a little girl, then he could dress like one as a punishment!

2000AD Progs 91, 92, 95, 101, 104

Perp Running

CRIME: Transport of wanted criminals into Deep Space

One of Mega-City One's many "Mega Rackets" is the practice of "Perp Running", where wanted criminals are offered passage off world to enable them to avoid capture. Perps pay large sums of money to begin new lives in Deep Space, although many find themselves sold into slavery on alien worlds instead! After all, the Perp Runners know that their clients are unlikely to expose their deception, so the opportunity to make some more credits is too good to resist.

See also CHUMP DUMPING

Introduced: 2000AD Prog 211

Judge Perrier

JUDGE: Mega-City One

Only the toughest of Judges could have survived on the decimated city streets during the Apocalypse War and provide an effective resistance against the Sov invaders. Judge Perrier acquitted herself admirably and was responsible for finding a batch of Stub Guns, which proved invaluable in the course of the battle. She survived and went on to prove herself a fine Judge many times over. Perrier was finally killed while she was supervising a Hotdog Run in the Cursed Earth. This training exercise for a group of Cadets coincided with Sabbat the Necromagus beginning his assault on the

Earth by reanimating zombies all over the world. While helping ensure that the Cadets in her charge all made it safely back into the city, Perrier was swamped by zombies and failed to make it home herself.

See also STUB GUN

2000AD Progs 255-258, 260, 263, 267, 778, 779, 785-788 (dies)

Judge Dredd the Megazine Volume 2: 4

Phantom of the Shoppera

ROBOT: Construction Droid, Mega-City One

Thousands of robots were employed by the Vycom Building Company during the construction of a huge shopping centre, the Shoppera, so when one went missing it was presumed stolen and given no further thought. In fact, its circuits had gone haywire and it hid out among the girders at the very top of the complex for three years before loneliness got the better of it. Believing itself to be the "Phantom of the Shoppera", the robot fell in love with and kidnapped a male shop assistant, then asked him to become its wife! Judge Dredd soon tracked down the Phantom and it finally plummeted to its doom from the roof after Dredd shot it to free its hostage.

2000AD Progs 494, 495 (destroyed)

YET MY JOY IS BLACKENED BY DESPAIR. OH, BITTER FATE THAT MADE ME A MONSTER! THAT BRINGS MY TRUE LOVE FOR ME TO GAZE UPON — BUT NEVER TO BE MINE.

The Phantom of the Shoppera

Pieromania

CRAZE: Pie-throwing, Mega-City One

When Judge Dredd was hit in the face by a custard-substitute pie on live TV, it not only got his attacker six months in the 'Cubes, but it also started a mad craze that swept through the city. "Pieromania" broke out everywhere with massive pie fights being waged between City Blocks and Judges became prime targets! Questions were asked at the highest level and severe penalties were suggested, but Chief Judge McGruder chose to ride out the craze with minimum measures to ensure that pie-production was kept to a reasonable pre-craze quantity and it soon died away.

Introduced: 2000AD Prog 350

Pinboing®

GAME: Giant pinball, Mega-City One

Encased in the miracle rubber, Boing, Mega-City One pleasure seekers can actually participate in a massive pinball game – as the ball! Completely protected inside the rubber, PinBoing players have a degree of control over their movements on the giant table and accumulate points in exactly the same way as they could when playing a regular pinball game.

See BOING

Introduced: Judge Dredd Annual 1981

P.J. Maybe

CITIZEN: Juvenile Perp, Mega-City One

Committing his first murders at the age of twelve – by unleashing a home made robotic bug loaded with deadly synthetic poison on two victims selected at random – Philip Janet Maybe was delighted with his ability to kill with no apparent danger of being found out. P. J. protected himself further by hiding his keen intelligence behind a mask of under-achievement.

P. J.'s next move was to carry out a series of murders which would profit him. He first killed his cousin Wilbur Yess by tampering with his hover-car controls, then his other cousin Watt by giving him a piece of candy containing a powerful hypnogenic drug. This made Watt completely susceptible to suggestion and P. J. was able to tell him to write a suicide note before jumping out of his office window! Finally, the psychopathic Juve injected his Uncle Fustas with the virulent Cursed Earth disease Purple Sore Fever. Fustas, who was the head of Emphatically Yess – the company which supplied the Justice Department with Judges' trousers – died within three months, but Judge Dredd's suspicions of foul play could not be proven. As a result of the twelve murders he had committed, P. J. had ensured that his family had inherited the Yess fortune and business.

P. J. Maybe was eventually captured when he became careless following major problems for the family business. Emphatically Yess had lost the Judges' trouser contract to Hoss Bros and P. J. was determined to win it back. To this end he fed a variant of his hypnogenic drug to Chester Hoss and instructed him to tell the truth at all times – a plan which very nearly worked, since truth and business rarely mix! Hoss Bros just hung onto the contract despite Chester, so P. J. decided to set up Chester's brother Alger Hoss. The boy's masterplan involved a robotic simulacrum of Alger standing in for him at an illicit meeting with a well-known drug dealer, but things went wrong when the real Hoss turned up to check out the deal! P. J. was apprehended by Dredd and soon found himself in a Psycho Cube.

P. J escaped while the Judges were trying to defend Mega-City One from the onslaught of the Sisters of Death. He found his parents so deep in despair that they were in the process of killing themselves, but the psychopathic boy was fortunate enough to find himself invited to hide out from the Dark Judges in a luxurious underground shelter belonging to the hyper-rich Urchison family. Having murdered their son, P. J. used a face change machine to make himself look like him and when the Judges released them from the bunker, P. J. had assumed the identity of Junior Urchison – the heir to an even bigger fortune than he would have been as a Maybe! P. J.'s homicidal tendencies continued in his new guise, but his acquisition of a Mock Choc factory seemed to provide an ideal place to dispose of any more dead bodies. This time, though, he was sloppy and Dredd was onto him a lot quicker, soon deducing his true identity. P. J. tried to flee to Banana City, but Dredd managed to intercept him and carted him back to the Psycho Cubes!

2000AD Progs 534, 592-594, 599, 632-634, 707-709, 820-822

Judge Dredd the Megazine Volume 2: 45 (cameo)

Plasteen

MATERIAL: All-purpose building material, Mega-City One

The miracle material of the 22nd Century, almost anything could be made with cheap and versatile Plasteen. Combining the adaptability of plastic with the durability of the toughest alloy metal, it could be as hard as a rock or as soft as tissue paper, so within a year or two of it coming onto the market it could be found all over the city. The only brake to its progress came when an alien virus was brought to the city accidentally by the giant corporation Inter-Space. All of Mega-City One's Plasteen was eaten away by the virus, causing all manner of catastrophes, but an anti-viral agent was soon developed to ensure that all new Plasteen would be resistant to the alien menace.

Introduced: 2000AD Prog 139

Police Bloodhound Robot

ROBOT: Justice Department Tracker Vehicle, Mega-City One

An early experiment in robotic help for the Mega-City One Judges, the Police Bloodhound Robot was unveiled at the Robot of the Year Show 0f 2099 – just before the outbreak of the Robot Wars. This event overshadowed the Bloodhound's launch and the ingenious tracking robot never became widely used in the city.

Introduced: 2000AD Prog 9

Power Board

DEVICE: Flying surfboard, Mega-City One

ONCE MORE THE SKIES BELONG TO **THE MIDNIGHT SURFER**.

Surfing in Mega-City One takes on a whole new dimension, since it is often done in the air, using special Power Boards! Sky Surfing is a popular sport in the city, although low-level flying is strictly forbidden by the Judges. Shaped like a traditional surfboard, a Power Board has a throttle pad in the middle area where a surfer puts his or her feet. The harder the pad is depressed by the user's foot, the more thrust is supplied and the faster the board goes. As soon as the foot comes off its throttle pad, a Power Board automatically returns to hover mode. For safety, all sky surfers must have a billycord firmly secured to their ankle, attaching them to the board should they be unfortunate enough to fall of it during flight!

Introduced: 2000AD Prog 424

Power Tower

BUILDING: Power Generating Complex, Mega-City One

Power Tower was an electricity generating complex, which supplied a vast amount of energy by converting lava from beneath the Earth's surface into power. It was also an ideal target for Father Earth and the Doomsday Dogs. Planting explosives in the Tower's pipeways, they turned it into a raging volcano, spewing forth molten lava on the city streets around it. Before the situation became absolutely critical, however, the Judges called in their specialist Holocaust Squad who managed to stem the lava and thereby save the city.

See also DOOMSDAY DOGS, FATHER EARTH, HOLOCAUST SQUAD

Introduced: 2000AD Prog 122

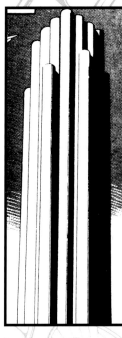

Mega-City One's engergy source – the Power Tower

Judge Prager

JUDGE: Retired, Mega-City One

Prager, having retired from active service, opted for the Long Walk. He knew things would be tough, but he didn't expect to find werewolves – least of all, one which had formerly been Judge Dredd! Rather than kill the creature, he Stumm gassed it and returned it to the city above, where the Judge was cured.

See also MED-JUDGE CASSIDY, WHITE WEREWOLF

2000AD Prog 329

Precious Leglock

ROBOT: Wrestling Droid, Mega-City One

In the aftermath of the Apocalypse War, thousands of robots were left without owners and looking for leadership. In South Sector 555, wrestler Precious Leglock declared himself King. When the Judges tried to retake the Sector from him, Leglock simply wrestled them to death. He believed he could beat anyone in the ring, but he reckoned without Dredd who hooked him up to an electrical source, transforming him into a giant magnet so that he was knocked down at last as dozens of droids slammed into him!

See also MEKA-CITY

2000AD Progs 271, 272

Project X

JUDGE: Renegade, East-Meg Two

Dredd faces off the Sov-Block's ultimate Judge: Project X

Pieced together from the dead bodies of a number of well-respected Sov-Judges who died at the hands of Judge Dredd during the Apocalypse War, Project X was intended to be East-Meg Two's "Ultimate Judge". Under the supervision of Sov-Judges Andropov and Yeltsin, the Project – or the "Frankenstein Division", as it came to be known – reanimated the hulking great frame of their artificially constructed Judge, but they had a problem with its synthi-brain. Obsessed with revenge on Judge Dredd, it escaped from their clutches and headed off to Mega-City One to begin the war anew. Invading Dredd's city, the Sov monster was responsible for the deaths of hundreds of citizens before it finally confronted the object of its hatred – but even East-Meg Two's "Ultimate Judge" was no match for Mega-City One's finest lawman and Project X was duly closed down!

See also SOV-JUDGE ANDROPOV, SOV-JUDGE YELTSIN

2000AD Progs 868-871 (dies)

Psi-Division

DIVISION: Mega-City One Justice Department

While Psi-Judges are called upon to use their abilities in times of great paranormal activity in Mega-City One, these kind of psychic combat situations are quite rare. In the normal run of events, Psi-Division is mainly concerned with the predictions of major crimes or disasters and the carrying out of mind probes on suspects who prove resistant to regular types of interrogation. In executive terms, Psi-Division ranks as one of the four key sections of the Mega-City One Justice Department – alongside Tek-Division, the SJS and the regular street Judges.

Introduced: 2000AD Prog 150

Psi Shield

DEVICE: Force Field, Deadworld

A rare synthesis between scientific hardware and accurately harnessed psi-power, Psi Shields are used by the Dark Judges to set up a virtually impenetrable barrier of variable size. Because this device is powered by their own psychic energies, it is impossible for a Psi Shield to be breached.

See also DARK JUDGES

Introduced: 2000AD Prog 225

Pug Ugly

CITIZEN: Pop star, Mega-City One

Famous for his terrible whining voice, Pug Ugly was one of Mega City One's most famous and best loved pop stars. With his backing group, the Bugglys, he took the city by storm during a hugely popular tour until he was gunned down during a gig. The band claimed ownership of his vocal chords and arranged for them to be transplanted into a new Pug Ugly selected from thousands of applicants. Unfortunately, the vocal chords were affected by cellulo psychic regenesis – where transplanted organs can somehow retain a piece of the intelligence of the donor – and so Pug's own voice was able to implicate them in his murder live on stage!

2000AD Prog 203

Puglies

GROUPS: Youth gangs, Mega-City One

During the craze inspired by Otto Sump's Ugly Clinics, a number of young perps had ugly treatment, becoming known as "Puglies". These vicious trouble-makers truly were the ugly face of the ugly business and added impetus to the Judges' determination to put an end to the ugly craze altogether.

See also UGLY CLINICS

2000AD Prog 186

Red has a spell in the Quarantine Bubble

Quarantine Bubble

DEVICE: Quarantine compartment, Mega-City Justice Department

Flexible but quite impervious, a Quarantine Bubble can be expanded quickly to contain the carrier of any contagious disease. It provides a completely sealed off and sterile environment in which to treat someone who is either suffering from or has been exposed to viral contamination.

Introduced: 2000AD Prog 61

Quasar Bike

VEHICLE: Lawmaster Mk2, Mega-City One Judges

The updated version of the Judges' Lawmaster, the Quasar Bike offers even greater power and efficiency. Improvements include a front and rear firing laser cannon and armoured undercarriage. The front of the Bike also bears a Justice Shield below the Eagle.

See also LAWMASTER BIKE

Introduced: 2000AD Prog 62

Tek-Judge Quiggly

JUDGE: Tek-Division, Mega-City One

One of Tek-Division's most brilliant engineers, Quiggly played a leading role in getting the Mechanismo programme off the ground. Working with Judge Stich, he designed, redesigned and maintained the robots, but couldn't prevent disaster when the Mark 1 robots went haywire. He was convinced that the Mark 2 machines were fine, however, and he was furious when Judge Dredd ensured they were decommissioned. Officially, Quiggly was demoted as the programme was closed, but Chief Judge McGruder secretly arranged for him to update the robots and pro-duce a Mark 2A version. When Judge Dredd discovered this deception at a carefully concealed Justice Department laboratory, the embittered Tek-Judge panicked and tried to kill him, but Dredd was too resourceful for him. He arrested Quiggly and his assistant, Tek-Judge Somes, before confronting McGruder over her clandestine re-commissioning of the Mechanismo project.

See also MECHANISMO, TEK-JUDGE DESMON STICH

2000AD Progs 892-894

Judge Dredd the Megazine Volume 2: 17, 22

SJS Judge Quincy

JUDGE: Special Judicial Squad, Mega-City One

One of Judge Cal's most trusted lieutenants in the SJS, Quincy was entrusted with the task of arresting Judge Dredd when the Deputy Chief Judge framed him for murder. When Dredd proved he was innocent of this charge, Quincy was ordered to take far more drastic action to further Cal's cause. First he led a group of undercover SJS officers in the murder of Chief Judge Goodman and then, acting as a lone sniper, he put a bullet through Judge Dredd's head! During the struggle with the Chief Judge, however, Goodman pulled an SJS button off his uniform, providing a vital clue as to who his assailants really were. Although Cal was unaware of this, he noticed the missing button and – enraged that one of his men could be dressed so sloppily – he made Quincy wear only his Judge's helmet and underpants from then on!

2000AD Progs 86, 87, 89-92, 95, 99, 101

Qususu Quq Ququuu

ALIEN: Ambassador, Planet Uq

Hailing from a little known planet where victims are punished for their part in a crime, Uqqan writer Qususu Quq Ququuu proved to be less than diplomatic when he made a "goodwill" visit to Mega-City One. Accompanying Judge Dredd as an observer on a regular patrol, the alien intervened once too often, trying to impose his own version of justice on the situation. Eager to carry out arbitrary executions on perps they

encountered on the Mega-City one streets, the forthright alien soon got the wrong side of the number one Lawman. Qususu found himself under arrest by the time the patrol was over and spent a while in the Alien Pound before being packed off home to the Planet Uq. Much to Chief Judge Griffin's dismay, Qususu Quq Ququuu's visit had done very little to promote goodwill between Mega-City One and the Planet Uq.

2000AD Prog 204

Rad Beast

CITIZEN: Mega-City One

Fueled by his desire to live forever, Bizmo Klux invested a great deal of his not insubstantial wealth in cyborg body parts when his own human organs began wearing out. Bizmo's plans were thwarted, however, when he was unfortunate enough to fall into an unguarded pit full of radioactive slime shortly after the Apocalypse War. An experience that would have killed any ordinary man saw Bizmo transformed into the gruesome Rad Beast, as his artificial organs refused to die, and he went on one last rampage through the streets of Mega-City One before he was finally laid to rest!

See 2000AD Progs 296, 297 (dies)

Radlands of Ji

LOCATION: Radioactive wasteland near Hondo City and Sino-Cit

Traditionally the place of conjoinment of all mystical Earth forces, the Radlands of Ji are the Eastern equivalent of America's Cursed Earth. Devastated by nuclear war, Ji remains an important area for mainly criminal elements who use mystical powers in their activities – though the significance of the place has been devalued by the wars and other crises which have beset the Earth. Many believe that these catastrophes have shifted the conjoinment to somewhere within Mega-City One, but Sabbat found the Radlands of Ji a sufficiently potent source of mystical energy to base his operations there when he was using the power of the Earth to boost his own Necromagical abilities.

Introduced: 2000AD Prog 451

The Rad Beast works up an appetite on a rampage through the city

Raggedy Man

JUDGE: Renegade, Mega-City One

Buzz Izzard was a Judge noted for being a hard-liner, but when he began to overstep the mark it got him into trouble. Frequently using excessive violence in the course of his duties, he was eventually suspended from duty and it was recommended that he should take the Long Walk into the Cursed Earth, rather than face the prospect of being brought up on criminal charge for his actions. Izzard did the sensible thing and left the city, but he soon became a bigger hazard than most of the other residents of the Cursed Earth – going completely crazy when a bolt became lodged in his head after one early skirmish. Calling himself the Raggedy Man and abandoning his Judge's uniform in favour of clothes made up of rags, he started killing anyone who dared to enter what he considered to be his territory. Feeling responsible for the rogue Judge, Chief Judge Silver dispatched Judges Dredd and Carlton to find him and bring him to justice, but Izzard was a difficult man to catch. He killed Carlton and badly wounded Dredd before moving on to slaughter a number of Helltrekkers. Dredd made a swift recovery, however, and managed to kill the Raggedy Man before he could finish the entire Helltrek off!

2000AD Progs 525, 526 (dies)

Judge Rameses

JUDGE: Luxor City

Generally regarded as Luxor's toughest Judge – especially by himself! - Judge Rameses was none too happy when he was selected to take part in a cultural exchange scheme which involved him swapping places with Judge Dredd for a week. Displeased at the prospect of leaving his own beloved city in the hands of a mere Mega-City One Judge, he was determined to make short work of any lawbreakers he met in the American city. Unfortunately, he ran into a gang of stray muties on his first night on patrol there, wound up in traction and was sent home to Luxor City in a wheelchair at the end of the week, facing a long period of convalescence!

2000AD Prog 859, 866

Random Physical Abuse Test

PROCEDURE: SJS, Mega-City One Justice Department

To curb any corruption amongst the Judges, the Justice Department set up the Special Judicial Squad (SJS). It employs a number of unusual tactics specifically designed to root out any criminal tendencies in a Judge before they become a problem. The Random Physical Abuse Test is their most potent and ruthless weapon, involving as it does the unyielding bullying of a Judge selected at random and without prior warning. The Judge under test is usually surprised at home and accused of any crimes the SJS Judges can come up with. They are lied to, beaten, strip-searched and forcibly cajoled into making an admission of some kind of guilt, on the assumption that any corrupt Judge would almost certainly crack under the strain. RPA Tests are an unpleasant but necessary evil according to the SJS, although the very act of surprising a Judge can be very risky indeed. It is not unheard of for SJS Judges to be killed while carrying them out, since Judges are trained to react quickly in instances of attack and are conditioned to take out their assailants if they are unidentified and appear to offer a mortal threat.

Naturally, the procedure is not something regular Street Judges are familiar with until they have actually experienced a Random Physical Abuse Test themselves. This secrecy is required to ensure the efficacy of the procedure, but also increases the element of risk for any SJS Judges carrying them out.

See also SPECIAL JUDICIAL SQUAD

Introduced: 2000AD Prog 518

Raptaurs

ALIEN: Unknown origin

The ultimate killing machines, these alien predators camouflage their movements by generating a psi fog and kill with ruthless efficienc. They are more than capable of ripping apart their prey at will, but Raptaurs prefer to leave their victims mostly intact until they wish to feed on them – although they usually consume their brains right away, since these contain the hormonal chemicals the alien creatures particularly need. They have appeared in Mega-City One, but little is know of their origins. A silica based lifeform, Raptaurs are vulnerable to sonic devices and these are the only kind of weapons that have proved effective.

Judge Dredd the Megazine Volume 1: 11–17

2000AD Graphic Novel: Raptaur

Ratty

ANIMAL: Mutant rat, Cursed Earth

Fink Angel's closest – and probably only – friend, Ratty was a vicious bowler hat wearing mutant rat from the Cursed Earth. Always at his master's side, he was a great help in any fight and he came to Mega-City One with Fink, when the Angel sought revenge on the Judges responsible for his family's deaths. When Fink was captured by Judge Dredd and put in an Iso-Cube, Ratty ended up living in Resyk, where there were rich pickings to be had for a rat like him. While living there, Ratty had an equally vicious son, but he left his family when Fink escaped from prison and the two friends were reunited. Fink and Ratty took on Judge Dredd once more, but this time the mutant rat didn't survive, as he was the accidental victim of one of Fink's quick acting poisons. Ratty's young son observed the whole tragic event and swore to get even with Dredd one day.

2000AD Progs 193-196, 283, 285-288 (dies)

Judge Dredd Mega-Special 1989 (flashback)

Red Razors

JUDGE: East-Meg Two, 2177

Formerly a member of the notorious "Red Deth" street gang, Razors was finally captured, tried and condemned to death for his heinous crimes. Instead of being executed, however, he was put forward for experimentation and, after neuro-surgery to remove his anti-social tendencies, he was controversially appointed as a Judge. His success in his new role was a credit to the doctors who re-engineered his brain, particularly when he was instrumental in the recovery of the holy corpse of Elvis Presley! Just as the East-Meg Two Justice Department was about to step up the programme that created Judge Razors, however, he went berserk and murdered a number of Judges, including his partner, Ed the talking horse. Razors was tracked down by a defrosted Judge Dredd clone from Mega-City One who sentenced him to death and carried out the execution without compunction.

2000AD Progs 908-917 (dies)

Judge Dredd the Megazine Volume 1: 8-15

Judge Dredd Yearbook 1993

Right:
East-Meg Two's
Judge Razors

Resyk

BUILDING: Human recycling plant, Mega-City One

In Mega-City One nothing is wasted − including human remains! In an average year, more than eleven million citizens die in the city and their corpses eventually find their way to Resyk. The massive body recycling plant processes over one thousand corpses per hour, dissecting and breaking them down into 107 useful constituents − providing valuable chemicals for Mega-City One's industries. The Resyk workers' proud claim is "We use everything but the soul!"

Introduced: 2000AD Prog 196

Rex Youens

CITIZEN: Mega-City One

When he realised that he was dying, Rex Youens knew that his only hope of survival was a full body transplant. Unfortunately, a human body was well out of his and his wife's price range, so he was forced to look at robotic alternatives. Even these seemed too expensive and Rex's wife suggested that they travel down to Mex-Cit and have his brain put into the body of a specially bred Rottweiler dog! Rex agreed, but his wife was having an affair and really wanted rid of him. By exchanging her husband for a Rottweiler, she was free to do pretty much what she liked, and poor Rex soon found himself leading a dog's life. When he heard his wife and her lover discussing having him put down, Rex Youens used his canine strength to kill them both, but subsequently confessed all to the Judges by typing up his story with his canine paws. The only question which remained was − would he be taken to the dog pound or spend the next fifteen years in an Iso-Cube for his crime?

2000AD Progs 648, 649

Med-Judge Rheinhart

JUDGE: Med-Division, Mega-City One

When Judge Dredd first had doubts over his judgement, he let his emotions cloud his mind for one fateful moment and assaulted Judge Winslow of Accounts. Although Dredd wasn't punished for this lapse, he was referred for psychiatric evaluation under Med-Judge Rheinhart. The psychiatrist explored Dredd's state of mind and discovered that the doubts were quite deep-rooted, so he recommended immediate psycho-surgery if Chief Judge McGruder wished to ensure that she didn't lose him. McGruder declined to take such drastic action, since she was sure it would diminish the man, and instead decided to rely on Dredd to overcome his problems.

2000AD Prog 389

Richard Magog

CITIZEN: Mega-City One, 2045

As a twenty year old in 1998, environmentalist Richard Magog blew up a nuclear power plant and the young prosecutor handling his case, Eustace Fargo, managed to convince a court of law to impose a massive fifty year sentence in solitary confinement on him – a judgement which made Fargo's name and introduced a new harsh code of punishment. Magog spent much of that time creating "The World", a virtual reality computer simulation of an idyllic world free from pollution of all kinds. Before he left prison, however, his computer game had been stolen and transformed into a dangerous cybernarc, but he was just happy to be free after almost half a century. The hapless environmentalist was rather less pleased when he realised just what a ghastly place Mega-City One was and he soon sought refuge back in his game. This time, though, he had Dredd with him in the environment of the game and things are never quite so ideal when there's a Judge around!

Judge Dredd #s 3-7

Rico Dredd

JUDGE: Renegade, Mega-City One

When Joe Dredd was training to become a Judge on the streets of Mega-City One, only one of his fellow Cadets could consistently outperform him. That Cadet was his own clone brother, Rico. Rico Dredd was considered to be the finest prospect of the Class of 2079, but his career as a Judge was to be very short indeed. While Joe was known for his seriousness and his strict application of the law, Rico's additional flair for everything he did came at the expense of a less noble aspect of his personality.

As soon as he hit the streets, Rico Dredd realised that he had a position of great power, yet stood to gain nothing in personal terms from his role as a Judge. He therefore turned his attention to putting this right and began accepting bribes and even assisted in a number of petty crimes. When his brother discovered the truth about Rico's activities, Joe was shocked by his crimes and had no choice but to turn him in. As a result, Rico was sentenced to a twenty year stretch at the Penal Colony on Titan.

Having served his time at the brutal Penal Colony reserved especially for corrupt Judges, Rico Dredd returned to Mega-City One seeking revenge on Judge Dredd. He confronted Joe at his home and challenged him to a shoot-out to settle their differences, knowing that he could always outdraw his brother. However, twenty years on Titan had slowed Rico to a fraction and Joe was forced to kill him.

See also VIENNA DREDD

2000AD Prog 30

Rinus Limpopop Quintz

ALIEN: Galactic Salesman

Picked up by the Justice 1 during the mission to find the Judge Child, Rinus Limpopop Quintz was desperate to trade goods with the Mega-City One Judges aboard. When they refused to have anything to do with him, however, he decided to capture them and add them to his wares. Using the amazing process of Terlian Warping, he was able to miniaturise his goods and store them in his carry case and he applied this technique to Judges Dredd, Hershey and Larter. Even at tiny size, the Mega-City One Judges proved to be a handful for the Salesman, though, and he soon found himself shrunken down and inside his own carry case, until they returned to Mega-City One and he could be sentenced properly for his kidnap.

2000AD
Progs 174, 175

Riot Foam

WEAPON: Solid Foam, Mega-City One

Riot Foam is a remarkable substance which expands and solidifies in seconds. The Judges sometimes use it on crowds when they are trying to quell a riot, since it traps people completely as it solidifies around them, yet allows them to breathe through it and so does not endanger theri lives. These people can then be released at the Judges' leisure, ensuring that crowd control can be a simple, safe and painless matter in Mega-City One.

Introduced: 2000AD Prog 18

The Robot Wars

EVENT: War between Robots and the Mega-City One Judges

Recognising the dangers of making robots too intelligent, Judge Dredd petitioned Chief Judge Goodman to outlaw all hi-grade robots. When his request was denied, Dredd resigned, but when Call-me-Kenneth began his rampage and declared war on the Mega-City Judges, the Chief Judge relented. Dredd immediately rejoined the Judges as the Robot Wars begun. Thousands of citizens and Judges lost their lives as robots revolted all over the city and it wasn't until Dredd himself infiltrated Call-me-Kenneth's secret factory hideout that the tide began to turn. With the help of a handful of loyal robots like Walter the Wobot and J70 Stroke 13, the Judge managed to reprogram a large number of Call-me-Kenneth's robot followers to oppose him. This signalled the beginning of the end for the robot leader, who was forced to mount one last-ditch attack on the Grand Hall of Justice, accompanied by a group of Heavy Metal Kid robots. An electrical storm, courtesy of Weather Control, put paid to that, but it took a massive explosion, as Judge Dredd blew up a Texas City Flying Oil Tanker, to finally destroy Call-me-Kenneth once and for all.

See also CALL-ME-KENNETH

2000AD Progs 10-17

Rookie Judges

SOCIAL CATEGORY: Trainee Judge, Mega-City One Justice Department

The position held by any Judge for the shortest time, Rookies wear white Judges' helmet and a half Eagle. Cadets are awarded these items when they are about to participate in their final street assessment.

Introduced: 2000AD Prog 27

Rowena

ROBOT: Waitress, Luna-1

Waitress robot Rowena was very fond of Walter the Wobot. The two robots became sweethearts while Walter and Dredd were on the Moon, which suited the Judge as it kept them out of his way.

2000AD Prog 47

Russell Muscle

CITIZEN: Bodybuilder, Mega-City One

When top bodybuilder Russell Muscle decided to market his tough muscular look he knew that people would be unlikely to train hard like him, so he came up with "inflatable biceps"! Guaranteed to impress girls and deter muggers, these strap-on muscles were hardly life-like, but – naturally enough – they made Russell Muscle a fortune. Unfortunately for the bodybuilder, his luck finally ran out when he was accosted by a gang of dissatisfied wimps who wanted to complain about the inflatable biceps. Angered by their invasion of Muscle Mansion, Russell set about the weedy intruders and beat them all up. Then he made the mistake of taking on Judge Dredd when he turned up to investigate, but the bodybuilder found the lawman a rather tougher opponent and was soon on his way to the 'Cubes.

2000AD Progs 432 (cameo), 480

Sabbat the Necromagus
See page 136

Judge Inspector Sadu
JUDGE: Hondo City

Hondo City's toughest Judge Inspector, Totaro Sadu commanded respect from his colleagues and the citizens of his city alike. As an investigator, Sadu had no equal in Hondo's Justice Department and his was a powerful voice in the running of the cit y. He was also eight times Hondo City champion in Ritual Combat with a Tendo Stave, so it didn't pay to cross him. When Judge Dredd visited his city, Sadu took him on with the Tendo Stave and bested the Mega-City One Judge with ease. On this occasion, the defeat suited Dredd's purposes – helping him cover up the potentially damaging Ueno Hama affair – but he was keen for a rematch at some future date to satisfy his bruised pride. Unfortunately, the opportunity didn't present itself until the two Judges met once more in the gravest of circumstances. Between them, Dredd and Sadu played leading roles in the defeat of Sabbat the Necromagus when he unleashed his massive zombie assault on the world. Both of the Judges took part in the attack on Sabbat's base in the Radlands of Ji and it was Sadu who made a vital breakthrough when he gained control over the madman's lodestone. Unfortunately, the Judge Inspector couldn't handle the awesome amount of Earth power channelled through the lodestone and the effort saw him mutilated and horribly killed in the process, but at least he broke Sabbat's hold over Judge Dredd and Johnny Alpha, so they were able to defeat the Necromagus and thereby save the world.

See also RADLANDS OF JI,
SABBAT THE NECROMAGUS, UENO HAMA
2000AD Progs 608-611, 787-790, 793, 795-799
Judge Dredd the Megazine Volume 2: 4, 8, 9 (dies)

Sagbelly the Toad
ALIEN: Toad-like creature, Planet Necros

An extremely old and vile monster, Sagbelly was the source of Murd the Oppressor's power on Necros. In fact, the highly potent hallucinogenic drug known as Oracle Spice – so important to the Necromancer – was produced by a wart on his hindquarters! Sagbelly's taste for live human flesh finally proved his undoing when he accidentally ate Murd himself, however, and he failed to recover from the resulting stomach pains.

See also MURD THE OPPRESSOR, ORACLE SPICE
2000AD Prog 171 (dies)

Satanus
ANIMAL: Tyrannosaurus Rex, Cursed Earth

When American scientists perfected the techniques for cloning dinosaurs from their ancient reconstructed DNA patterns in the middle of the 21st Century, their first success was a Tyrannosaurus Rex they called Satanus. The creature was cloned from the offspring of Old One Eye, a beast who had almost single-handedly wrecked a Time-Travelling operation to farm dinosaurs for meat back in the Cretaceous Era. Satanus was her most vicious progeny and he even challenged her for the leadership of their pack. Old One Eye responded by breaking every bone in his body and Satanus breathed his last.

Back in the 21st Century, the newly cloned Satanus was true to his heritage when, as a new-born baby, he took his first bite of human flesh out of the finger of his scientist "creator". He grew very quickly and consumed a vast quantity of meat – usually in the form of live animals he could kill himself – so much in fact that he almost bankrupted the whole dinosaur cloning project. In order for the project to survive, the scientists behind it decided to clone found the Dinosaur National Park. Satanus soon became the Park's star attraction, but his taste for human flesh made him by far the most dangerous animal there. When he escaped and killed a number of the Park's guests, Satanus was soon recaptured, but he managed to escape a second time before the surgery could be carried out. This time he remained free, hiding out high up in the mountains, and the Atomic Wars of 2070 saw the Park close down.

As the years passed, he became known as "Satanus the Unchained" to the people of the Cursed Earth town Repentance, who appeased him by tying human sacrifices to a rock for him to eat. This arrangement suited Satanus until Judge Dredd arrived in the town on his way to Mega-City Two. When the local towns-folk tried to feed the Judge and Spikes "Harvey" Rotten to the dinosaur, they evaded the monster and Satanus, enraged by the loss of his meal, vented his fury upon the town. During the ensuing battle, the Tyrannosaurus Rex was buried in the rubble and left for dead. However, the son of Old One Eye was not so easy to kill and he emerged relatively unscathed.

See also DINOSAUR NATIONAL PARK

2000AD Progs 73-76, 85

Judge Dredd the Megazine Volume 2: 45

Sector Houses

BUILDINGS: Justice Department Control Stations, Mega-City One

Hundreds of Sector Houses are situated around Mega-City One and each one is a miniature version of the Grand Hall of Justice itself. A Sector House comes equipped with its own interrogation cubes, holding pens, medical facilities and even a forensic lab. All the routine judging for an entire Sector is carried out there and citizens have to endure the frenetic, hothouse environ-ment of a Sector House if they wish to report any non-major crime. Commanded by Sector Chiefs, these control stations are in constant contact with the Grand Hall of Justice via M.A.C., the Judges' powerful base computer, and they ensure the Justice Department can maintain law and order throughout the entire Mega-City One.

See also GRAND HALL OF JUSTICE, M.A.C.

Introduced: 2000AD Prog 359

Psi-Judge Shenker

JUDGE: Chief of Psi-Division, Mega-CityOne

Having been one of Mega-City One's outstanding Psi-Judges for many years, Shenker was pro-moted to Chief of Psi-Division when his predecessor, Psi-Judge Omar, sacrificed his life to save the city. Shenker soon established himself as an important voice on the Council of Five and heartily endorsed Chief Judge McGruder's decision to resign over the incident which had led to Omar's death. He went on to run Psi-Division with considerable success under Chief Judge Silver and was one of very few Senior Judges to survive the horrors of Judge Death's Necropolis several years later. He was dubious about the return of McGruder in the wake of this crisis and was unhappy about the dis-solution of the Council of Five, but he was in no posi-tion to object at the time. After a while her judgement became increasingly erratic, however, so he helped organise a delegation of Senior Judges to challenge her autonomous rule. McGruder was unmoved and declined their requests to reform the Council of Five, but by the time she returned from her near-fatal trip to Hestia – during which a Mechanismo robot tried to kill her, thus putting an end to her robot Judge project – she had changed her mind. Resigning her position, she put Shenker, along with Judges Niles and Hershey, in temporary charge of the city until a new Chief Judge could be elected.

2000AD Progs 457, 671, 675, 676, 678-681, 789, 842, 844, 891, 915-918

Judge Dredd the Megazine Volume 2: 24, 57, 68

Judge Inspector Shimura

JUDGE: Hondo City

Very much a loner in the Hondo City Justice Department, Shimura followed his own personal honour code and fought tirelessly against the Yakuza gangster societies, but was betrayed from within the Justice Department. Forced to go "ronin" – becoming an outcast leading a one-man crusade against the Yakuza societies and the city authorities themselves.

See also JUDGE INSPECTOR AIKO INABA

Judge Dredd the Megazine Volume 2: 37-39, 50-55

Sabbat the Necromagus

CITIZEN: Osborne's World, Borealis System

Young Soppi Walters was frequently bullied by school tough guy Dennis Mennis until he met Baggie, an old witch. Soppi killed her and stole all her dark secrets, then used them to kill Dennis and bring him back as a mindless zombie. As he grew older, Soppi learnt more about black magic and he eventually left his home of Osborne's World and travelled to Necros. Once there, he studied under Murd the Oppressor himself and he left the planet as Sabbat the Necromagus – one of the most dangerous and evil men in the galaxy. He moved on to the paradise planet of Bathsheba in the Blessed Nebula in 2178 and transformed it into a hell-hole. With its two billion settlers turned into zombies, the planet had to be nuked, but Sabbat escaped and stole a time displacement unit, so that he could travel back in time to 2114 and continue his terrible work on Earth!

Having established a base in the Radlands of Ji, Sabbat used a lodestone to tap into the Earth power there and set about reanimating corpses all over the world. The scale of death and destruction he caused was dreadful – billions were killed as several massive cities were completely overrun by his zombies and had to be nuked out of existence. Judges from all over the world got together to combat the threat of the Necromagus and Johnny Alpha, a Search and Destroy Agent from Sabbat's own time, arrived to help them. In one last desperate bid to stop him, an elite squad of Judges attacked Sabbat at his base, but they found themselves helpless against his power until Judge Inspector Sadu managed to gain control of his lodestone. The effort killed Sadu, but Sabbat's power was broken and Judge Dredd took his chance to kill him. Somehow, the head of the Necromagus survived and it took the mutant skills of Johnny Alpha, along with Dredd's brute force to defeat it and strand Sabbat on the top of his own lodestone! This meant he would live on for eternity, so the lodestone was taken to Mega-City One to be safeguarded by the Tek-Judges there. They found that he was powerless in this predicament, but the odd side effect of his existence was that zombies would appear occasionally in the city For this reason, all workers at Resyk have been issued with pump-action shotguns!

2000AD Progs 787-790, 793, 795-799, 816

Judge Dredd the Megazine Volume 2: 4, 8, 9, 45

Shojan, Warlord of Ji

CITIZEN: Criminal Warlord, Radlands of Ji

As a Psi-Mystic of the Tenth Dan, Shojan had earned himself a big reputation for his activities around the Radlands of Ji before he turned up in Mega-City One. The self-styled Warlord of Ji had decided that the centre of Earth power had shifted from his homeland to the Mega-City, so he made contact with a number of psi-criminals there in order to carry out a plan he believed would see him become the master of the World. He managed to summon up the Seven Samurai and they began a rampage through the city that the Judges seemed powerless to stop. Shojan himself proved an easier target than his supernatural creations – even if his psi-power was strong enough to deflect oncoming bullets! – and Judge Dredd mortally wounded him with a ninja star. It still required the supreme sacrifice from Psi-Judge Omar to neutralise the psychic power of the Samurai after Shojan's death – he quite literally "squeezed" them out of existence using a user-fatal psionic amplifier to increase his normal psi abilities.

See also PSI-JUDGE OMAR, RADLANDS OF JI

2000AD Progs 451-455 (dies)

Chief Judge Silver
See page 138

Slick Dickens

CITIZEN: Fictional character, Mega-City One

A debonair master criminal, Slick Dickens was the only perp Judge Dredd actually feared, and with good reason – he murdered the Judge on two separate occasions! Unfortunately for Slick, he was merely the creation of hack author Truman Kaput who made the mistake of trying out his character's crimes before he wrote about them. Lacking Slick's undoubted élan and skill, Kaput was easily apprehended by Judge Dredd while trying to commit a burglary and got five years in an Iso-Cube for his trouble. Though, when Dredd realised just how many crimes the author had written about in his books, he increased the sentence to fifty years – just to be on the safe side!

2000AD Prog 505

Judge Dredd the Megazine Volume 2: 34, 35

Sisters of Death

ALIENS: Death Cultists, Deadworld

The weird sisters, Phobia and Nausea, were already Death Cultists and devotees of the dark arts when they met up with the then living Judge Death. They had both been taking flesh-rotting poison for some time and were well on their way to their own state of "living death" when they offered the Judge a similar deal. Judge Death and his fellow Dark Judges agreed to undergo their treatment and so became the undead creatures who finally wiped out all life on their planet.

When Judges Death, Fear, Fire and Mortis failed to return from Mega-City One, the Sisters used their powers to help them. With the unwitting aid of Xena Lowther and Psi-Judge Agee, they formed a Psychic Bridge between Deadworld and Mega-City One, then used their mental powers to manipulate Judge Kraken to free the Dark Judges. Phobia and Nausea then combined their power with that of the Dark Judges to turn the city into a Necropolis. Judge Dredd finally returned and broke the Sisters' Psychic Bridge between dimensions. This released Phobia and Nausea's hold on Mega-City One and they were no longer able to assist the Dark Judges, who were soon defeated.

See also JUDGE DEATH, DARK JUDGES

2000AD Progs 661, 662, 673-684, 687, 692-695, 707, 734

Judge Dredd the Megazine Volume 1: 10, 11

The Sisters create their Necropolis

Slick Willy

MUTANT: Undercity, Mega-City One

Slick Willy was the leader – or "Prime Cat" – of the Troggies, a group of mutants who lived in the disused subway system below Mega-City One, part of the vast Undercity. Bitter and twisted by the experience of life in this dark underworld, Willy swore vengeance on the city above and was determined to blow-up Mega-City One's underground support struts, in order to bring the entire city crashing down! Fortunately, while investigating a number of other crimes perpetrated by the mutant Troggies, Judge Dredd was able to thwart their leader's masterplan and arrest him, following a remarkable chase through the tunnels in an old subway train.

See also TROGGIES, UNDERCITY

2000AD Progs 36, 37

Chief Judge Thomas Silver

JUDGE: Chief Judge, Mega-City One

Mega-City One's Chief Judge Silver

Even as a young Judge, working the streets of Mega-City One in the 2070s, Thomas Silver acquired quite a reputation as one of the Justice Department's hard-liners. In fact, when Morton Judd proposed the idea of cloning a more docile population to make the city easier to control, the idea appealed to the tough-minded Silver. His first duty was always to the Chief Judge, however, and he came round to Fargo's view when Judd was discredited. After more than twenty five years on the streets, Silver was injured and forced to retire from active duty. He opted to take a teaching post at the Academy of Law and spent twelve happy years there as the Principal Lecturer in Applied Violence.

When Chief Judge McGruder resigned for the first time, Judges at the top of the Justice Department were inclined to appoint a Chief Judge known for his tough views and Judge-Tutor Silver seemed the ideal man for the job. His selection was never a popular one with the citizens of Mega-City One, but he had the full backing of his Judges, which was far more important to him. Silver's term as Chief Judge was a difficult one: he had to cope with the surprise return of Morton Judd, who tried to take over the city with the help of his cloned army of Judda; he crushed the growing democracy movement in Mega-City One by controversial means; and, worst of all, he had to decide what to do when Judge Dredd resigned and took the Long Walk. Having prepared for such an event, Silver had arranged for Kraken – a member of the Judda who shared Dredd's bloodline – to be re-educated at the Academy of Law. Rather than let Mega-City One's most potent symbol of the law go, Chief Judge Silver hushed up his resignation and actually put Kraken on the streets wearing Dredd's badge.

This proved to be Silver's biggest mistake, since Kraken's deep-down resentment for the Judges was used by the Sisters of Death to help them control him. This enabled them to set up a psychic bridge between their world and Mega-City One and they also made Kraken release the Dark Judges from limbo. Catastrophe followed for Mega-City One and Judge Death killed Silver, then reanimated him as a pathetic zombie, so that he could torment him further. When Judge Dredd returned to the city and defeated the dark Judges, the zombie Silver hid out in a mass grave while he decided what to do. Several months later he came back to the Grand Hall of Justice and asked for his job back, but in view of his failure to protect Mega-City One in its direst hour of need, his request was denied. Judge Dredd invoked Judicial Indictment 4 against him for dereliction of duty, but spared Silver twenty years on Titan by executing his zombie form with an incendiary shell.

See also JUDGE KRAKEN, SISTERS OF DEATH

2000AD Progs 457, 530, 531, 533, 541, 552, 563, 572, 584, 585, 643, 644, 662, 668-671, 675, 681, 684, 700 (cameo), 702, 733-735 (dies)

Judge Dredd Mega-Special 1989

Judge Dredd Annual 1988

SJS Judge Slocum

**JUDGE: Special Judicial Squad,
Mega-City One**

Probably the man closest to Chief Judge Cal, SJS Judge Slocum was remarkably loyal to his leader, despite the fact that he understood what a madman his boss could be. In fact, Slocum's influence ensured that Cal's administration stayed on track more than once, as he curbed the most insane policies of the tyrant. When Cal sentenced the whole population of Mega-City One to death, it was Judge Slocum who – under pressure from Judge Dredd – killed the Chief Judge's goldfish. Since the goldfish held the position of Deputy Chief Judge at the time, Cal was easily convinced that this was a sign, indicating that "if the citizens die, the Judges die". So, thanks to Judge Slocum's action, Cal put a stop to the executions. Treading a very fine line, the SJS Judge prospered as Cal's right hand man, but his luck ran out when he rashly called the Chief Judge "crazy" for trusting Walter the Wobot, who was well-known for his loyalty to Judge Dredd. Slocum covered himself by explaining that he "worried" for Cal, but he knew he was in trouble. When he discovered Walter's true purpose in feigning hatred for Dredd – the robot wanted to steal a briefing tape, so that Cal's brainwashing of the Judges could be subverted – Judge Slocum hoped that he could get back in the Chief Judge's good books. Before he could report Walter's indiscretion, however, he found himself poisoned and paralysed by Cal in preparation for being pickled to stop his "worries" giving him wrinkles!

See also CHIEF JUDGE CAL

2000AD Progs 91, 92, 94–96, 98–101, 104, 105 (dies)

Smokatorium

BUILDING: Designated for smoking cigarettes

Smoking is illegal and trade in cigarettes is rigidly controlled in Mega-City One, but citizens are allowed to attend the Smokatorium, where they can smoke under special license. Every smoker in the building has to wear a helmet which protects them from the deadly smoke-filled environment of the building while they inhale their own cigarette, free from the additional hazards of "passive" smoking.

Introduced: 2000AD Prog 23

Sov-Judge Snekov

JUDGE: East-Meg One

Snekov contemplates the conquest of Mega-Ctiy One

As a member of East-Meg One's ruling Diktatorat, Snekov played a leading role in the planning and launching of the Apocalypse War against Mega-City One. The Sovs' key strategist, he came up with the idea of inducing Block Mania in the American city before a full-scale nuclear attack was launched, in order to weaken the enemy in preparation for the real battle. Sov-Judge Snekov was killed before he could enjoy the full fruits of his labours however, when War-Marshal Kazan organised his putsch to overthrow the Diktatorat and assume the position of Supreme Judge himself.

See also BLOCK MANIA,
WAR-MARSHAL "MAD DOG" KAZAN

2000AD Progs 245–247, 249, 250, 259

Sons of Erin

**ORGANISATION: Liberation group,
Emerald Isle**

Opposed to the exploitation of their country by its being turned into a giant theme park – pandering to all the corniest stereotypes about Ireland and the Irish people – the Sons of Erin were dedicated to putting a stop to the tourist industry. They were generally tolerated by the Judges since their methods were usually non-violent and ineffectual, but things changed when they brought in professional blitzer Bonny Staples from Mega-City One. He masterminded a massive campaign of violence, which saw the Sons of Erin wielding their spud guns – firing full potatoes, chips or even mash! – to deadly effect. To an extent their action was successful, in that it caused a temporary decline in the tourist industry, but the price of that small victory was great. Staples' radical tactics resulted in the death or capture of almost every member of the Sons of Erin, so their future as an effective political movement was virtually wiped out in one bloody and completely futile gesture.

See also BONNY STAPLES

2000AD Prog 727–732

Sov-Block

COUNTRY: Formerly Russia

Following the Atomic Wars of 2070, Russia and its neighbouring states were reformed into two vast Mega-Cities called East-Meg One and Two, making up what became known as the Sov-Block. The premier city was very much the region's political power base until the Apocalypse War against Mega-City One saw it all but annihilated, so the Sov-Block and East-Meg Two are now more or less synonymous.

See also EAST-MEG ONE, EAST-MEG TWO

Introduced: 2000AD Prog 50

Special Judicial Squad

DIVISION: Mega-City One Justice Department

Mega-City One's Special Judicial Squad was set up shortly after the Judges acceded to power in the city to ensure that corruption never took hold in the Justice Department. SJS Judges were trained to curb the excesses of their colleagues and a number of Judicial Indictments were laid down to cover Judges who were convicted of any criminal act. In almost all non-trivial cases, Judicial Indictment 4 is invoked – condemning the guilty Judge to a twenty-stretch at the harsh penal colony on Titan.

Introduced: 2000AD Prog 86

SJS Judge Spiegl

JUDGE: Special Judicial Squad, Mega-City One

One of the SJS's toughest Judge investigators, Spiegl specialises in carrying out Random Physical Abuse Tests. His RPA Test on Judge Dredd was so thorough that Dredd actually wondered whether the SJS had turned bad again, like they did under Judge Cal. When a later RPA Test on Judge Reeves went tragically wrong because she shot and killed two SJS Judges, believing them to be intruder, Judge Spiegl demanded she be sent to the Titan Penal Colony, but she was suspended from duty for a year.

See also RANDOM PHYSICAL ABUSE TEST

2000AD Prog 518, 826

Spikes "Harvey" Rotten

CITIZEN: Leader of the "Muties" Bike Gang, Mega-City One

Spikes first came to Judge Dredd's attention when the punk took part in the illegal and terrifyingly dangerous Mega-City 5000 Bike Race. Of the thousands of entries, only Spikes and Zoot Smiley, the leader of a rival Bike Gang, made it anywhere near the finishing line and Spikes was within inches of reaching it before the Judges stopped him and sent him off to the Cubes. The punk had impressed Dredd with his biking skills and his determination to succeed, however, so when the Judge was asked to lead a mission across the deadly territory of the Cursed Earth to Mega-City Two, he insisted that Spikes should join him. The vicious criminal had knowledge of the Cursed Earth from when he had engaged in gun running to some of the mutants there, so he knew a bit about the hazards the area had to offer. Naturally enough, then, Spikes was none too enthusiastic about helping out, but Judge Dredd was very persuasive indeed.

In fact, Spikes proved to be a highly dependable and invaluable member of Dredd's crew – not because he owed any allegiance to the Judges, but mostly because he knew that sticking with the team represented his most realistic hope of surviving the mission. Although he was seriously tempted to betray his comrades on several occasions, such a course of action would probably have turned out to be suicidal in the nuclear wasteland of the Cursed Earth. Certainly the gambling-obsessed lifestyle of Las Vegas appealed to Spikes, but he stuck with Judge Dredd against the Mafia Judges there. Sadly, Spikes "Harvey" Rotten failed to see the mission through to its end, as he was shot when Dredd's group were attacked by the robotic Legion of the Damned. Just before this fatal encounter in Death Valley, he had learned of the spectacular mineral deposits on Tweak's home planet, and the alien – who was aware of Spikes' coming death, due to his precognitive powers – had kindly signed over 50% of the mining profits to the doomed punk. Thus, Spikes died in a blaze of glory, shooting down dozens of robots as they finished him off, but he died happy in the knowledge that he was no longer a two-bit punk. He was a billionaire ... he owned half a planet ... and, as Judge Dredd put it, he was the greatest punk of all time!

See also LEGION OF THE DAMNED, ZOOT SMILEY

2000AD Progs 40, 41, 62-84 (dies)

Stan Lee - "Death Fist"

CITIZEN: Radlands of Ji

Generally thought to be the best martial artist ever to come out of the Radlands of Ji, Stan Lee – also known as "Death Fist" – belonged to a Sino-Cit Kwoon and was their most dangerous assassin for hire. He proved this when he managed to defeat Judge Dredd in hand-to-hand combat during his first visit to Mega-City One, but he made the mistake of returning for a rematch just over a year later. This time, Judge Dredd was determined to even the score and he was even able to ensure live TV coverage of the fight. The fact that he had been beaten once smarted with Dredd and he wanted to publicly demonstrate that you can't take on a Judge and win. He duly defeated Stan Lee and put him away in the 'Cubes for a long time.

See also WU WANG

2000AD Progs 484, 540, 541, 764

Judge Dredd the Megazine Volume 2: 45 (cameo)

Starborn Thing

ALIEN: Unknown origin

Highly intelligent and adaptable, these parasitic alien lifeforms landed on Earth out in the Cursed Earth. Capable of possessing a person or any other animal and implanting their progeny inside them, the Starborn Things proved to be a major threat to Mega-City One. Having already defeated one of the aliens, Judge Dredd tracked down and destroyed the remaining creatures in their spacecraft, but in the process he became the host for one of their offspring. The young alien was subsequently born safe and secure in a Mega-City One Tek Lab and kept under carefully controlled conditions for study. The fact that Judge Dredd had just become a mother was the source of considerable amusement among the Judges present, but "Old Stoney Face" himself could not see the funny side!

2000AD Progs 310-312

Judge Becky Steel

JUDGE: Brit-Cit, transferred to Pan African Judges

Rebecca Steel and her sister both chose to become Judges in Brit-Cit, but while Treasure joined the plainclothes homicide division, "Becky" trained as a Street Judge. What she hadn't reckoned on was the racism running through the Brit-Cit Justice Department and, being of mixed descent, Becky Steel came in for more than her fair share of abuse. When she was assaulted and hung upside-down for more than three hours, she decided enough was enough. She demanded a transfer and her superiors complied by packing her off to join a Pan-African Judge Squad. Assigned to a patrol led by Judge Kwame Assengai, she soon found out how tough things could be in a country where Judges are afforded little or no respect by lawbreakers and independent states alike. A brutal encounter with an ivory poacher called Van Buesen saw her badly injured, but she was unbowed and – following her conversion to Islam – Becky Steel felt able to look forward to the future with a new optimism.

See also ROOKIE JUDGE TREASURE STEEL,

JUDGE KWAME ASSENGAI

Judge Dredd the Megazine Volume 2: 45-49

Rookie Judge Treasure Steel

JUDGE: Rookie, Brit-Cit

Treasure Steel was one of two sisters of Afro-Caribbean descent who became Judges in Brit-Cit, though their careers diverged widely. While Becky trained as a Street Judge and was eventually transferred to Pan Africa after experiencing no end of racist taunts, Treasure joined the plainclothes homicide division after a successful period of training at Hendon. She then began a year-long assessment as a Rookie Judge, assigned to the idiosyncratic Detective Judge Armitage, and she took an instant dislike to the unconventional but highly experienced officer. Gradually though, Steel began to respect Armitage and she developed from an uptight, by-the-book Judge into a firebrand who flouts authority and breaks the rules just as freely as he does. In turn, he has come to see her as an excellent Rookie, although he was sceptical about her marriage and he warned her that it wouldn't last. Treasure's husband Terry has certainly had to put up with a lot, since her job can be frustrating, unrewarding and often involves long hours, but they have stayed together through all of her many trials and tribulations as a Brit-Cit Judge.

See also DETECTIVE JUDGE ARMITAGE,
JUDGE BECKY STEEL
Judge Dredd the Megazine Volume 1: 9-14
Judge Dredd the Megazine Volume 2: 10-19, 21, 35, 36, 63-70
Judge Dredd Yearbooks 1993, 1994

Tek-Judge Desmon Stich

JUDGE: Tek-Division, Mega-City One

When Chief Judge McGruder asked Tek Chief Greel to secretly initiate a special project to create reliable Robot Judges, the task was passed on to robotics expert Desmon Stich. For Stich, the Mechanismo Project became an obsession and he worked long and hard to develop a fully working Mark 1 model. He was delighted when the machine performed efficiently on the streets but when ten units were put into action, the machines soon malfunctioned and Stich was horrified as he tried to shut them all down, some failed to respond. Stich's mind became extremely unbalanced when the robots had to be brought in by force. When Number 5 escaped into the city's sewer system, Stich's career was in ruins and was soon admitted to the Psycho-Cubes. He later escaped himself and began a manic search for the lost robot in the sewers. As luck would have it, he did encounter Number 5 there, just as it was terminated by a Mark 2 Judge Robot. Judge Dredd was on the scene, too, and he was able to destroy the new Mechanismo robot. He then managed to convince Stich that his Mark 1 machine had done the deed, in order to close down the project.

See also MECHANISMO, TEK-JUDGE GREEL
2000AD Prog 892-894
Judge Dredd the Megazine Volume 2: 12-16, 22, 24-26, 37, 40, 42, 43, 57

Stookies

ALIENS: Planet Stook, Deep Space

When it was discovered that the Adifax Gland of the Stookie – a gentle and rather friendly alien race – possessed anti-aging properties that made it a highly effective youth drug, the wholesale production of Stookie Capsules began on Earth. Stookies bred quickly and they meekly went to their deaths, but further investigation revealed that they were an intelligent alien lifeform and so were classified as a protected species. The manufacture of products made from Stookies therefore became illegal and the existing "Glanding" operations swiftly moved out to Cursed Earth factory farms. The potential for profit by supplying anti-aging drugs to rich Mega-City One citizens was huge, so the Judges found the racket extremely hard to stamp out. Judge Dredd did close down one huge farm when he was tipped off by an escaped Stookie and thousands of his fellow aliens were saved. As a measure of their gratitude to him, they made Dredd an "Honorary Stookie", but no-one was likely to get any younger chewing on his glands!

2000AD Progs 220, 221

Strato-V Assault Craft

VEHICLE: Flying assault craft, East-Meg One

East-Meg One's standard strike aircraft during the Apocalypse War, the Strato-V was a multi-purpose flying vehicle. Heavily armed with various kinds of nuclear and conventional bombs and missiles, their major and primary role was to prepare for a ground assault by blitzing targets beneath them, but they were also manoeuvrable and well-equipped for dogfights with any airborne enemy craft. Furthermore, the Strato-Vs were capable of terrific speeds, making them useful troop carriers and one even made an extremely mobile base of operations for War-Marshal "Mad Dog" Kazan as he commanded the Sov forces in Mega-City One.

Introduced: 2000AD Prog 245

Stub Gun

WEAPON: Hand-held Laser Rifle, Mega-City One Justice Department

The most devastating hand-held weapon ever devised, Stub Guns were stuck at the development stage for a long time, due to a problem with their Las-booster Barrel. Prone to overheating thanks to the high-intensity laser beam the gun fires, the barrel could easily explode – meaning that the gun had to be classified as "dangerous to user". Despite this, Stub Guns provided the Mega-City One Judges with their only truly effective weapon against the East-Meg One invasion forces during the Apocalypse War.

Introduced: 2000AD Prog 254

Stumm Gas

WEAPON: Gas, Mega-City One Justice Department

Stumm gas is a last resort weapon used by the Judges, typically to quell highly dangerous riot situations. The gas's choking vapours cause nausea, unconsciousness and, in one case in every 250, death.

Introduced: 2000AD Prog 237

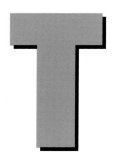

Tactical Command Bunker

BUILDING: Justice Department Emergency Ops Bases, Mega-City One

In times of war or any other extreme emergency, control of Mega-City One can be transferred to three Tactical Command Bunkers. These Bunkers are heavily fortified operational bases in top secret locations beneath city bottom and are designed to be as self-contained as possible, while providing maximum protection against any attack.

Introduced: 2000AD Prog 248

The Taxidermist

CITIZEN: Jacob Sardini, Mega-City One

In Mega-City One it is legal to have a loved one stuffed after their death. This has led to the setting up of a large number of taxidermy firms and one of the longest established belongs to the double Mega-Olympic medal winner Jacob Sardini. Sardini first made his name when he took bronze at the 2078 Games for his work entitled "Explosion at a Bus Q", but he still needed some help in setting up in business as a taxidermist. He sought the help of Don Giovanni - a Mega-City One gangster - who recommended him to a few rich friends and Sardini's business soon took off.

Unfortunately, the Don called in the favour many years later when his son was killed in a gang fight. Although he lacked the proper death certificates, Giovanni asked Jacob Sardini to stuff his son and the attackers responsible for killing him. The taxidermist found this an offer he couldn't refuse, but while he was working on the illegal stuffing, the Don himself was the

Teddy Choppermitz

CITIZEN: Teddy Krunk, Mega-City One

When Teddy Krunk was jumped by a group of drunken unemployed surgeons he woke up to find that they had removed his fingers and replaced them with deadly motorised knives for a joke. Teddy's parents wisely kicked him out of their apartment and poor Teddy was left to fend for himself. When he met Winnie Flapwapper he thought his luck had changed and that they could build a life together, but instead he chopped her and her family up by accident, before mistakenly slicing his own head off! Oops.

2000AD Prog 760

Judge Tex

JUDGE: Judge-Marshal, Luna-1

Basically honest, but for a long time rather an ineffectual Judge, Tex was the deputy to a string of Judge-Marshals who came to Luna-1 for six month periods to fulfil the agreement between America's three Mega-Cities to police the moon colony. Most of these Marshals were happy to see out their terms without controversy and so avoided upsetting the regular way of life in a city where the law meant little. Judge Dredd's appointment to the post saw things change very quickly in Luna-1 and, after an edgy start, Judge Tex seized this opportunity to help clean up the colony. He so impressed his mentor that when Dredd reached the end of his six month term as Judge-Marshal, he recommended Tex for the post on a permanent basis. Judge Tex was duly appointed and was able to offer Luna-1 the kind of stability it had never enjoyed since its foundation in 2061.

2000AD Prog 42-44, 48, 49, 54-59

Texas City

CITY: Formerly the State of Texas, U.S.A.

Although the smallest of the three American Mega-Cities, everything in Texas City is big! Boasting some of the tallest buildings in the world and an enormous monument to its symbol of freedom, Tex, the city is an awesome sight indeed. Originally named Mega-City Three, the Texans fought a short but bloody civil war against the Judges from the other cities in order to win their independence a few years after the Atomic Wars of 2070. Their success saw the place renamed and Texas City soon developed its own individual character, though it remained allied with Mega-Cities One and Two.

Introduced: 2000AD Prog 17

Titan Penal Colony

BUILDING: Prison Colony on Titan

In Mega-City One, the harshest penalty for any crime is reserved for Judges who break the law. The mandatory sentence for any Judge found guilty of any crime is twenty years on Titan, after first undergoing drastic surgery to enable them to survive the inhospitable atmosphere there. The Penal Colony is infamous for its tough conditions and many Judges sent there don't live long enough to complete their term.

Introduced: 2000AD Prog 30

Near left: Rico Dredd arrives on Titan

145

Supreme Judge Josef Traktorfaktori

JUDGE: Supreme Judge, East-Meg Two

After the Apocalypse War relations between Mega-City One and the surviving Sov-Block city, East-Meg Two, were decidedly frosty. Eventually efforts were made on both sides to build bridges and Supreme Judge Traktorfaktori was a key mover in this process. In 2113 he became the first Supreme Judge of a Sov-Block city to visit Mega-City One and he held historic talks with Chief Judge McGruder and a rather sceptical Judge Dredd. Later, when Sabbat threatened the future of the entire world, Traktorfaktori joined the council of Judges which met in Hondo City to try and thwart his plans. This futhered cemented relations between the cities, but the Supreme Judge's days were numbered, however, since less than a year afterwards he was murdered by professional assassin Jonni Kiss.

2000AD Progs 743-745, 793, 830

Trapper Hag

ALIEN: Bounty Hunter, origin unknown

When the alien bounty hunter Trapper Hag realised that a number of outlaws on his bounty list were humans hiding out in Mega-City One, he thought nothing of flouting local laws in the pursuit of his quarry. Naturally enough, the Judges were none too happy about the alien's activities, but apprehending him proved to be a tough proposition, thanks to the incredible technology Hag had access to. His weaponry, spacecraft and teleport beam were like nothing ever seen before in the city and the monstrous Bounty Beasts he brought with him were not only helpful to the alien in sniffing out his prey, but they doubled up as fearsome "guard dogs" for his spaceship. Trapper Hag's luck finally run out when Judge Dredd fooled him into dropping his personal force shield long enough for the Judge to take out the alien mano-a-mano and put him under arrest.

2000AD Prog 305-307

Troggies

GROUP: Mutant Cult, Undercity, Mega-City One

The Troggies have a night on the town

EYES BULGING LIKE DEAD FISH. FACES GREY... DECAYING. THEY CREPT OUT AT NIGHT TO PREY ON THE INNOCENT CITIZENS OF MEGA-CITY 1.

HELP!

AAAGH!

Descendants of a group of people in the 20th Century who sought refuge from the modern world by hiding underground, the Troggies slowly mutated to survive in their new environment. Their occasional forays into Mega-City One above to kidnap citizens eventually drew the attention of Judge Dredd, who entered the subway system and managed to arrest the entire band of Troggies, including their crazed and vengeful leader, Slick Willy.

See also SLICK WILLY, UNDERCITY

2000AD Progs 36, 37

Two Ton Tony Tubbs

CITIZEN: Fattie, Mega-City One

Having spent three years in a Segregation Block, Tony Tubbs was finally released as food rationing was officially ended. Free at last to pursue his dream of becoming the fattest man to ever walk the Earth, Tony started training for the Fatty of the Year Contest and actually surpassed the two ton mark before his big day! His enormous bulk was actually too much for the stage the competition was held on and the resulting collapse saw several of his competitors killed in the crush. But nothing could mar Tony's triumph and he became a superstar following the contest, going on to guest regularly on vid-shows and even making an appearance in the Fatties' events in the Mega-Olympics!

2000AD Progs 440, 441 Introduced: 2000AD Prog 381

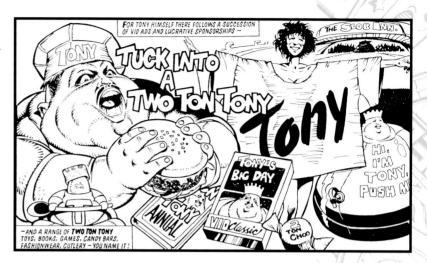

Tuskerosa The Vicious

JUDGE: Covert operations, East-Meg One

Heavily disguised as a mutant pirate, East-Meg agent Nikita Kramm became Tuskerosa the Vicious and joined the crew of Captain Skank. He quickly became Skank's most trusted lieutenant and manipulated the madman into launching a nuclear attack on Mega-City One. The attack saw the destruction of a City Block and Kramm's mission was complete. The Judges soon boarded and captured Skank's undersea vessel, however, and Tuskerosa was unmasked and killed.

See also CAPTAIN SKANK

2000AD Progs 197-199

Judge Dredd the Megazine Volume 2: 45 (cameo)

Tweak

ALIEN: Unnamed planet, Deep Space

When humans arrived on Tweak's home planet, he arranged for his people to go underground and hide from their visitors until he could discern more about them and their intentions. Using sophisticated mind probes, he was able to determine that human history was littered with violence, exploitation and hatred – so, as President of his world – he decided that no contact should be made with the humans at all. Unfortunately, Tweak's own children strayed onto the surface and were captured by the earthmen, along with his mate who had gone up to retrieve them. Although he could have rescued all three, Tweak chose to accompany them in captivity and pose as a "dumb alien", rather than betray his race's intelligence and risk the humans returning to his planet, exploiting it and contaminating his people with their diseases. The place was rich in precious minerals – which Tweak's people ate! - but his power of precognition told him that the humans would think nothing of mining the planet to exhaustion and leaving his people to starve.

On Earth, Tweak refused to reveal his true intelligence, despite the most stringent of testing, and the humans were finally convinced he was as dumb as they thought he looked. He and his family were then sold into slavery in the Cursed Earth – Tweak was bought by the Ferry-Master who operated on the burning and highly polluted Mississippi, while his mate and two children went to live with a rich land-owner and his spoilt daughter. When the little girl became bored with her new "pets", her father shot them in cold blood and Tweak, who had escaped from the Ferry-Master, arrived too late to save them. Instead, he was forced to bury them under rocks which – according to the customs of his people – provided them with the food they needed on their journey into the after-life.

Tweak was soon recaptured, but could not accept life as a slave and so escaped again. This time, the Alien Catcher General and his Slay-Riders were set on him to kill and make an example of him, but Judge Dredd stepped in to save his life from the mad mutants. The Judge sensed the intelligence in Tweak's eyes and asked him to join his mission to deliver the 2T(FRU)T antidote to Mega-City Two and the alien was only to happy do so, since Dredd was the first human he had met whom he could really trust. In fact, apart from Judge Dredd himself, Tweak was the only survivor of the trek across the Cursed Earth and his back-pack full of vaccine was of immeasurable value to the plague victims of Mega-City Two when the pair arrived there onfoot. In gratitude, Dredd arranged for him to be returned to his home planet, insisting that there should be no further interference with the alien's home world but keeping quiet about the mineral deposits there. At his own request, Tweak remained a "dumb alien" and his planet a worthless globe – his secret safe with Judge Dredd.

See also ALIEN CATCHER GENERAL,
SPIKES "HARVEY" ROTTEN,
2000AD Progs 69, 70, 72, 74-76, 78, 81-85

U

Ueno Hama

ROBOT: Mark IX Simulacrum, Hondo City

Placed as a "sleeper" robot spy in Hondo by the Mega-City One Justice Department, Ueno Hama was assimilated into the city's population and he was given employment as a scaffolder. Unfortunately, a building site accident damaged his circuits and switched him into "Attack Mode", so he began killing Hondo City officials with ruthless efficiency. Programmed to kill or be killed, the robot would not give up until it was completely deactivated or destroyed, though it soon sustained terminal damage from the Judges on its tail. Before he ceased functioning, Ueno Hama tried to kill Judge-Inspector Totaru Sadu, but Judge Dredd stepped in to save his Hondo counterpart. Dredd then engineered a massive explosion to destroy the robot – and therefore the evidence of Mega-City One's involvement in the whole sordid affair.

2000AD Progs 608-610 (destroyed)

Ugly Clinics

BUILDINGS: Uglifying salons, Mega-City One

The sum of 60 million credits was more money than the newly-rich Otto Sump could ever hope to spend, so he decided to invest in a chain of Beauty Clinics. Unfortunately, Otto's dreams turned to disaster when his beauty treatments kept going wrong and he ended up creating a string of ugly customers! Luckily, the look caught on and his Beauty Clinics soon became Ugly Clinics, as an ugliness craze took hold in the city. The Clinics made more money for Otto and he soon became the target of a blackmail attempt by some small time villains. Judge Dredd dealt with the blackmailers, but he also wanted the Ugly Clinics closed, since he believed that Sump's range of products was unhealthy. Otto was unwilling to comply, but Dredd got his way, thanks to a new Ugly Tax that saw all the Clinics shut up shop – apart from a few exclusive salons which catered for very wealthy clients.

See also OTTO SUMP, UGLY TAX

Introduced: 2000AD Prog 186

Ugly Tax

TAX: Levy on all Ugly Products, Mega-City One

Having decided that Ugly Products were unhealthy, Judge Dredd recommended the levying of a new Ugly Tax. In Mega-City One you have to be very rich to be really ugly!

See also OTTO SUMP, UGLY CLINICS

Introduced: 2000AD Prog 188

Umpty Baggers

CRIMINALS: Umpty Candy dealers, Mega-City One

Although 22nd Century science has permanently eliminated all known addictions, there is one exception – candy made to the recipe of Uncle Ump. Umpty Baggers deal in such candy in Mega-City One.

Introduced: 2000AD Prog 213

UMPTY CANDY SOLD IN ALL SHAPES AND SIZES. IT WAS THE MOST POPULAR CONFECTION OF THE EARLY 22ND CENTURY...

A selection of Justice Department approved Umpty goodies

Umpty Candy

FOODSTUFF: Candy, Mega-City One

Sold in all shapes and sizes, Umpty Candy is the most popular confectionery in Mega-City One. Naturally, it must be completely sugar-free and it has to pass standard nutrition tests, but otherwise most Umpty Candy is fully legal. The one exception to this is the banned candy formerly produced by Uncle Ump, which proved to be so good it was addictive.

See also UNCLE UMP

Introduced: 2000AD Prog 145

Uncle Ump

CITIZEN: Candy manufacturer, Mega-City One

Poor Uncle Ump's only crime was to produce the greatest taste of all time. His Umpty Candy was so good, that it was addictive and even the analyser machine used to examine the stuff demanded extra samples! Withdrawal from the candy had terrible side effects so the Judges were forced to act. With regret, the Judges arranged for Uncle Ump to be put on a spacecraft and sent off into exile in space, taking the secret of his candy with him. Unfortunately for the candy maker, his ship was tracked by ruthless criminals who followed it and killed him for his recipe, so that they could sell his special Umpty Candy on the black market to addicts at hugely inflated prices.

See also UMPTY BAGGERS

2000AD Prog 145, 213 (dies)

Undercity

LOCATION: Beneath Mega-City One

When the old cities of the USA's Eastern Seaboard became too polluted and too crime-ridden to live in any longer, the government's solution was to slap a big sheet of concrete over them and to build a fantastic new city on top of them. This city was to become Mega-City One, while the remnants below soon became known as the Undercity. Although most people took up residence in the new City Blocks of Mega-City One, a few people remained. By the start of the 22nd Century, the Undercity was almost exclusively populated by mutants who had adapted to live in the cold, dark environment. The place is an attractive place for criminals to hide out, however, since the only Judges who operate there are the few who have taken the Long Walk and elected to serve in the Undercity.

Introduced: 2000AD Prog 36

Undertone Hankok

CITIZEN: Vid-slug author, Mega-City One

As the author of illegal vid-slug "Rough Guide to Suicide", Undertone Hankok was responsible for an horrific trend, as suicide became fashionable in Mega-CIty One. The Judges were determined to make him appear on air and denounce his philosophy in an effort to discourage citizens from taking their own lives, but by the time they found him, Hankok had killed himself!

2000AD Prog 761

Urk

ALIEN: Mutant Klegg

The last Klegg left in Mega-City One, Urk had all the raw viciousness of his race, but lacked intelligence. He was found by two citizens who fed him and kept him like a pet. Unfortunately, the alien proved too much for them once he was fully grown and Urk killed them. When he was discovered by the Judges, he was terminated under the standard execution order applying to all Kleggs in the city.

2000AD Prog 138

Vanilla Batcave

CITIZEN: Vid-star, Mega-City One

When her vid "Planes, Trains and Democrats" came out, popular actress and film-maker Vanilla Batcave became identified with the democratic cause. She understood that preaching revolution would make her very unpopular with the Judges, so she merely implored people to see her film and think about the issues it raised. Unfortunately for Vanilla, she was stunned and kidnapped by an extreme right wing group called "The Sons of the Iron Lady' – actually a front for undercover Judges – during her publicity tour for the film. By the time she awoke, the actress found herself in the Justice Department facing electro-shock therapy, face-change surgery and deportation to an off-world colony for daring to delve into the dirty world of Mega-City One politics!

2000AD Prog 656

Varks

ALIENS: Proxima-Proxima, Deep Space

Vampire-like reptilian creatures, Varks are dangerous parasites who think nothing of swallowing an entire human in one gulp! They replicate by injecting their own cells into a selected host animal and the cells gradually multiply until they take over the host body. So when this metamorphosis is finally complete, the host actually becomes the new Vark. Mainly restricted to large fenced off "Varkeries" on their home planet, they have been known to infect tourists from Mega-City One and so have made it back to earth inside unsuspecting hosts.

2000AD Prog 503

Vienna Dredd

CITIZEN: Mega-City One

Judge Dredd's niece, Vienna was his corrupt brother Rico's daughter, and was orphaned when Joe was forced to kill her father. Vienna loved her uncle, but was unaware of the exact fate of Rico until she was kidnapped by electronics genius Harry Carmen. Carmen had a grudge against Dredd since the Judge had put him away for six years for a computer swindle previously, and he chose to seek his revenge through the child. Dredd managed to rescue Vienna, but not before Harry Carmen had revealed that the Judge had killed her father himself. Vienna forgave him, but Dredd vowed to see her less often in future and asked her guardian, Mrs Pasternak, to ensure that the girl would forget him, rather than risk the heartbreak of her hearing about his death on the streets of Mega-City One.

2000AD Prog 116

Virus Strain 2T(FRU)T

AFFLICTION: Deadly virus, Mega-City Two

A virus strain left over from the short-lived Germ War which followed the outbreak of the Atomic Wars in 2070, 2T(FRU)T proved so lethal that it afflicted millions of people in Mega-City Two thirty years later! Causing its victims" skin to turn grey and scrambling their brains so that they became kill-crazy cannibals, it was so contagious that it overran the city in days. A cure for the virus was available in Mega-City One, but when pilots arrived with the vaccine they found Mega-City Two's airport swarming with plague victims and were unable to deliver it. The cure was finally brought to the stricken city by Judge Dredd after an arduous trek across the Cursed Earth and millions of citizens were saved from a lingering death. Unfortunately, the death toll was still to rise, since statistically some 10% of the "TOOTY-FRUITY" plague's victims are unresponsive to the cure.

Introduced: 2000AD Prog 61

Vito Colletta

CITIZEN: Mega-City One

With "thought theft" becoming a lucrative business in Mega-City One, Vito Colletta was determined to acquire some very special memories – Judge Dredd's! He offered 5 million credits to anyone who could steal a copy of the Judge's thoughts, but when he tried out the merchandise, his brain could not handle all the bad memories the Judge had accumulated in a career on the streets of Mega-City One and it quite literally exploded!

2000AD Prog 836, 837 (dies)

Sov-Judge Vlad

JUDGE: Diktatorat member, East-Meg One

WE WILL HIT THEM WITHOUT WARNING – WITHOUT MERCY! WE WILL REPAY THEM FOR ALL THE INDIGNITIES THEY HAVE HEAPED UPON US! BEFORE THIS DAY IS OVER, I PROMISE YOU– MEGA-CITY ONE WILL BE CRUSHED AND ITS DECADENT CITIZENS WILL BE SLAVES TO THE MIGHT OF OUR GLORIOUS EAST-MEG!

As a leading member of East-Meg One's ruling body, the Diktatorat, Vlad was one of the key architects of the Apocalypse War that saw the Sovs launch a massive nuclear attack on Mega-City One. Sov-Judge Vlad disliked the Judges of the U.S. city and was a zealous proponent of the war, desiring no less than the complete annihilation of his enemies. He found the so-called "acceptable casualties" of around 12% of the population in his own city hard to stomach, however, when he had to face up to the consequences of the Diktatorat's actions. He had not expected such an effective counter-strike, especially since East-Meg One possessed the remarkable Apocalypse Warp to quite literally "warp" their enemy's missiles into another dimension. Perhaps it was fortunate for Sov-Judge Vlad that he never saw his city destroyed by Judge Dredd at the end of the Apocalypse War, since he became a casualty of war himself long before then. Vlad and his fellow Diktatorat members had reckoned without the ambition of their War Marshal. "Mad Dog" Kazan was from satisfied with being the one who put his own life and the lives of the Judges under his command on the line while East-Meg One's rulers were safely back at home, so he organised a coup to overthrow them during the conflict with the American city. Vlad was outraged by this betrayal, but was killed before he could do anything about it!

See also APOCALYPSE WARP, APOCALYPSE SQUAD,
WAR MARSHAL "MAD DOG" KAZAN,
2000AD Progs 245-247, 249, 250, 259 (dies)

W

Wally Squad

DIVISION: Undercover Squad, Mega-City One Justice Department

It is very rare for a regular street Judge to go under-cover on an operation in Mega-City One – this sort of task is usually left to the specialists of the "Wally Squad". These Judges dress like ordinary citizens and often act like them in order to establish false identities, but can prove invaluable in the detection of crimes that regular, very high profile Judges can miss. Nonetheless, Wally Squad operatives are viewed rather suspiciously by their colleagues, since their association with the citizens makes them far more susceptible to going off the rails than any other Judges.

Introduced: 2000AD Prog 390

City Father Washington

CITIZEN: City Father, Mega-City One

Occupying the mainly ceremonial post of City Father of Mega-City One, Washington was well thought of by the Judges and citizens alike. When his son was kidnapped by the Cursed Earth mutant group, the Brotherhood of Darkness, Judge Dredd himself effected a rescue. City Father Washington's popularity took a nose dive, however, when he presided over the disastrous opening of the Komputel and he declined nomination for the new post of Mayor when it was contested shortly afterwards.

See also KOMPUTEL

2000AD Prog 32

Watchers

ALIENS: Servants of Murd the Oppressor, Planet Necros

Described as "obscene creatures of unparalleled vileness", the Watchers were animated by the pure and plentiful source of evil provided by Murd the Oppressor, the Necromancer of Necros. It has been suggested that they were merely extensions of the Necromancer himself, rather than individuals in their own right and indeed, when their master was killed, they expired too.

See also MURD THE OPPRESSOR

2000AD Progs 170, 171

Weather Control

DIVISION: Mega-City One Justice Department

The smallest section of Mega-City One's Justice Department, but one of the most important, Weather Control regulates all of the city's weather. Based on the "Atmosphere Control" floating strato-station, they ensure that weather conditions are maintained at a moderate level throughout the year.

Introduced: 2000AD Prog 3 (term), 16 (concept)

Walter the Wobot
See page 154

Walter the Wobot

ROBOT: Free citizen, Mega-City One

During the Robot Wars of 2099, Walter fought bravely on the side of the Judges against Call-me-Kenneth and he played a vital role in helping quell the revolt. He developed a nervous mechanical lisp in the course of the struggle, so he was known as Walter the "Wobot" by the time the vending droid was awarded his freedom following the war. Despite receiving this historic honour, he sought nothing more than total subservience to his new hero, Judge Dredd, and at one point he even burned his freedom papers and filed ownership details in the Judge's name instead. Dredd refused to accept this and had Walter's freedom documents replaced, much to the Wobot's disappointment.

Over the years, Dredd's faithful robo-servant shared many dangerous adventures with him and proved to be both a help and a hindrance. He even stowed away on the shuttle to the Luna-1 moon colony when Dredd was appointed Judge-Marshal there for six months. Walter met Rowena on the moon, however, and he grew quite fond of the female robot. Back on earth, Walter nearly committed suicide when he thought the Judge no longer wanted him around, but he did prove very helpful in the struggle against the mad Chief Judge Cal. Unfortunately, when Mean Machine turned up at Rowdy Yates Conapts looking for revenge, poor Walter was on the receiving end of an almighty head butt that smashed him to bits. As a free robot, he had to be rebuilt as the city provides basic medical services to all its citizens, but he convinced himself that he was no longer welcome at Dredd's apartment.

Having wandered around Mega-City One aimlessly for several years, Judge Death's Necropolis turned out to be great news for Walter. He started filing lost property slips on abandoned robots he found and, after three short weeks, their ownership reverted to him if they weren't claimed. The Wobot made a fortune running Walt's Used Droid Lot and he even splashed out on having his mechanical lisp fixed, so he became Walter the Robot again. Unfortunately, when one of his second-hand droids went berserk, Judge Dredd had to investigate his former robo-servant. Convinced that Walter had nothing to do with the murders carried out by the machine, Dredd was still forced to close him down and Walter not only went bankrupt, but his mechanical lisp returned as well!

Still devoted to the Judge, Walter popped up during the renegade Judge Grice's attack on Mega-City One to rescue Dredd, but he didn't even get a proper thank you. This was the last straw for the poor Wobot and something snapped in his programming. Walter set about organising a small-scale robot rebellion, and he tried to kill his former hero. Dredd survived, however, thanks to the actions of Rookie Judge Giant, who was on his final street assessment, and – as a free robot – Walter ended up facing a thirty-stretch in the Iso-Cubes.

2000AD Progs 10, 13-18, 25, 26, 29, 33, 34, 42-44, 46, 55, 56, 58-60, 86, 87, 89, 90, 93, 96, 103-106, 114, 115, 119, 121, 126, 191, 252, 253, 255, 256, 259, 262, 263, 285, 286, 611, 847, 848

Judge Dredd the Megazine Volume 2: 45 (cameo), 51, 52

2000AD Annuals 1979, 1980 2000AD Sci-Fi Special 1978

White Werewolf

MUTANT: Werewolf leader, Undercity

Some of the after effects of the Apocalypse War were felt in the Undercity when a pool of radioactive chemical sludge turned some of the people there into werewolves. The substance, which later came to be known as Cassidium, saw one particular mutant Undercity dweller become the White Werewolf, recognised widely as the leader of the pack. Ultimately, the White Werewolf was killed by Judge Dredd, but not before he had infected the Judge with the "werewolf disease" by biting him!

See also MED-JUDGE CASSIDY

2000AD Progs 325-327 (dies)

"Whitey" Logan

CITIZEN: Criminal, Mega-City One

A vicious criminal, William "Whitey" Logan soon became one of Mega-City One's most wanted perps when he killed Judge Alvin. He was apprehended by Judge Dredd and imprisoned on Devil's Island, but vowed to escape. Whitey – who sometimes went under the alias of Randolph Whitely – did indeed engineer not one, but two breakouts during his first year of imprisonment. First, he got away when a fellow prisoner, an electronics wizard calling himself "Einstein" built a machine that could override Mega-City One's Weather Control and create snow – forcing traffic to stop around the Island. After a chase through a terrible blizzard, however, Dredd took him back to his prison. Shortly after this, Whitey's brother, Welch Logan broke him out, only to be killed as Judge Dredd recaptured Whitey for a third time.

Security was tightened at Devil's Island following these escapes and Logan was stuck there for ten years before a mass breakout gave him the opportunity to get out yet again. This time he holed up in a Munce-Co Plant and took a number of hostages, demanding that Dredd be handed over to him. The Judge barely remembered Whitey, but he still entered the plant unarmed. Once inside, Dredd was forced to kill the Judge killer to protect the hostages.

See also DEVIL'S ISLAND

2000AD Prog 2, 31, 520 (dies)

2000AD Annual 1978

William Wenders

CITIZEN: Juve, Mega-City One

When Judge Dredd found a letter addressed to him in the hand of a young murder victim, he had no idea it would serve to shatter his own faith in the Justice he was supposed to represent. In the letter, William Wenders raised some questions about the way in which the Judges worked that Dredd found himself unable to answer. If the Judges came to power to "combat a tidal wave of lawlessness", why has Mega-City One got the worst crime rate anywhere? How come, according to statistics, a citizen is almost as likely to be killed by a Judge as by a criminal? Don't Judges ever worry about making mistakes? And why was the Democratic March broken up in a flood of violence when it had seemed to be a peaceful protest? Young William was sure that Dredd could explain everything, but he didn't live long enough to discover that the Judge had grave doubts of his own.

2000AD Prog 661 (dies)

Judge Winslow

JUDGE: Accounts, Mega-City One Justice Department

Originally assigned to the crew of the Justice 1 when Judge Dredd led the mission to find the Judge Child, Judge Winslow was determined to ensure that costs were kept within reasonable limits. Dredd himself removed the accountant from his team, since he believed that the mission could not become too expensive, with the future fate of Mega-City One.

Winslow felt the wrath of Judge Dredd a second time when Winslow questioned his authorisation of 130,000 creds spent on medical treatment for a sick girl whose parents were unable to afford it. Dredd had taken pity on Bonny Crickle, the victim of a terrible accident in a chem pit, but her cure had ironically led to her death. He was not in the mood for criticism and the accountant found himself on the wrong end of mighty punch for his trouble! Demanding the ultimate penalty of twenty years on Titan for Dredd, Winslow was to be disappointed as Chief Judge McGruder dismissed the case against him without punishment.

See also BONNY CRICKLE

2000AD Progs 162, 388

Judge Winslow brings Dredd to account

XYZ

Xanadu

PLANET: Johannsen Cluster, Deep Space

A barren volcanic rock on the edge of the Johannsen Cluster, Xanadu was declared an "Open Planet" in 2078 and soon became a refuge for fugitives and law-breakers from all over the Galaxy. It also provided a safe haven for renegade robots who could go there and live in the world's Robot Free-State, "Grunwald's Kingdom". It was to this area on Xanadu that the Angel Gang brought the Judge Child, with the intention of doing a deal with the mysterious robot ruler of the Kingdom, the Grunwalder. The Angels' arrival on Xanadu might have gone unnoticed on a planet which was a haven for criminals, but they were super-bad and managed to lower the tone even there! In the event, the Angels were all killed by Judge Dredd when he caught up with them on Xanadu, having tracked the criminal gang halfway across the universe. First to fall were Mean Machine and Link Angel, while Pa and Junior made it all the way to Grunwald's Kingdom before they died. Ironically, Owen Krysler, the so-called Judge Child was left on the planet anyway, in the care of the Grunwalder. The mysterious robot then set about using the Judge Child's strange powers to help him spread his influence on Xanadu. Within two years the planet was almost completely under his control, so he renamed it "Grunwald's World" and declared the place a robot-free planet. Where it had been a safe planet for human renegades, Xanadu was suddenly a very dangerous place for any human to visit. The Grunwalder was happy with the new arrangements as well as his custody of the Judge Child, however, since he rather enjoyed being the ruler of an entire planet!

See also THE ANGEL GANG, GRUNWALDER, GRUNWALD'S KINGDOM, THE MUTANT,

Introduced: 2000AD Prog 176

Xena Lowther

CITIZEN: Dunc Renaldo Block, Mega-City One

When the Dark Judges took over the City Block she lived in, Xena Lowther was attacked by Judge Death, but not killed. The evil Judges were quickly defeated by their Mega-City One counterparts on that occasion, but Xena's wounds were not easily healed. She lost the use of her right arm and started to become cold and distant – despite the fact that there was no physical evidence of any injury. Obsessed by death and the darker life, she was a changed woman. Slowly, Xena became more estranged from her husband, until she rejected him completely and declared her love for Judge Death!

Having turned their home into a shrine to the Dark Judges, Xena found herself under the control of the Sisters of Death who possessed her mind even though they were still in their own dimension on the planet of Deadworld. They promised to summon Judge Death for her if she would provide a psychic bridge, enabling them to come across the dimension to Mega-City One. To do this she had to stab and kill her husband, the sacrifice completing the bridge and unleashing the forces of death on her city. The Sisters of Death kept Xena alive until they found a much stronger psychic substitute in Psi-Judge Kit Agee to maintain the psychic bridge and then they were quite prepared to let her die.

Finally, though, they did summon Judge Death as promised, with the unwitting help of Judge Death, so that she could die in the Dark Judge's arms as the "Bride of Death"!

See also PSI-JUDGE KIT AGEE, JUDGE DEATH, JUDGE KRAKEN, SISTERS OF DEATH

2000AD Progs 672, 673, 676, 678, 679 (dies)

Yassa Povey

CITIZEN: Bubbletown, Cursed Earth

Coming from the God-fearing community of Bubbletown, a remote Cursed Earth town, young Yassa Povey was rather disturbed when he stumbled across an apparently dead body while out walking. He was even more shocked when he realised that the gnarled and wizened "Dead Man" he had found was actually still alive! The boy's parents took the man into their home to tend his injuries, fully expecting him to die soon anyway, but he proved to be a tough customer.

The Dead Man had lost his memory, but he refused to die – certain that there was a very important reason for him to stay alive. When he set out across the Cursed Earth in search of the scene of whatever trauma had overcome him, Yassa went along with him. They discovered the shocking truth in the ruined town of Crowley, where the Dead Man remembered that he was actually Judge Dredd! He recalled a terrifying encounter with the Sisters of Death there, only for the Sisters to manifest themselves again. Poor Yassa bore the main brunt of their attack this time – he was blinded by their psychic assault and was beset by terrible nightmares that made his life a misery when he returned home to Bubbletown.

Judge Dredd travelled on to Mega-City One and ultimately banished the evil Sisters, but Yassa's terror continued. He was not forgotten, however, and Dredd soon made arrangements for him to come to his city for an operation to replace his eyes with a bionic pair. It was the least the Judge could do for the boy who had been instrumental in saving Mega-City One from complete disaster. Yassa was also treated by Psi-Judge Anderson, who managed to exorcise the demons plaguing his mind, so the boy's nightmare was over at last and he went home a hero, fully recovered from the dreadful influence of the Sisters of Death.

See also DEAD MAN, SISTERS OF DEATH

2000AD Progs 650-663, 702-706, 712

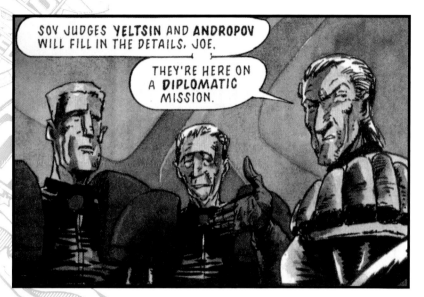

Sov-Judge Yeltsin

JUDGE: EAST-MEG TWO

Along with Sov-Judge Andropov, Yeltsin was responsible for unwittingly unleashing a monstrous "Ultimate Judge" on Mega-City One, seeking revenge on Judge Dredd. Yeltsin and Andropov visited the American city to warn Chief Judge McGruder of the impending danger, but they both wound up as the victims of diplomatic executions – with the full backing of the East-Meg Two Chief Judge – in retribution for the actions of the monster.

See also PROJECT X

2000AD Progs 868-871 (dies)

Yu-Tsu

CITIZEN: Sage and traveller, Cursed Earth

Hailing from Philadelphia, Yu-Tsu was a wise and spiritual soul who travelled the land in search of enlightenment, but he was met with considerable suspicion when he tried to gain passage into Mega-City One. The Judges tested him, prodded him and interrogated him mercilessly, but the Sage submitted patiently to their cruel treatment. Finally satisfied that he posed no threat to their city, they still refused him admittance and Yu-Tsu realised something very important as Judge Dredd escorted him to the City Gate – even a man whose entire life has been dedicated to understanding and non-violence has a limit to his tolerance – and so he bopped the Judge on the nose! At least Yu-Tsu's desire to stay in Mega-City One was fulfilled, but ten years in a Kook Cube was not what he'd been hoping for.

2000AD Prog 577

Zachary Zziiz

CITIZEN: Mega-City One

Rather luckier than Aaron A. Aardvark, his counterpart at the very beginning of the Mega-City One Vid-Phone Directory, Zachary Zziiz was the last named person in the book. Hence he survived when millions of citizens were executed by Chief Judge Cal and, indeed, he could have ended up as the last citizen left alive in the city.

2000AD Prog 93

Zipper Bike

VEHICLE: Flying Squad Judges standard issue bike, Mega-City One

In a multi-levelled city like Mega-City One, a regular Lawmaster Bike is not always enough and so the Zipper Bike was created. The Zipper shares most of the features of its ground-based counterpart, except that it flies. Although not used often, these "bikes" can be extremely valuable in certain tactical situations and provide their user with the kind of speed no ordinary Lawmaster can match. Because of their specialist nature, Zipper Bikes are almost exclusively used by the specially trained Judges of the Mega-City One "Flying Squad", although many of the Judges have opted to use Power Boards in recent years.

See also FLYING SQUAD

Introduced: 2000AD Annual 1981

Zombies

ANIMALS: Genetically engineered "humanoids", Mega-City One

A zombie is released from the misery of its life

With experimentation on animals an ethical minefield, a supposedly humane solution to the problem of vital research was the breeding of genetically mutated animals with only minimal brain functions. In theory, these creatures – which are disturbingly humanoid in form – are insensitive to pain, have no feelings, no thoughts and no personality. They are merely Zombies, ideal subjects for any kind of gruesome experimentation . . . or are they?

Introduced: 2000AD Prog 470

Zoot Smiley

CITIZEN: Leader of the "Spacers" Bike Gang, Mega-City One

A leading participant among the 5000 contestants in the Mega-City 5000 bike race of 2099, Zoot Smiley was the leader of the "Spacers" bike gang and was among the last four left in the illegal competition before the Judges put a stop to the race altogether.

He was narrowly edged out by Spikes "Harvey" Rotten, though neither of them crossed the finishing line and both ended up in the 'Cubes!

See also MEGA-CITY 5000

2000AD Progs 40, 41

Zoot Smiley (left) takes on Spikes "Harvey" Rotten in the Mega-City 5000

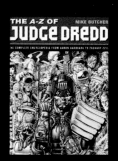